Moses Asaah Awinongya

The Understanding of Family in Ghana as a Challenge for a Contextual Ecclesiology

Studien zur systematischen Theologie und Ethik

herausgegeben von

Band 64

LIT

Moses Asaah Awinongya

The Understanding of Family in Ghana as a Challenge for a Contextual Ecclesiology

LIT

Bibliographic information published by the Deutsche Nationalbibliothek
The Deutsche Nationalbibliothek lists this publication in the Deutsche Nationalbibliografie; detailed bibliographic data are available in the Internet at http://dnb.d-nb.de.

ISBN 978-3-643-90314-3
Zugl.: München, Univ., Diss., 2012

A catalogue record for this book is available from the British Library

Klosbachstr. 107
CH-8032 Zürich
Tel. +41 (0) 44-251 75 05
Fax +41 (0) 44-251 75 06
E-Mail: zuerich@lit-verlag.ch
http://www.lit-verlag.ch

LIT VERLAG Dr. W. Hopf
Berlin 2013
Fresnostr. 2
D-48159 Münster
Tel. +49 (0) 2 51-620 320
Fax +49 (0) 2 51-23 19 72
E-Mail: lit@lit-verlag.de
http://www.lit-verlag.de

Distribution:
In Germany: LIT Verlag Fresnostr. 2, D-48159 Münster
Tel. +49 (0) 2 51-620 32 22, Fax +49 (0) 2 51-922 60 99, E-mail: vertrieb@lit-verlag.de
In Austria: Medienlogistik Pichler-ÖBZ, e-mail: mlo@medien-logistik.at
In Switzerland: B + M Buch- und Medienvertrieb, e-mail: order@buch-medien.ch
In the UK: Global Book Marketing, e-mail: mo@centralbooks.com
In North America: International Specialized Book Services, e-mail: orders@isbs.com

Dedicated to
my grandparents Asaah and Awinpoka (of blessed memory)
for the gift of education and selfless love.
To Roger Ajene (of blessed memory) who came to my aid as an angel.
To my mother, Alice Asaah, who taught me how to sacrifice for the comfort of other people.

TABLE OF CONTENT

PREFACE

Community, communal life and solidarity are as old as the human race. They have taken on different proportions according to the society and culture in question. The human person has learnt to live in such a constellation. He shares his life with others. He relates with his fellow community members and they also do the same with him. Through their interaction and activities they construct what one may call human community and culture. According to the Judeo-Christian tradition it is the nature of the human being to build and live in a community. This took place through the creation of Adam and Eve, a man and a woman, who formed a community from the very beginning of creation. In the first book of Moses, this act is said to have taken place on the sixth day of creation. God saw that "it was good, it was very good". The statement could be interpreted to either mean that the creation of man and woman in the image and likeness of God was very good or that the fact of companionship or the building of community through these two creatures, man and woman, was very good. The basis of the second version of interpretation is that before God created Eve (the woman), Adam was lonely and unhappy. Upon reception of his partner he (Adam) said this is at last "bone from my bone and flesh from my flesh, she will be called woman". The two of them formed the basis for conjugal relations, which in turn became the foundation for family formation. God remains the source of life and sustainer of the unit called family.

I am grateful to God for giving me life and making me to be born into a family. The members in this unit gave me warmth, love, moral support and a home at various stages in my life. I have learnt to love and be loved, to relate and be related to and to experience selflessness from many people and I have learnt to sacrifice for the comfort of other people. My life in the Church-family, family of friends, family of academia and in the Arnoldus family is the more lively because of the experience gained in my family of origin. I thank God for the life of all those in the above mentioned families, who have contributed immensely to help me live a fulfilled life.

My sincere thanks go to Prof. Dr. Peter Neuner, who took keen interest in the topic of my dissertation and the research work as a whole. I remember with heartfelt gratitude all the encounters with him. They were very hearty and filled with Christian brotherliness. The moderation of the thesis was undertaken with competence in the subject and meticulousness. However, I am wholly responsible for all errors, misstatements and limitations that may be found in this work. The time spent in the Catholic Theological Faculty of the Ludwig-Maximilians-Universität was very fruitful and enriching. My sincere gratitude goes to all the professors and students with whom I interacted during this time.

My sincere thanks go also to the Provincial Superior of the German province of the Divine Word Missionaries, Rev. Dr. Bernd Werle SVD, and his council for granting me the necessary condition and fraternal support for my doctoral studies.

In the same way I say thank you to the parish-family of St. Canisius, Großhadern/Munich and the parish team thereof under the pastoral headship of Rev. Fr. Johann Georg Lechner, my brother in priestly ministry. I am equally grateful to all members of my family of friends in Cologne, Ebersbach-Musbach and Munich for their encouragement and prayer support. I had the opportunity to discuss my views with some of them. The critical remarks sometimes made from them helped me to rethink or sharpen my thoughts on certain issues.

I am also indebted to Gilbert and Margaret Mary Awinongya (Mr. and Mrs.), Vivian and Irene for granting me the opportunity to experience what is family solidarity and support. Without their financial, moral and prayer support I could not have gone this far in my academic career.

I also thank Tobias Schmitz, Rev. Fr. Ludger Feldkämper SVD, Prof. Dr. Gerhard F. Straßer, Dr. Werner Störzbach and Katja Legner, who read the manuscript at various stages of its development. Michaela Bauer took over part of the work of my foundation, Stiftung Regentropfen, so that I could have enough time for the write-up of this research. I owe her a lot of heartfelt gratitude. She is not only a friend and co-worker in the foundation but more so she has become my "Bavarian sister". Similar thanks goes to my "Bavarian mother", Mrs. Maike Heckenstaller.

The implication of a large family network is that the individual in question cannot mention all members thereof who have touched and influenced his life. I also find myself in such a situation that I cannot mention the names of all those I would have loved to due to lack of space but also for the fear that I may forget someone. All my friends and relatives are very special to me and I am grateful to all for being part of my life. May God, the father of the great human-family bless and protect all people of good will. May he help the Church-family gather the whole of humanity together into the one fold called kingdom of God.

Munich, 29th September, 2012 Moses Asaah Awinongya SVD

GENERAL INTRODUCTION

0.0 It Began with Jesus

The question as to whether or not Jesus intended to form a Church has won intensive theological discussions. The views on this topic are as many as the schools of thought. A good summary of the various positions and interpretations is offered by Joseph Ratzinger in his book *Zur Gemeinschaft gerufen. Kirche heute verstehen*[1]. He describes three theories with their respective world views. As would be expected, the adherents of the different schools of thought provide answers to the question above based on their thought pattern. Ratzinger mentions three mainstreams of exegetes or what he calls "three generations of exegetes", namely the liberal exegesis, cultic exegesis and the neoliberal exegesis. He links the three exegetical generations to the particular epochs and socio-political factors at the time.

Notwithstanding the diverse views on the form and character of what Jesus intended to create, the general consensus is that he and those who followed him formed a community in which domination and its supporting structures were abhorred. It was a community in which the principles of fraternity and service ruled, regardless of whether it was within the inner circle of disciples who built a fixed group around Jesus or without it, namely, with the group of followers who remained with their families in anticipation of the reign of God but felt bound to Jesus and the followers who moved with him from place to place. This second group had the task of announcing the good news of the Lord among their own life-communities. For instance, Mark 5,18-20 narrates that "as he [Jesus] was getting into the boat, the man who had been possessed begged to be allowed to stay with him. Jesus would not let him but said to him, 'Go home to your people and tell them all that the Lord in his mercy has done for you.' So the man went off and proceeded to proclaim in Decapolis all that Jesus had done for him. And everyone was amazed"[2]. The closest of his followers were the twelve disciples who later got the title apostles. He lived in a community with them and illustrated here the outlook and practice of the true family of God.

It could be concluded from the reports in the New Testament that the gathering around and living with Jesus as a family formed the basis for the future mission of the disciples. The gospel of Mark illustrates this aptly: the disciples were with him so that he can send them out to proclaim the message of the Kingdom of God (Mark 3,14). Jesus went further on to give prominence to the theme family of God in his teachings. Joseph Ratzinger observes that among

---

[1] Cf. Joseph Ratzinger, Zur Gemeinschaft gerufen. Kirche heute verstehen, Freiburg i. Br., Basel and Wien [2]2005, pp. 12-20.

[2] Cf. Gerhard Lohfink, Jesus and Community. The Social Dimension of Christian Faith, (*Wie hat Jesus Gemeinde gewollt? Zur gesellschaftlichen Dimension des christlichen Glaubens*), translated into English by John P. Galvin, London 1985, pp. 31f. See also Joachim Jeremias, Neutestamentliche Theologie, Gütersloh [2]1973, p. 164.

the many images used by Jesus to describe the "new" people of God the most recurring concept is family of God[3]. As will be observed in later analysis of this research Jesus uses the concept family as a metaphor which is not to be seen as an analogy but includes perceiving the concept as a lived-reality. Since the followers were not born of the same mother and father, it would be biologically impossible to call them brothers and sisters, except that one decides to make reference to Abraham. Through and with Jesus the biologically unrelated persons, who now build a new family, were to treat each other truly as brethren.

After his death and resurrection the disciples kept on the spirit of brotherhood and spread the gospel message. The effect was the birth of many communities. Even though each unit had its own dynamics and autonomy, all of them formed the universal family of faith and supported each other in various ways (cf. Acts 11, 27-30). These communities kept their divine character and mission. Since the composition was human they existed within a given cultural and societal set-up. The remarkable features, however, are that God remained the father of these communities and as already mentioned above the believers were brothers and sisters to one another. Notwithstanding these ideals there were tendencies towards ethnic extremism and biases within the early Christian community. In Acts 6, 1-7 a report is given about a complaint of the Hellenists (disciples) against the Hebrews, that the widows of the former were overlooked in the daily distribution of food. A meeting was thus called to solve this problem. The consensus was that seven men of good reputation, filled with the Spirit and with wisdom should be elected to take up the task of sharing the food, so that the twelve apostles could devote themselves to the proclamation of the word. Another report is given in Acts 11 about the protest of the "circumcised believers" against the apostle Peter, because the latter had been visiting the "uncircumcised" and eating with them. He defended his action by explaining the work of the Spirit among the gentiles and the fact that God does not discriminate against a particular race or ethnic group. He treats all people as his children. The report states that the Hebrew Christians were satisfied with the account given by the apostle Peter. The community gave glory to God and said: "God has clearly granted to the gentiles too the repentance that leads to life"[4]. Despite the above-made experience the Hebrew believers had the temptation to package the gospel message with the wrappers of Jewish culture and religious tradition. What ensued was the "convocation" of the Council of Jerusalem[5]

---

[3] Cf. J. Ratzinger, Zur Gemeinschaft gerufen, ^{2}2005, p. 21.

[4] Acts 11,18. The translation is taken from *The New Jerusalem Bible, Standard edition,* London 1985.

[5] Some of the brothers who formerly belonged to the Pharisees' party insisted that the gentile-Christians should be circumcised and instructed to obey the Law of Moses. The reason for their action can be traced to the Jewish religious practice. They were equating the belief in God with being circumcised or as it were becoming a Jew. For them it was unimaginable that a person could be chosen by God without circumcision and instruction in the Law of Moses. The response given by the apostle Peter offers a guideline even to modern day Christians, namely that salvation comes through the grace of God and not through the observation of the Law. He says: Why do you put God to the test now by imposing on the disciples the very burden that neither our ancestors nor we ourselves were strong enough to support?" (cf. Acts 15,10).

which clearly distanced itself from anything that will put burden on the gentile-disciples. The summary of the arguments is that even though Jesus could be seen as the founder of the Church, he did not expound on the nature and structure that the latter should take. The future development of the *ecclesia* was thus left to the imaginative power and creativity of the followers, guided by the Holy Spirit. In the event of the creative construction of the structures and life of the Church the cultural values of the particular Christians could not be neglected[6].

The two factors – ethnic extremism and exportation of cultural elements to other societies found expression again and again in the evangelization mission of the Church. After Greek imperialism, Latin was imposed on many societies as the language for civil administration and of the Church. Civil structures of the Roman or Western society were assumed by the Church and exported to other parts of the world. Church laws were sometimes made using the Roman civil constitutional standards, without considering their suitability or otherwise in other cultural situations. It must be remarked here that canon law is neither bad in itself nor does one question the usefulness of laws that could enjoy universal acceptance and suitability: they provide common grounds for the affected members thus providing order and discipline. The problem arises where uniformity is placed higher than appropriateness and suitability. It is doubtful whether uniformity promotes good Christian living and the growth of faith. A solution to this problem could be the provision of a canonical stipulation that allows the particular Churches to reinterpret certain canon laws to suit the life situation of their faithful[7]. This has the possibility of helping the Church circumvent the risk of putting burdens on certain members or possible members of the Church. An example of such a burden is the feeling of guilt that somebody may have, when he is made to understand that all the partners of a

---

[6] Cf. Emmanuel Orobator, Perspectives and Trends in Contemporary African Ecclesiology, in: Studia Missionalia, Vol. 45, Rome 1996, p. 269.

[7] Jonathan Hildebrandt, who has made an extensive study of the history of the Church in Africa, illustrates this issue aptly in his book *History of the Church in Africa*, Achimota [4]1996, p. 68. He attributes one of the failures of the Portuguese missionaries in Africa to their lack of understanding of the African culture in which they were working. One of the burning issues which still exist today was the problem of monogamy. They demanded their converts to practice this form of marriage without making provision for the “unwanted” wives. It is not only the failure to provide social security for the above-mentioned women but more so no regard was made to address the issue of social stigma, embarrassment and the resulting conflicts between families. In traditional African societies as much as I am aware marriage is between families and not just between two persons. A divorce brings a rift between the affected families and clans, just as marriage brings union and friendship. If one does not pay attention to such an important issue, his work is bound to be a failure. Notwithstanding the hope expressed by the Special Assembly on Africa of the Synod of Bishops, which took place in 1994, that Episcopal Conferences in cooperation with Universities and Catholic Institutes would establish study commissions to look into the matters concerning marriage, the veneration of ancestors and the spirit world, not much has be done in this area. Cf. John Paul II, Post-Synodal Apostolic Exhortation *Ecclesia in Africa* on the Church in Africa and its Evangelisation Mission towards the Year 2000, (14th September 1995), no. 64 (hereafter *Ecclesia in Africa*). See also *L’Osservatore Romano* Weekly Edition, 20th September 1995, p. VII (hereafter OR).

polygamous relationship except the first wife are living in perpetual sin and so cannot be baptized. How can this problem be solved? It is important to remark here that if the Church as a community of believers does not undertake a step to give a solution to the status of such people living in polygamous relationships, the situation could lead to the feeling that there are two classes of children of God: those who are lucky to be baptized and those who are refused the sacrament because of a particular traditional and cultural value. The affected people may even think that God does not love them as they are. Since the Church has the mission of proclaiming God's love and living it, one would expect that such people would also be led to experience the unconditional love of God. A former catechist, who is now a marriage counsellor in a parish in Ashaiman/Ghana once narrated an experience he had on the pastoral field: A couple wanted to have the child baptized, although the marriage was not yet solemnized in the Church. The above-mentioned catechist prepared the couple for the baptism of the child in the mother language of the couple. Some days before the baptism, however, the mother of the child went to see the priest-in-charge. The said pastor told the lady, whose child was to be baptized, that she will go to hell because she had asked him to baptize a child whose parents were not married in the Church. This is a demonstration of pastoral sensitivity. To the best of my knowledge there is also no clear cut canonical stipulation that forbids the baptism of a child, regardless of the "marital status" of the parents. Even if the code of canon law would support the action of the said pastor, it is worth questioning the pastoral orientation of the shepherd and the law itself, especially in the above-mentioned case. This raises the question of the issue of the proclamation of the gospel message and the construction of ecclesial life, which were coloured by culture and tradition of a "dominating" society at a time. It also means that the ecclesial language and image(s) are also those of the Christians, evangelizers or missionaries in a particular era. Are the native believers participating in the Church of the "foreign missionaries" or can they call themselves Church in the real sense of the word? This is the question worth asking when one considers the development of and in the Churches in Africa.

0.1 The Cry of the Church in Africa

From the very beginning of the Church (after the advent of Pentecost) Africans got involved in the leadership of the Church and in the evangelization on the continent. The baptism of the Ethiopian minister through Philip (Acts 8, 24-38) marked the commencement of Christian presence in Africa. Since he was an official in the palace of the queen of the Ethiopians[8], it was seemingly certain that he would have influenced many more people to get converted to the new religion. The second important person is John Mark, who is said to be the one who evangelized Egypt, beginning with the conversion of a cobbler called

[8] In the first century AD the term Ethiopia was not applied to the present day Ethiopia. The general consensus is that he was an official of Nubia. Cf. J. Hildebrandt, History of the Church, [4]1995, p. 6.

Anianus and his household[9]. Before John Mark's martyrdom in the year AD 68, five Churches were established in Egypt and Libya. From this time onwards the Church grew in number despite the Roman persecution. Ecclesial districts or episcopates were erected and the number stood at almost 600 in the year 430, with each bishop being responsible for the affairs of his Episcopal See.

The Church flourished very well but was, however, beset at various stages with external attacks and/or internal rivalries. The Constantine era brought Christians unprecedented freedom, which was not devoid of negative effects in Christendom: state and Church affairs, politics and religion got mixed up. "Thus when church leaders had an argument, instead of seeking God's guidance to settle the matter, they would ask the Emperor to help solve the problem"[10]. It was a time of loose fraternal cohesion caused partly by the new political constellation. Before this period, the brethren came together to fight the common enemy, who persecuted them and they were also vigorous in the proclamation of the word. With the absence of an external antagonist, the brethren got themselves entangled with theological discussions and power-struggle. Splits within the Church and heresies were the mark of the time. Not even the first Council of Nicaea (A.D. 325) and later the Council of Chalcedon (A.D. 451), represented by the national Churches in the world at that time, were able to eradicate the spread of heresy and splits. The end result was that many Church leaders dedicated more time to fighting among themselves than to spreading the gospel message. The scene was thus well prepared for successful external attacks. When the vandals attacked Numidia they accepted Arianism as their religion and expelled the priests of the Christian Churches. The fraternal unity characterised by the breaking of the Word of God and the one bread of life was sacrificed on the "altar" of divisions and power based presumably on theological differences. The Church in North Africa thus became weaker and weaker and experienced its extinction through the Arab Muslim invasion, which started around 643 and ended with the capture of Carthage and Ceuta in 698 and 709 respectively. During the Pontificate of Pope Gregory VII (1073-1085) one could count only three bishoprics in the whole of Africa, which all disappeared entirely around the 13th century.

Renewed attempts to evangelize the continent in the 15th and 16th century, respectively, did not produce lasting results. The Churches founded at this time on the African continent also disappeared. Some of the factors accounting for this lamentable situation were the disinterest of the Portuguese and Spaniards at the time to open up the region to missionaries from other parts of Europe and their failure to create an ecclesial body that considered the culture and context of the people as two important components necessary for a deep-rooted evangelization and Christian life. The consequence of such an attitude was that the efforts to rekindle the Christian faith in Africa did not yield much fruits. The mission was therefore stopped.

---

[9] Cf. Iris Habib Masri, The Story of the Copts, Cairo 1978, p. 14.
[10] J. Hildebrandt, History of the Church, [4]1995, p. 12.

The third evangelization effort took off in the 19th century under the guidance of the Sacred Congregation *de Propaganda Fide*. The practice was that a particular missionary territory was handed over to a mission society or congregation. It is worth anticipating that the structures of the Western Church and the theologies thereof were brought along to the various African countries. The expectation is not far-fetched since even in the political arena most African states were under colonial rule. Apart from the late Cardinal Malula, who expressed his wish for a truly African Church in an independent Africa in 1959, there are no further records of any resistance to the prevailing Church structure and ecclesial self-understanding on the continent. His position was rather an exception than the norm. The other successors of the missionaries judiciously protected the tradition handed over to them in a so-called "prudential obedience to authority" set up through the feudal Church structure of the period before Vatican II. In the year 1969 Paul VI made a statement, namely, that Africans should be their own missionaries. This could be perceived as new wind blowing in the African ecclesial arena. Some African theologians construed the statement to mean that the Church in Africa should be African. A response to this situation which represents the sentiments of many African theologians today is the statement from the Nigerian exegete and Spiritan priest, Elochukwu E. Uzukwu. He writes *inter alia*: "the church in Africa is born old. The midwives awaited the birth and the child itself really had no choice in the matter"[11]. The child (here the Church in Africa) was neither given the opportunity to make a choice nor did its leaders think that they had a choice. What came from Rome was final. One experiences a similar situation prevailing in many seminaries on the continent. The consequence was the inability to establish a Church that paid attention to the culture and context of the affected faithful, a Church that gave the people – the brothers and sisters – the feeling of being at par with their counterparts in other parts of the world, and a Church whose members would dare to want to interpret the signs of the time and live them in the Spirit of the gospel.

It is important to remark that the Christian missionaries of the 19th Century brought an antagonizing Church to Africa. Evangelization was no longer the preserve of the Catholic Church. This time round protestant missionaries also participated in it. Schools and hospitals were built by the different Churches. The confession of an individual also determined to a large extent which school he or she attended and vice versa – families were sometimes torn apart due to this phenomenon.

The hunger for a model which reflects the cultural values and the sentiments of the people and one that promotes unity thus arose naturally in the course of time. The answer to this quest for contextualization was given at the first Special Assembly for Africa of the Synod of Bishops in the year 1994.

---

[11] Elochukwu E. Uzukwu, The Birth and Development of a Local Church. Difficulties and Signs of Hope, in:Africa Faith and Justice Network, The African Synod. Documents, Reflections, Perspectives, Maryknoll – New York 1996, p.3. The article was originally published in Concilium 1992/1, pp. 17-23.

Even though a detailed analysis of the history and content of the above-mentioned Synod will be done later in this study, it is important to mention that the Synod served as propeller for the various Churches on the African continent to re-examine their life as such and to interpret the image of the Church-as-Family of God in their various cultural contexts.

0.2 The Ghanaian Response

The Churches in Ghana took up the proposals of the African Synod 1994 and organized their respective diocesan synods. An intensive study of the documents of four dioceses – Accra Archdiocese (Acts of the Synods published 1997 and 2009), Koforidua Diocese (Acts published 2004), Navrongo-Bolgatanga Diocese (Acts published 2002) and Wa Diocese (Acts of the Synod published 1999) – demonstrates the desire of the local Churches to contextualize the content of *Ecclesia in Africa* to suit their particular situations. It is worth remarking that only the Synod of Koforidua Diocese explicitly took the theme *The Church as Family of God and its Evangelising Mission in the Catholic Diocese of Koforidua*. The three other synods were based on themes particular to their situations, for instance, *Walking together in Christ* – Navrongo-Bolgatanga Diocese, *Renewal of Evangelisation in the Archdiocese of Accra* (1996/1997) and *Renewing the Church and Fulfilling our Vocation and Mission in the Catholic Archdiocese of Accra in Preparation for its 125th Anniversary (2009)* – Accra Archdiocese. There is no title in the Acts of the Wa Diocesan Synod. Issues such as local Church – unity in diversity, marriage and family, youth in the Church, laity in the Church, Justice and peace, social communication and inculturation – specifically liturgy and culture, appeared in almost all the acts published by the four dioceses.

Accra Archdiocese uses the term Church-family[12] to express its self-understanding and the principle of the Small Christian Communities/Basic Christian Communities to achieve the ideals thereof, namely communion,

[12] Charles Gabriel Palmer-Buckle, Acts of the Second Synod of the Catholic Archdiocese of Accra 2009 (Renewing the Church and Fulfilling our Vocation and Mission in the Catholic Archdiocese of Accra in preparation for its 125th Anniversary), Accra 2009, p. 31. The formulation "Church-family of God" illustrates the self-understanding of the Church as a program of action. It is a contextualization of the ecclesial image of the Church in Africa: "Church-as-family" of God, thus making the faithful know what they are, namely a Church-Family. In Chapter Six of the Acts entitled "Pastoral care in the metropolis (Church-Family of God)" we read: "Coming from the wake of the first Special Assembly for Africa of the Synod of Bishops, the first Synod of this Archdiocese adopted the model 'Church-Family of God' from the Post-Synodal Apostolic Exhortation Ecclesia in Africa 63. Even though this model was not mentioned explicitly, the very many references made to this exhortation of Pope John Paul II in the final document 'Challenges and hopes for a new millennium' did imply the desire to build the Church in the Archdiocese as Family of God. A decade after the first Synod of the Archdiocese, and looking at the challenges of pastoral care in the metropolis of Accra and Tema and their environs, it has become imperative to accept and implement the model Church-Family of God as 'the guiding idea for the evangelization of' the Archdiocese of Accra. It will be simply ideal if we could indeed build the Church in the Archdiocese as Church-Family of God".

solidarity and sharing between different ethnic groups and societies. The document praises the work of the laity but shows neither the authority structure nor the type of family that it is dealing with. Is it the extended family or the nuclear family? It is taken for granted that the individual members know what family means to them. In considering the Church structure, no mention is made about how the diocese, parish and the Small Christian Community should be understood, even though each one of them could be perceived as a family in its own right. An attempt is made by the above-mentioned Synod of the Navrongo-Bolgatanga Diocese to portray how one should understand the diocese. According to the Acts of the Synod, the diocese is an extended family[13]. No other structure is been talked about. It could, however, be deduced that the parish is the nuclear family. The document is self-critical and not silent on the complex nature of the diocese, which is said to be made up of many tribes with similarities and dissimilarities. Their diversities are praised but also the dangers of conflict are acknowledged. An important ecclesiological consideration is the depiction of the diocese as "the **Local Family Church** with the Bishop as the father of the family", whose responsibility it is to administer the "rich patrimony judiciously for the benefit of all"[14]. The priests are described as his closest collaborators. This concept is borrowed from the language of Vatican II. It is thus not clear enough, which relational position the priests occupy in the "local Family Church". Are they the fathers of the nuclear family called parish? The document goes further to state that the religious men and women in the diocese have the vocation to live their evangelical perfection of the vows of chastity, poverty and obedience. "The lay faithful have the vocation to live their faith in the midst of the world activities. They are active co-workers in the mission of the Church"[15]. The formulation of the text brings to mind the differentiation that hitherto existed in the Church between clerics and the laity. The latter had the duty of participating in the life of the Church and providing financial resources for the upkeep of the clerics and the poor. They had nothing to do with administration and leadership[16]. The suggested administrative structure of the diocese of Navrongo-Bolgatanga can be seen thus as a tacit institutionalization of hierarchy, which is neither the intention of Vatican II nor that of ***Ecclesia in Africa***. It is not also the spirit of the family structure in Ghana. Fatherhood within the traditional Ghanaian cultural value system is one of service and not of hierarchy or lordship. The father has the role to coordinate life within the family and to ensure that all feel integrated into the network of relations. If the bishop would see himself as the father of the diocese in terms of

---

[13] Cf. Lucas Abadamloora, Acts of the first Synod Navrongo-Bolgatanga Diocese 2002, Navrongo 2002, p. 35.
[14] Ibid., p. 32.
[15] Ibid.
[16] Cf. Hans Bernhard Meyer, Liturgischer Leitungsdienst durch die Laien. Eine liturgiewissenschaftliche Grundlegung, in: Wie weit trägt das gemeinsame Priestertum? Liturgischer Leitungsdienst zwischen Ordination und Beauftragung, edited by Martin Klöckener und Klemens Richter, Freiburg i. Br. 1998, pp. 107-144 and Sabine Demel, Zur Verantwortung berufen. Nagelprobe des Laienapostolats, Freiburg i.Br. 2009, p. 21.

making himself available to all the faithful without discrimination, it would correspond to the spirit of Vatican II and also bring out the sense of fatherliness as a value within the Ghanaian family system. Otherwise there is the danger that some bishops could assume that they are fathers of their dioceses, thereby demanding that all the faithful in their dioceses should do what the bishops say and want. The Church has the Holy Triune God as its foundation. The fatherhood therein belongs only to HIM. All others are brothers and sisters with varied roles and responsibilities. The bishop, therefore, could be seen as a brother who has been entrusted with the responsibility of uniting the family of God with its varied structural elements.

For a better understanding of this research, it is important to clarify the parameters of the terminology. This will be undertaken with the help of the synod documents of two dioceses in Ghana which depict how the *Ecclesia in Africa* is variedly received and interpreted in the different ecclesial contexts. Whereas the Accra Archdiocese understands itself as a **Church-Family**, the Navrongo-Bolgatanga Diocese identifies itself as **Family-Church**. An examination of the second formulation illustrates a certain amount of nuances inherent in the concept Family-Church: it is one of possessiveness and evokes the sense of exclusion and exclusivity, which could be a disservice to the promotion of unity. It implies that the Church is being owned by the particular family and possesses or should possess, as a matter of course, the character thereof. The danger of such a model is its inability to promote "catholic communion" with the universal Church. One "Family-Church" may also want to feel superior to the other, thereby creating deeper drenches among the local Churches rather than building bridges of unity. Another aspect that can be deduced from the concept Family-Church is the desire to model the family as a domestic Church. It is the wish of the entire Church, that Christian families will be places of prayer and lived-faith. A study of the synod document of the Navrongo-Bolgatanga Diocese, however, does not make such a deduction a probable intention. In any case Family-Church as an ecclesiological metaphor of a local Church has untold consequences and does not correspond to the spirit of the African Synod 1994. Within the context of this research, the concept Church-as-family is not to be understood as Family-Church. The Synod of the Accra Archdiocese describes the local Church as Church-family. This concept acknowledges the identity and programme of the Church – it is a family. Further to that it implicitly portrays the goodwill to relate to other families, since no family stands alone in society and is not possessive in its character. The Church as an establishment is presented here as the environment within which life finds its expression.

The analysis made so far leads us to the question, what is the Church in Ghana: a Family-Church or a Church-Family? The question can be answered based on what one wants to achieve with the proposed image of the Church in *Ecclesia in Africa*. The discussions in this research will lead to the conclusion that the most appropriate and contextual self-identity of the Church in Ghana is the "Church-as-family of God". This image contextualizes itself in the form of "Church-Family of God" in the spirit of the early Christian communities.

0.3 Purpose of the Study

At various places in this work the image "Church-Family" is used alternatively with "Faith-Family" or "Church-as-family of God". They carry the same meaning, namely, the "Church-as-family". The study sets out to analysis the significance and implications of making a socio-cultural concept a *locus theologicus*. The central issue at stake is to undertake an examination of the ecclesial image "Church-as-family" in Ghana and its implications. In the discourse ecclesiology negotiates with sociology and anthropology; a theological concept, Church, engages itself in a trade-off with a sociological term in a mutual interpretation of values. Cultural background and contexts become enrichment rather than hindrance to ecclesial life. By so doing contours will be constructed for the Church to navigate into the future.

In all the Acts of the four diocesan Synods discussed above the relationship among the dioceses in Ghana and the corresponding solidarity amongst them is conspicuously missing. All the documents mention (financial) self-reliance. However, there is no discussion on how the parishes as nuclear families help one another in the extended family, such as the diocese. The glaring absence of such a highly praised cultural value in the Ghanaian society is an invitation to scepticism and suspicion. Why are they all silent on it? This study aims at highlighting the *Sitz im Leben* of solidarity within the framework of a contextual ecclesiology.

Since family exists in a particular society at a time and is made up of individual human beings, an analysis will be undertaken of the person in his cultural communal context, his relationship with others and his place in the community – taking the family as his starting point. The person is assumed to be someone who wants to be included and who has the right not to be excluded. How does the understanding of person and personhood in Ghana challenge the Christian view of the human person and vice versa?

Despite the fact that the topic "Church-as-family of God" is as old as the Church, its richness has not been exhausted: it is the beacon of hope for those yearning for solidarity and fraternal unity without reference to race and tribe. The research is undertaken with the proposal that if the Church in Ghana will succeed in any way in its evangelising mission and in the building up of healthy communities, which promote national unity and social transformation, the socio-cultural context of the society becomes a necessary ingredient. History, social institutions and the human being can be observed within the framework of a particular time and situations. The same is true of theology and ecclesiology for that matter: the thought patterns therein are intrinsically connected with eras and circumstances. It is the reason for the premise in this research, namely, that ecclesiology has always been undertaken in context of culture and/or time.

0.4 Methodology and Limitations of the Study

The study has phenomenological, analytical and contextual theological dimensions in its approach to family, religion and Church and is inter-disciplinary in character. Support is thus lent from the fields of sociology, anthropology, exegesis, Church history, canon law and systematic theology, respectively. Of equal importance is an examination of the synod documents of four dioceses in Ghana. The personal experience of the researcher, especially his ability to speak and understand a number of Ghanaian languages backed by his knowledge of the ecclesial life in Ghana are also relied on in expounding the cultural and linguistic nuances associated with certain thought patterns contained in words or sentences in the Ghanaian languages used in this study. An important source of literature has been the interventions and statements of the fathers of the African Synod 1994 as published in the weekly editions of *L'Osservatore Romano*. They present a wider picture of the Church in Africa and the various ways in which the concept "Church-as-family" is understood by the various bishops on the continent. An analysis of the views of the synod Fathers would help to a great extent in the development of the theology of the Church-as-family. The respective Vatican II documents and the relevant encyclicals have been duly quoted. Unless otherwise stated, the biblical quotations are taken from the New Jerusalem Bible, Standard edition.

Limitations cannot be ruled out. There is not much literature available on the subject, probably because it does have the same prominence in the theology in Europe and North America as other models in Vatican II documents. The limited available literature may also be caused by the fact that Church-as-family of God is not the outstanding image of the Church in the documents of Vatican II.

Furthermore, Ghana is a complex society in all aspects of life and the period allocated to a doctoral thesis does not allow for an in-depth study of all the languages and cultures in the country. Some of the dioceses were also created after the first African Synod 1994 and are still mapping out their pastoral and ecclesial structures. Conclusions made are also valid to the extent of their applicability in the various cultures and life situations of the affected ecclesial bodies.

The bishops of Africa observe in their deliberations at the African Synod 1994 that "Africa is a huge Continent where very diverse situations are found". It is, thus, "necessary to avoid generalizations both in evaluating problems and suggesting solutions"[17]. It must be stated here that just as one cannot talk about the African culture and family, it is also difficult to talk about the Ghanaian *Ghanaian culture and family* as such. The country has a heterogeneous cultural landscape. One would thus talk about Ghanaian cultures. The phenomenon poses a problem to the research under consideration. The above analysis notwithstanding, it is possible to make generalisations due to the availability of conceivable common cultural elements in the society.

[17] *Ecclesia in Africa*, no. 40. Cf. also OR, 20th September 1995, V.

The research is also undertaken with the perception of the Church as an organic establishment and not as a hierarchically structured institution. It is not the working out of a mathematical problem by which set of rules are applied. Rather proposals are made that will help the Church in its role as a catalyst of social transformation and in the proclamation of the Word of God in Ghana. This is achieved through living the ideals of the Church-Family which has the potential of supporting national unity and solidarity.

0.5 Outline of the Study

In consonance with the deliberations above and with aim of achieving its set-out goal, the dissertation is divided into seven chapters, which are logically structured to depict their connectivity to one another. Chapter one looks at the family as one important social institution that has enjoyed an enviable place in the life of human kind. In times of social uncertainties it serves as the anchor for intense personal and social relationships. Very few fields of study have been so burdened with political, economic and emotional sensitivity as the family. Its importance can be felt in every sector of society. For instance, the decision to belong to a certain religion, political party or the ability to belong to a certain economic class is influenced in some cases by the family background of the individual(s) concerned. Some people are baptised in and belong to a particular Christian confession because of family tradition. This applies to (general) religious affiliation and ways of life, too. It has also been observed that developments in the family institution (in many cases) are an indicator of the changes in society. At one time, a stable society was seen as originating from stable families and vice versa. The family thus has a symbolic character here and signals in many respects the pulse in the wider society[18].

A report on families to the Church of England illustrates that because families are so fundamental to society they easily become its centre of attention especially any time it (society) is anxious about itself. The report observes trends of the 20th century such as "the increase in female employment in the 1970s, the question of authority and new experience of affluence and freedom in the 1960s, the emergence of a teenage culture in the 1950s, and wartime displacement in the 1940s"[19] which all aroused fears for the future of families. The anxieties are not baseless: a disoriented family life takes its toll on society. In the same way rapid uncontrollable developments in spheres outside the family have the potential of causing instability therein. This again will have an effect on other areas of life. The crux of the matter is that family plays a pivotal role in the social structure of every community, since it serves as life-centre and the starting point of relationships *ad intra* and *ad extra*. It is, therefore, no wonder that family as an institution and as a unit of economic and biological

[18] Robert Hettlage, Familienreport. Eine Lebensform im Umburch, München 1992, p. 14.

[19] General Synod Board for Social Responsibility, Something to Celebrate. Valuing Families in Church and Society, London 1995, p. 1.

reproduction is of great interest to most people. An examination of the interplay between religion and family forms the concluding part of the chapter.

In chapter two a further treatment of family is undertaken with the concentration on the Ghanaian understanding of it, wherein the human person in relation is given special attention. He mirrors family life and dynamism to the outside world – he relates and is related to. In the same way family does not stand in isolation but rather belongs and relates to similar social units in the bigger community called society. The parameters of the family will also be examined: what does it mean when a Ghanaian calls someone brother or sister? Can a non-brother or non-sister later on bear the title? How does that take place? Family is characterised by growth. It is thus worthwhile considering the place of new-members and strangers in the family in the various Ghanaian societies and the nature of authority structure therein.

To be able to appreciate the Christian conception of the Church as family, it is important to trace its biblical and historical origins. Chapter three thus concentrates first of all on the analysis of Israel as family of God. The use of kin terminologies in the Hebrew Scriptures will also be undertaken. This forms the bedrock for understanding Jesus' view of his community of followers as family. Jesus lived with them in such a constellation. It is the reason why it would not be wrong to say that the concept Church-Family finds its roots in the teaching of Jesus himself and is to be conceived as one of the basic self-understanding of ecclesia. An examination of the Pauline communities shows that the members therein did not only see themselves within their particular community as brothers and sisters but rather crosses their territorial boundaries to treat those of other Christian communities as members of the one family of God, the Father. There is no conceptual disputation in Scripture over the term brother or sister. Fraternal solidarity and love were the hallmark and identity of the early Christian communities. A kin terminology that did not, however, find usage was mother. This situation found change in the life of the Christians in North Africa, where motherhood was attributed to the Church as a body, first of all by Tertullian and then later on by Cyprian. The latter somewhat subjugated the fatherhood of God to the motherhood of the Church by saying that no one can call God father if he does not have the Church as mother. Belonging to the mother Church then became the criteria for appropriate fraternal gesture. Only those who were baptised in the Catholic Church also received the needed help from Cyprian. He complicated the relation by referring to non-Catholic Christians as children of the step-mother in his latter works. One could term this scenario as a negative revolution for the Christian fraternity as a whole.

After over 2000 years of its existence the Church can be perceived as having gone through various stages of development. Over the years it has offered images for its self-understanding. None of these images was without nuances. These nuances should, however, not be seen as reasons to throw a model or the models overboard. Rather they should serve as challenges which can help sharpen the model(s). An examination of the most essential models presented in the Vatican II is undertaken in Chapter Four. The section is concluded by looking at communion and its relation to hierarchy. A good mix of the two concepts greases the dynamic relations between the members in the Church and between the communities.

The element of Church-as-Family as contextual ecclesiological model is analyzed in chapter five. The Church has experienced different theologies at the various stages in history. The different theologies can be described generally to be contextual in nature. It can thus be said that no theology is undertaken in a vacuum. It always has a point of reference. This could be in respect of an era or epoch, in respect of a cultural setting, a thought pattern or a socio-political issue. The study investigates this phenomenon through the response of the local Church of Burkina Faso. An examination of contextual ecclesiology in the contemporary time cannot ignore the place of Vatican II and the self-identity the Church has set-out for itself. The analysis of the rich ecclesial images presented in the Dogmatic Constitution of the Church *Lumen Gentium* illustrates, on the one hand, the inexhaustible beauty associated with the various models. On the other hand, the analysis demonstrates that even though the self-understanding of the Church as "the People of God" has received general acceptance in the universal Church, certain local Churches still hungered for an ecclesial image particular to their situation and context. An example is the Church in Africa which proposed the ecclesial model of "Church-as-family" of God to be the way it understands its life and mission on the African continent. The official "rebirth" of this model took place in 1994 at the Special Assembly for Africa of the Synod of Bishops. The historical development of the Synod and the model in Africa and by Africans are examined, paying attention to the different thoughts presented by the Fathers of the Synod. A cry for change implies a certain amount of discontent with the existing state of affairs. It is the same with the various evangelization methods such as adaptation, accommodation, indigenisation which were used in the past in the Churches in Africa. These methods together with their inappropriateness for evangelization are analyzed in this chapter. The alternatives to the above mentioned evangelization models are also discussed, namely, incarnation and inculturation. Especially the last concept is the one that gave birth to the self-image of the Church in Africa – Church-as-Family of God. It must be stated that whereas inculturation is the way the Church in Africa can live out its self-identity, the theology or ecclesiology in question falls under the rubric of contextual ecclesiology – the latter entails also the former.

Chapter six considers the theology of Church-as-family of God. It borrows elements from Vatican II, Post-Vatican II ecclesial documents and the cultural values of the family in Ghana. The first important element is the place of God in the model under consideration. He is considered in the traditional Ghanaian society as the giver of life and the natural head of the community. There is only one God and above him is no other. He is also the ultimate recipient of the libation and offerings of the family, clan or village. The individuals, however, do not have personal relationship with him. Ancestors bring the offerings of the worshiping community to God. The Christians on their part believe in three persons in one God. They can and do have a personal relationship with him. He is also the head of the Church. This thought is the foundation of the image of the Church-as-family of God. The relationship between the three persons in one God serves as an example for communion in the Church. As community of believers the faithful stand in a particular position to one other and participate variously to building up the Church. Also of great importance is the element of dialogue. There can be no good communion without communication among the members. Since every human community has relationship with others of its kind, the nature of such a relationship is worth investigating. In many theological discussions emphasis is placed mostly on ecumenical and inter-religious dialogues, respectively. Equally important, however, is intra-ecclesial dialogue, that is, the dialogue within the local and/or universal Church itself. The amount of dialogue among the parishes and dioceses in the Church in Ghana will serve as living witness to the Gospel message of unity in the Lord. It will also enhance the common identity of the communities.

The last chapter of the study falls under the general term "Epilogue" – a way into the future. It undertakes an examination of the salient elements in the study that could serve as bedrock for the life of the Church-family of God in Ghana. It is in this chapter that the discourse takes place between the socio-cultural unit called family and the religious institution called Church. The similarities and dissimilarities of the two concepts are undertaken with the aim of highlighting the challenges that the understanding of family in Ghana can pose to the Church that takes the former as a model for its being. An important question here is, what is the place of Jesus in the Church-as-family and how does the Christological view here correspond to the generally accepted perception of the role of Jesus in the Church as mediator, redeemer/savior, Lord? Not of less importance is the element of membership in the Church, which is associated with baptism. Who may belong to the Church-as-family? How does the understanding of family in Ghana help the Christians understand the place of the saints, the baptized and the catechumens in the life of the Church? The thorniest issue is the case of polygamous couples in the Church. The examination of this issue has the purpose of awakening the interest of the Church to the plight of people living in such situations. It is also aimed at making the Church in Ghana re-examine the wrong image of God that it probably unwillingly and/or unconsciousness transmits to some of its members and non-members alike. Since the Church and the family in Ghana both stand for the love of life, it is imperative on the Church to ensure that all those who come seeking God, the giver of life, will be received with love and fed with the Word of God and Bread of life. They need to experience that God does not discriminate against anybody. He loves all his sons and daughters. His desire is that all will live under his guidance and headship. Their duty is to honour him and love one another as he loves them. The study ends with a brief summary of the issues already discussed, by repeating some of the ideas that bring out the appropriateness of the concept “Church-as-family” as the most appropriate contextual ecclesiological model for the Church in Ghana today.

CHAPTER ONE

THE FAMILY IN SOCIETY: SOCIO-ANTHROPOLOGICAL ANALYSIS

1.0 Introduction

When confronted with the market place question as to whether the interviewees have families or not, most people may give "yes" for an answer. The face value of this answer can, however, be very deceptive. Each person gives the answer with a set of categories known to him or her alone. For instance, a religious missionary sees his/her religious congregation as a family although he/she may also have parents and/or siblings, who are his family too. Other people would give yes for an answer to this question but with categories in mind, which may not meet the expectations of the questioners. In reporting his experience with this question, Halvor Moxnes[20] narrates that he usually gives the answer "yes", implying that his parents are still alive, he has two brothers and a sister, who also have children etc. In his view, the questioners are not usually interested to hear about his family of origin, in which he grew up but rather, they want to know whether he has a "family of procreation" - whether he is married with children[21]. The story above hints to the existence of hidden meanings appropriated to the word "family". Whereas the general notion may be that of family of procreation – conjugality and consanguinity – it may also be understood as family of orientation thereby depicting the relational element in the concept. In other words, different emotional elements also influence our conceptualization of what family is: the intensity depends, however, on the individual in question and in some cases on his cultural background.

In short, experience shows that most human beings are born into a family and most of them either want to build or they actually have their own families[22], others live in family-like structures. It is regarded in this sense as a cultural universal phenomenon based on the assumption that every "culture of any society will contain a general normative expectation that all adults who are mentally and physically capable of doing so should marry and should have children"[23]. Life is not based on assumptions but on reality. Therefore, it is

---

[20] Halvor Moxnes is Professor of New Testament at the University of Oslo, Norway, and is author of many studies of social relations in early Christianity.

[21]Halvor Moxnes knows from experience that there are different types of families. He does not want to pin himself to one answer. He says that his answer to the question whether he is married and has children is "no, and that would appear to end the conversation". Halvor Moxnes, What is Family? Problems in Constructing Early Christian Families, in: Halvor Moxnes (ed.), Constructing Early Christian Families. Family as Social Reality and Metaphor, London and New York 1997, p. 13. This situation portrays the problematic that confronts us when considering what a family is: there are a variety of ways emanating from this question. The categories associated with it are as many as various groups that consider themselves as family.

[22] Cf. Robert Hettlage, Familienreport, 1992, p. 16.

[23] David Cheal, The One and the Many, 1999, p. 61. See also Sarah B. Taubin and Emily H. Mudd, Contemporary Traditional Families: The Undefined Majority, in: Eleanor D. Macklin and

important to consider the fact that some religious practices may make it impossible for young and able persons to marry. Further to that, more and more people in contemporary times choose single life as a form of living. Notwithstanding these components of abstinence and/or asceticism in religious practices and single life, which cause that some members in the society do not have their own families of procreation, most people if not all, have their own understanding of what they consider family. Added to that, the concept itself has maintained its universal character through its community dimension, its relationship to other social institutions and its historical component. Also important in the concept of family is that it goes through changes[24] without losing its basic structural elements: family still functions as a unit of production, generative reproduction and consumption. For this reason, it is better to consider family as a lived reality rather than just as a cultural universal phenomenon. This view pays the needed attention that should be given to the developments in modern social theory and to the reality of modernization.

From the analysis above and added to the fact that the family institution is of great interest to politics, economics, social and religious life, it would be expected that the concept could be defined easily[25]. This is surprisingly not the case. Experts in this field of study have been in search of a consensus as to what family really is. Jan Trost in his conclusion of a research he undertook on this topic posits that "evidently no one 'knows' what a family is; our perspectives vary to such a degree that to claim to know what a family is shows a lack of knowledge"[26]. Trost makes a difference between family as a term and family as a concept. Drawing from his findings he says that "apparently, what is familiar is the term only, certainly not the concept"[27]. The lack of consensus in the definition of family is sharply formulated by Barbara H. Settles. She claims that "it is not likely that the job of specifying what is meant family will progress rapidly. Consensus would be [...] improbable by scholars"[28]. Some scholars on family do not only doubt the amount of knowledge on what family is, but go further to ask whether such a thing called family really exists[29]. These questions arise as a result of the divergence of views on the part of the professionals engaged in the study of family and the different categories that lay people provide when they talk about family. Furthermore, the questions are reflective in nature: to the lay person they are rhetorical questions that do not need to be

---

Roger A. Rubin (eds), Contemporary Families and Alternative Lifestyles, Beverly Hills 1983, pp. 256-68.

[24] Cf. Friedrich Bechina, Die Kirche als „Familie Gottes". Die Stellung dieses theologischen Konzeptes im Zweiten Vatikanischen Konzil und in den Bischofssynoden von 1974 bis 1994 im Hinblick auf eine „Familia-Die-Ekklesiologie", Rome 1997, pp. 462ff.

[25] Cf. R. Hettlage, Familienreport, 1992, p. 17.

[26] Jan Trost, Do We Mean the Same by the Concept of Family?, in: Communications Research, (1990), 17/4, p.
442.

[27] Ibid., p. 431.

[28] Barbara H. Settles, A Perspective on Tomorrow's Family, in: Marvin B. Sussman and Suzanne K. Steinmetz (eds.), Handbook of Marriage and the Family, New York 1987, p. 161.

[29] Cf. D. Cheal, The one and the Many, 1999, p. 61.

answered – "everybody knows what family is". To the professional, the questions serve to spur him to delve deeper into the phenomenon. Katja Boh, who has written extensively on the family in European societies, demonstrates that even though there is no indication in the analysis of those who undertook the study "the evolution of family life patterns in European societies would follow a certain pattern to become the model for family modernization in Europe"[30]. In her view, a variety of family patterns are lived by people based on their respective needs and living conditions. Despite these diverse family patterns in Europe and despite the different living conditions and social forces that impact upon the respective European countries, however, "there is at least one uniform trend in the overall development of family patterns, and this is the trend towards recognition of diversity" [31]. She describes the family life pattern in Europe as convergence to diversity. The conclusion to be drawn from the analysis above is that that there are many appropriate definitions of family with social and cultural variations. A desire to win a holistic view of the concept demands its examination as perceived by the various players and stakeholders. Such a methodology enables a crystallization of common features, thereby allowing for a certain amount of generalization.

In this chapter, the etymology of the family and the associated nuances in it will be examined. This paves the way for an analysis of the concept as a relational category or as a lived reality. One of the important functions of family as a unit is that relationships are created. As a relational phenomenon, however, it allows the various members in the society to choose whom they want to be related to emotionally as a family member – family of orientation is considered here. The relational category is important so that the element of surrogate or fictive family can be appreciated as a form of family, which will be treated under section 1.1.5. A socio-anthropological analysis of the family with its function as engine of society ensues. This leads to a further conceptual examination of the social unit as one determined by biological ties or one that allows residence and other factors, which determine its boundaries, such as the case of the extended family.

As a social institution the family also goes through changes as a result of transformation and modifications in the other areas of life in society. The family is part of a social complex and its relation to the large system is important, even though one does not underrate its existence as an independent social institution. It is observable that change in the vocabulary of people in society also affects the life style in families. For instance instead of using the word "spouse" people now opt for "partner"; "adultery" has been replaced by "affair"; a person no longer "lives in sin" but rather "cohabits"[32]. Since

[30] Katja Boh, European Family life Patterns – a Reappraisal, in: Katja Boh et al. (eds), Changing Patterns of European Family Life: A Comparative Analysis of 14 European Countries, London 1989, p. 295.

[31] Ibid., p. 296.

[32] Graham Allan, Introduction, in: Graham Allan (ed), The Sociology of Family. A Reader, Oxford 1999, p. 4.

language is indicative of the attitude of people, it shows that the changes in society hint to non-static family life. The question is whether the family as an institution changes or it only goes through phases of adaptation? Do the changes and/or adaptations within the family institution reversely affect the life in the wider society? Is it possible to find common features within the unit which make it to be called a lived-reality in all cultures?

The main aim of this research is to map out the challenges that the concept family poses to the particular Church in Ghana when the former is used as a model for the life of the latter. Chapter one is concluded by looking at the term religion and the role it plays in the life of the family. Most religious activities, including the Christian religious activities, are of a corporate nature, where group identity as well as the sense of belonging is created by participation. These dynamics may be better understood if they are traced back to their very origin, namely family, where community life and solidarity set a pace for life, especially in societies where kinship ties are strong.

1.1 Clarification of the Term Family

Since family has a long standing in the history of humankind and is experienced every day, the average person expects to find words in every culture that clearly define it. A thorough examination of many non-western languages as well as ancient western ones such as Greek and Latin reveals, however, the unavailability of a single word that carries with it the meaning that connotes the present Western European and North American understanding of family: that is, husband, wife and one or two children or what is called the nuclear family. In Greek literature the word *oikonomia* is found, which connotes the management of households (or economics). Economics and house were thus put under one umbrella called O*ikos*. This term was thus used to mean two different things: it implied in respect of property to imply the material possessions of the head of the household. Other writers, like Aristotle, employed it to include all the members of the household under the authority of one headship, which included husband, wife, children, and other blood relatives, not forgetting slaves and servants.

A similar situation applies to Latin. Two terms *familia* and *domus* which are used to refer to family do not convey this strict connotation. As was the case with *oikos* in Greek, *familia* was used on the one hand to indicate things and possessions. On the other hand, it was applied to persons and meant all those who were under the authority of the *pater familias*, namely, "wife and children as well as slaves, and also all agnates (related through male blood from the same house), or all those related through males to a common ancestor"[33]. *Domus* on its part implied household and comprises of husband, wife, children, slaves and others living in the house. The meaning of the term could even be extended to imply a descent group, which is not restricted to the descendants through the males only but included also those through the females. There are

[33] H. Moxnes, What is Family?, 1997, pp. 20f.

still societies, cultures and languages in our times which present situations similar to that of Greek and Latin. That is to say that they do not have a single word that indicates a "family" of parents and their children. Ruth Westheimer reports of a native group in southern Mexico which has the "house" as the key social unit[34] and does not have a word for our concept "family" – as primary descent group. Further examples to this will be offered in chapter two of this study. Considering the difficulties involved in finding a generally accepted terminology that means the same thing in all languages and cultures, the study will examine some of the ways of perceiving the social category or unit called family.

1.1.1 Family as a Relational Category

Nobody can say for sure when exactly family started in human life. However, it is not an exaggeration to assume that some form of family organisation must have always existed among peoples and in history. The observation of human life, for instance, indicates the helplessness of the human infant at birth which demands the creation of an essential condition of life, namely a family unit, permanent enough at least for both the bearing and the "rearing" of children[35]. The family in this sense would be understood basically as an organised network of socio-economic and reproductive interdependence and support, grounded in biological and kinship ties and marriage. As the basic unit in the organisation of society family is composed of persons closely related by marriage or blood and principally but not compulsorily sharing common residence[36]. Each member of this smallest community of society plays his or her respective role for the sustainability of life in all its forms. In respect of the above-mentioned point, family may be defined as a "small kinship structured group with the key function of nurturant socialisation"[37]. To fend for the children is usually the first level of interaction between parents and children, and nurturant socialisation encompasses all that the youngsters need – love and warmth, food, shelter and the necessary training to adulthood etc. In short, family comprises all that children need from their parents for proper socialisation and growth. The children on their part give the parents the feeling of fulfilment that they have passed on life to them through procreation. Older siblings also take care of the younger ones by protecting them from harm till they are grown enough to take

---

[34] Cf. Ruth Westheimer and Ben Yagoda, The Value of Family. A Blueprint for the 21st Century, New York 1996, p. 12.

[35] Cf. Gerald R. Leslie, Family, in: Edward Humphrey et al (eds.) The American Peoples' Encyclopedia. A Modern Reference Work, New York 1970, p. 437.

[36] James Dahir, Family, in: William D. Halsey and Louis Shores (eds.), Collier's Encyclopedia, [9]1969, p. 545.

[37] Ira L. Reiss, Family System in America, New York 1971, p. 17. Ruth Westheimer stresses the need for every species – human and animal – to have a certain form of nurturing its young ones during the period prior to their being able to fend for themselves. She observes, however, that "what separates human beings from animals is that we go beyond procreation and minimal care and construct families into intricate, clearly defined, and powerful social organizations". R. Westheimer and B. Yagoda, The Value of Family, 1996, p. 12.

care of themselves. These roles are determined in the given structures of the kin group called family. Unity and harmony among the siblings could even fall under the rubric of nurturant socialisation.

The interactions between the siblings, that is, brother-sister relation and those between parents and children, namely, mother-child or father-child relations, are biological ties of common descent. The husband and wife, who are joined together through marriage, relate to each other in a social bond with a conjugal character. These arrangements and ties existing within a social setting called family lead to the thesis that life begins and ends as *relatio*[38], which finds its beginning in the smallest cell of society.

The intensity of these relationships among the various members of the family may differ from one cultural setting to the other and may also depend on the family unit in question. In a modern western society the relationship between husband and wife is more often than not taken for granted as "the most important social and familial relationship"[39]. This is, however, not the case with all societies, both present and historical. In ancient Greece, for instance, it was observable that friendships of a man were placed higher than his relationship with his wife. Similarly, the relationships within the family structure itself were weighed differently. Prominent among them was the father-son relation, which dominated the dynamics in many kinship groups. This might have been caused by the right of the son to inherit the father's property as well as the role and authority that he takes on upon his father's death. As long as the father lives, the son remains son and "this relationship takes precedence over his relationship with his wife"[40]. The mother is important. Her relationship with the son, however, has the character of emotional affinity and support from the son. The relationship among the siblings is supposed to be one of mutual love, solidarity, unity and harmony[41]. In some cultures, however, an imbalance is perceivable in such a relational constellation. The relationship between brothers outweighs that between brothers and sisters. It is not uncommon to observe that the relationship with the wife comes second to that between brothers.

Ernest W. Burgess described "the 20th-century family as a dynamic interactional system"[42]. The family identity is formed out of the individual interacting personalities. In his view

---

[38] Cf. Karin Barber, Anthropology of Texts, Persons and Publics. Oral and Written Cultures in Africa and Beyond. Cambridge 2007, p. 104. She argues that "anthropologies have criticised the idea of the autonomous, atomistic individual defined in contradistinction to society (as in 'the relations between the individual and society'), and have shown that other cultures' models often turn out to be relational rather than atomistic. Rather than starting from a unit – the individual – and building up from this towards a structured aggregate – society – indigenous theories often start and end with a relationship, often of mutual dependence". The person in this theory is seen to be part of other people and stands in relation to them.

[39] H. Moxnes, What is Family?, 1997, p. 31.

[40] Ibid., p. 35.

[41] Cf. ibid., p. 31-34.

[42] See Alexandra Loukas et al., The Family as a Unity of Interacting Personalities, in: Luciano L'abate (ed.), Family Pschopathology. The Relational Roots of Dysfunctional Behavior, New York 1998, p. 35.

> the actual unity of family life has its existence not in any legal conception, not in any formal contract, but in the interaction of its members. For the family does not depend for its survival on the harmonious relations of its members, nor does it necessarily disintegrate as a result of conflicts between its members. The family lives as long as interaction is taking place and dies only when it ceases[43].

Against the backdrop of dwindling family sizes and the changing roles of family members[44] of the 20th century, a dynamic interactional system shows that every human being has a starting point called family which enables his or her communal life. It consists of a man, a woman and their children who stand in emotional and social relation to one another. There is a giving birth of children, through which the offspring receives its blood relation to the parents and a biological descent. The children on their part find their relation to each other through the mother, but there is someone called the father. Between the parents there is a relationship based on social bond. This leads us to the categorisation of family relations under two headings: biological and social[45] or biological family and family of orientation. Whereas the former is a given fact, the individual may choose the latter. The amount of interaction or the intensity of the relationship between the individual members of a family unit varies from person to person and from one situation to the other. This underscores the fact that the dynamic interactions of the family members give birth to what is known as family identity.

1.1.2 Family: Conjugal unit with Children

The family is commonly observed as a community, its size varying from one unit to the other. It may thus be seen in general terms as "the biological, economic and spiritual life community of the married couple and the children"[46]. The emphasis here lies in three factors, namely, generative reproduction, production and religiosity – which are performed within a unit comprised of a married couple and their children. The primary group of husband, wife, and children may exist alone[47] or as part of a larger group which may span several generations. To this end, the family could be seen as a primary socio-biological group, which is created through the coming together of

---

[43] See Ernest W. Burgess, The Family as a Unity of Interacting Personalities, in: The Family (1926), 7: p. 6f.

[44] Ibid., p. 8.

[45] Cf. Gerald R. Leslie, Family, in: Edward Humphrey et al. (eds.), The American Peoples Encyclopedia. A Modern Reference Work, New York 1970, p. 437. Cf. also H. Moxnes, What is family?, p. 33.

[46] R. Hettlage, Familienreport, 1992, p. 20. The definition here is a free translation undertaken by the researcher.

[47] The Oxford Advanced Learner's Dictionary provides five definitions of family, four of which relate to human beings. The first definition confines the membership of family to be made up of "one or two parents and their children". It is a definition that pays attention to a situation of contemporary times. So it avoids the use of the word married couple.

the couple and the giving birth of children. The following is provided in *A Dictionary of the Social Sciences*, namely that

> the human family may be defined as an institutionalized bio-social group made up of adults (at least two of which, unrelated by blood and of the opposite sex, are married), and children, the offspring of the maritally related adults; the minimal functions of which are the providing of satisfactions and control of affectional needs, including sexual relations, and the provision of a sociocultural situation for the procreation, care, and socialization of offspring[48].

The definition above clearly sees the family as comprising a married couple, that is, a man and a woman and their children. Scholars like Giddens soften the strings on marriage and go on to define family as two adults living together in a household with their children. The difficulties with both definitions are that the first one recognises only married couples and their children as a family, which would, however, go to discriminate against partners, who are not yet legally married but have children. It also excludes single parents with their children as being capable of building a family. Consequently, Robert Hettlage argues that in speaking about family, one should bear in mind what type of family one is talking about[49]. Hettlage is surely not only talking about a nuclear or an extended family, but rather he is also paying attention to other forms of family. The second definition – two adults living together in a household with their children – may have acceptance in the Western society because of its open-ended and neutral character. It may be rejected in societies where family formation takes place within a marital setting, even though its existence as a lived reality is tolerated. This is testified by the increasing number of lone or single-parent households. In Britain just as in many other Western countries, for instance, this phenomenon has experienced ascendancy: single-parent households grew from under 600,000 in 1971 to 1.4 million by 1992. From these figures it is estimated that 20% of dependent children are living in such households[50]. Due to the increased rate of divorce there are more and more second marriages and more and more step-families. A child in such a situation will thus have to decide what its family is: mother, biological father and children or mother, step-father and children or both forms. Although marriage is perceived in most societies as the most basic form of building a family and as a contractual manner of uniting kin groups, through which social and economic relations are managed, modern trends show other forms of cohabitation which also enable the creation of family without marriage contracts. Since there is no illegal human being, everybody has the right to call his socio-biological unit a family. The unanswered question is what role kinship plays in the definition of family considered so far.

---

[48] Quoted in: R. Westheimer and B. Yagoda, The Value of Family, 1996, p. 11.
[49] Cf. R. Hettlage, Familienreport, 1992, p. 21.
[50] Cf. G. Allan, Introduction, 1998, p. 4.

Kinship denotes affiliation through reproductive lines. This definition is in virtually all cultures and signifies the value of the body and of essential material needs when dealing with the functions of the family. Elizabeth Ardayfio-Schandorf, who has among other things done research in the field of gender, family and development, stresses kinship as an important element in the concept of family. She perceives it as an important determining factor in the organisation of life among the members of the society especially in the political and economic spheres, the division of labour and in social stratification[51]. The ties between the kin members are made possible through the spouses who build the conjugal unit. In this case family can be seen as a spousal unit with kinship ties - conjugal or nuclear family.

Family is the smallest cell in society in which "all the warmth of those social relations that would otherwise have embraced a wide range of kinfolk, neighbours and friends is now seen as being focussed more narrowly and more intensely on the [...] close relatives"[52]. With the nuclear family there seems to be more flexibility, and economic decisions can be made without undue external pressure. In this sense the family enjoys an unprecedented air of freedom and autonomy.

1.1.3 The Extended Family System

The analysis made above betrays the thought that there is another system of family which differs from the nuclear or conjugal family. The situation depicts the existence of a family system which stretches its tentacles beyond the fringes of the unit in question and introduces "the sense of being connected in a strong and irreplaceable way to past and future generations, to ancestors and descendants"[53]. Karl Olav Sandnes writes in his book, *The New Family. Conversion and Ecclesiology in the Early Church with Cross-Cultural Comparisons*, *inter alia* that the understanding of family by Cicero in the Hellenistic era considered bonds at various levels. Cicero talked about the first bond of union as being the one between husband and wife; the next level is that between parents and children; between siblings; and "we find one home (*una domus*), with everything in common (*communia omnia*)"[54]. The first two bonds of relationship correspond to the knowledge gained so far about the nuclear family. The addition of *una domus* and *communia omnia* opens a new chapter for discussion. How is the membership in this *una domus* constituted and what is the relational dynamic among the individuals therein? Cicero went on to explain that, "the bonds of common blood hold men [and women] fast through goodwill and affection; for it means much to share in common the same family traditions, the same forms of domestic worship, and the same ancestral

[51] Cf. Elisabeth Ardayfio-Schandorf, (ed.), Family and Development in Ghana, Accra 1994, p. 1.
[52] Martine Segalen, Historical Anthropology of the Family, Cambridge 1986, p. 2.
[53] R. Westheimer and B. Yagoda, The Value of Family, 1996, p. 12.
[54] Cicero is quoted in K.O. Sandnes, A New Family, 1994, p. 47.

tombs"[55]. The sharing in common is part of expressing their relatedness to each other. The text is a demonstration of the nature of an urban family especially at the time of Cicero. The consideration of the bond of union in Cicero's text, namely that between relatives and cousins, is a hint to the existence of a family form which seems wider than the nuclear one. Since members of a kin group in ancient times worshiped and shared their life together either in the same or different households – through the provision of social support and obligations - the prevalence of the extended family can be deduced from the text above[56]. Of paramount importance in such a setup was the feeling of being related to each other.

Although the extended family may generally be defined as "a combination of primary nuclear-family units with other relations"[57], there are different types of it. We have the *three-generation family*, the *kinship family* and the *polygamous family* respectively. In the three-generation family system grand-parents, parents and children live together. The kinship family consists basically of larger units than the three-generation family and includes other relatives belonging to the same household, who are regarded as members of the family. The last form is the polygamous family, where a spouse lives with two or more partners and their children. In most cases it is a man living with more than one wife. It is also possible that the man lives with the most recent wife, with the other wife or wives living somewhere else with their children[58]. The practice of one man marrying more than one wife is called polygyny and its product is composite kinship forms, whereby two or more otherwise nuclear families are connected together through the common parent, in this case the father. The same is true when one woman lives with more than one husband. That is called polyandry. In a polygamous family, one has a lot of half-brothers and half-sisters.

Due to the fact that the individual members of the extended family owe a certain amount of responsibility towards their "relatives", some people see it as an unwanted system. It is, however, a disservice to the family institution and to the society at large to disregard the extended component of the family or to see it as a matter of the oblivion. This is because the family is not only a house community and an economic unit but also provides the grounds for the nurturing of relationships. The extended family is also a fertile soil to live out such bonds or relationships.

An important element within the extended family system is the ability to delineate its boundaries. This is especially the case when one goes beyond the generational boundaries and begins to consider all those who relate to the individual in question either through the mother or father and those who also

---

[55] Ibid.

[56] Cf. ibid., p. 48.

[57] Cf. Oluwole Adegboyega, James P. M. Ntozi and John B. Ssekamate-Sebuliba, The African Family: Data, Concepts and Methodology, in: Aderanti Adepoju (ed.), Family, Population and Development in Africa, London 1997, p. 30.

[58] Cf. ibid.

relate to these other relatives. It is not uncommon sometimes to be addressed as brother or sister even though the person does not know at which level he is related[59] to the other. The positive side of it is that members experience a greater amount of solidarity, especially in times of difficulties. In this way the individual person experiences that family is wider than he can perceive it. This can influence the way the members in society open up to encounter other people in their daily lives. The individual is a member of a nuclear family, which is a unit of the extended family system. This in turn is part of a wider economic and social formation.

1.1.4 Common Residence and Family Membership

The family has been observed up till now to be composed basically of persons related to one another either through marriage or birth/adoption or at least they are persons with the same family traditions and ancestral tombs. In the light of the above argument, the family could be described also as a tremendously variable social organism with differences in size, authority patterns, modes of determining residence and descent, and of the number and types of functions that it performs[60].

What has not yet been considered in detail is the relationship between "shared residence" – household or cohabitation – and family. A household depicts "a unit of people, consisting of two or more persons – related or not related by blood – usually living under one roof and/or making common provision for food and other living arrangements"[61]. It can be expressed in simple words as a domestic group and an economic unit. This is because living together and mutual economic interdependence are part and parcel of belonging to a household.

The concept is precisely defined as far as location is concerned. However, when the occupants are too many, some members may break up to re-form other households, thus giving it a variation. There can also be seasonal reorganisation due to economic activities as the case may be in some communities.

In comparing family with household, it is observable that even though the former is also an economic unit, does not necessarily refer "to persons occupying a particular dwelling"[62]. It is role play rather than placement that determines what a family is and who belongs to it. Children may move to form their own households, and in some societies deceased members of the family

[59] This issue will be encountered many times in this study, since it is also a central theme in Ghana when dealing with matters pertaining to family and social development.
[60] Cf. G. R. Leslie, Family, 1970, p. 437.
[61] O. Adegboyega, J. P. M. Ntozi and J. B. Ssekammate-Sebuliba, The African Family, 1997, p. 28.
[62] G. K. Nukunya, Tradition and Change in Ghana. An Introduction to Sociology, Accra, 1992, p. 47.

are still considered as belonging to the family[63]. What remains is the fact that roles are unchanged. Parents and children still maintain their relational status even when one or the other family member moves to form his or her own household.

Furthermore, the members of a household may include other persons such as workers, visitors and friends. These might have attained the title of family members or not. If the former is the case, then there is a situation similar to that of ancient times, in which family meant more than closer relatives and distant kin. The meaning derived from *oikos, oikia, domus* and *familia* contains the element of friendship. These terms, among other meanings, connote those living under the same roof as well as those united by the bonds of blood or even friendships[64]. In the opinion of Aristotle and Strabo[65], friendship means living, eating and drinking together. A friend or worker may be termed as a member of a household but not necessarily of the family, if he or she shares common residence and eating arrangements with those members who share kin or conjugal ties. When the relational bond allows, a good worker or a sympathetic friend could be seen as a brother. Even in some societies people coming from the same homestead (village or town) may also be attributed with kin terms or be called family members especially when the respective persons live outside of their place of origin[66]. Therefore, whereas family has its basis in kin ties and relation, household is spatial in character. Other members in a household may be incorporated into a family, thereby causing an increment. The occupants of a household may reduce due to resettlement. This must not necessarily affect the bond of relationship within the kin group or the number therein.

1.1.5 The Surrogate Family

It is striking to observe that beyond the boundaries of family and household family-like structures emerged in the course of history. In his investigation of the ancient Church as family, Joseph H. Hellerman put the concept under the umbrella of "voluntary associations"[67] comprising political parties, brotherhoods and other associations, which in ancient times played a compensatory role by providing "fictive families for those uprooted from clan or family and fictive polities for those excluded from political power"[68]. The issue at stake is the so-called surrogate family, which, per the definition above, serves as fictive family for those alienated from their clans or families and as fictive polities for those who were dislocated from their respective towns and cities. The surrogate family's is a social group and the members are neither

[63] This point will be looked at again in chapter two of this work when reflecting on the understanding of family in Ghana.
[64] Cf. K. O. Sandnes, A New Family, 1994, p. 48.
[65] Cf. ibid., p. 49.
[66] O. Adegboyega, J. P. M. Ntozi and J. B. Ssekamate-Sebuliba, The African Family, 1997, p. 3f.
[67] Joseph H. Hellermann, The Ancient Church as Family, Minneapolis 2001, p. 4.
[68] Stephen G. Wilson, Voluntary Associations: An Overview, in: John S. Kloppenborg and Stephen G. Wilson, (eds.), Voluntary Associations, London 1996, p. 13.

related by birth nor by marriage. They, however, use family terminologies to describe their relationship to one another. The group members expect reciprocal family-like behaviour in their interactions[69]. This caters for social and relational stability in their lives, especially of those who are away from their towns and cities of birth. Stephen G. Wilson associates this phenomenon with the natural desire of the human person to socialise with others of his like in "devotion to a deity, a trade or skill, a similar background, or even just a love of eating and drinking in a group company"[70]. He categorises this desire as basic and instinctive, which should not be underestimated. The idea of surrogate family highlights the longing of people to relate and be related to in a family-like atmosphere. Its validity neither belongs only to ancient times nor should it be placed in oblivion. Various social groups in our times including the Church still use such a system: Kin terminologies exist, such as father, brother and sister as it was with the earliest Churches.

It must be added that the surrogate family has its own difficulties: depending on the amount of loyalty demanded from the group members, it could lead to a scramble for attention. For instance, how true is the loyalty of the Christian when it comes to the point of making a decision either for the biological family, clan or tribe on the one hand and the Church on the other hand? The participation in the life of the Church is of a free will based on personal conviction. Does one have the moral obligation to require that a member of a surrogate family pays more loyalty to him and to other members than to those of the biological or adoptive family? If yes, what would be the motivation behind it? This issue will be looked at in detail in the ensuing chapters. It suffices, for now, to say that the natural family served as a model for other institutions and associations in ancient times and this has perpetuated to modern times.

It is important at this point to highlight that the building of family through kinship and marriage is basic. It prevails across cultures all over the world as an important social institution and provides the fundamental working concept of family for most individuals and societies. Despite this fact it is not the exclusive or only legitimate form of satisfying emotional needs. Other types of human alliances, necessary for mutual economic and domestic support analogous to the basic kin- and marriage-based family also exist without an automatic implication to biological ties.

1.2 Changes in Society and the Family Institution

Change in society of all forms is a phenomenon that can neither be bracketed out nor be prevented. The phenomenon corresponds with the old adage that nothing is static. The observation of life indicates that today was the future of yesterday and will be the past of tomorrow. The lesson to be drawn out of this occurrence is that what seems current and actual today is or will become the

---

[69] Cf. Ibid., p.14.
[70] Ibid.

history of tomorrow. In short, changes occur in every sphere of life and have impact on theories and models developed in the various fields of study. The same is true for the family. Changes in society have led to changes in family life and this in turn affects the theories on family[71]. The effects thereof carry seeds of ambivalence, which are of positive and less positive nature. Trends of change in the wider society are sensed by a great number of people and are thought to have a significant consequence on family life in the way fundamental family decisions are taken, buttressing the premise made earlier on that changes in society do affect family life and dynamics. For example, an uncertain, chaotic society may lead to a change in the behaviour pattern of the members in the society. One of such could be the preference of casual relationships to permanent ones. Somebody may not want to enter into a long-lasting relationship or commit himself or herself by making a once and for all promise to someone. This behaviour can in the long run lead to temporary marriage, broken homes and a fall in the birth rate. Jacques Grand'Maison contends that the consequence for the family institution as a result of the changes in other social institutions is that the structures of the family no longer shape and serve as models for society and its institutions. This is because it now performs only limited functions and its influence in modern society seems weaker than ever before. In his view, the family has gradually been emptied of its contents and has merely become a "sounding-box"[72]. It is true that many of the social functions which the family hitherto performed – education, security, social status, leisure etc. have been passed to a considerable extent on to other state institutions. Married and family relations have been weakened in some cases and the divorce rate is high in certain societies; some old people are "dumped" together in old-folk's homes; many adolescents meet one another outside the family; and for some members of the society the family has a short life lasting only as long as childhood. Other factors such as "geographical, vocational and social mobility…and the upsets of urban life have seriously affected […] the foundations of stabilisation and continuity in the family"[73]. These factors, however, do not make the family institution a sounding-box but rather they support the thesis that changes in other social institutions affect the dynamics in family life and cause changes therein. These changes can be positive or negative. Adaptations may also take place thereby helping the family play its cherished role as the very cell of society, or as demanded by the whole big system.

Another aspect of societal change which has a bearing on the family is the "*short-term society*" which has had a constantly corrosive effect on long-

[71] The relationship between family theories and the changes in family life is vividly captured by Giovanni B. Sgritta. He says: "studies and research on the family carried out in the last decade may be interpreted as an answer – in the area of knowledge – to the transformations that have occurred in the structure of society". See Giovanni B. Sgritta, Towards a New Paradigm, in: Katja Boh et al. (eds.), Changing Patterns of European Family Life. A Comparative Analysis of 14 European Countries, London 1989, p. 90. See also D. Cheal, The One and the Many, 1999, p. 56.
[72] Cf. J. Grand'Maison , The Modern Family, 1979, p. 47.
[73] Cf. ibid., p. 48.

lasting relationships in the married and family cosmos. Examples characterising such a society are transitory fashions, impulse buying with credit cards, all kinds of tranquillisers, the stimuli of advertising, and above all short-term relations in shops, at school, at work, in leisure pursuits and so on. The correlation is that the family adopts the same split and erratic way of life. Consequently marriage and family life seem to be scary long-term commitments. The option is to "enjoy the freedom that allows one to change one's partner, job, motor car or dwelling"[74]. The system analysed above is typical of a consumer or pleasure society, which sentences the family to be principally a social unit of consumption that shows its inhumanity to the institution[75].

In her speech presented at the IXth International Congress for the Family in Paris, Angela de Malherbe remarked that the family in Europe is "wounded"[76]. Rosario Gortazar de Oraa, speaking in Madrid at the Xth International Congress for the Family, also observed that "the family in Spain is very deep-rooted". She, however, goes on to say that they (in Spain) are struggling, "like all other countries in the world – under the influence of currents"[77] which have been emerging over many years. This view of Rosario Gortazar de Oraa establishes the fact that exogenous strains on the family institution exist but distances herself from the thought that these elements make the family lose its role as a catalyst in society, as some schools of thought propose[78].

In conclusion, it would be said that changes in a social institution are inevitable. Some of them leave lasting imprints behind and others exert only temporary impressions. Whatever the changes may be, they demand creativity and flexibility, which allow for adaptation and reorientation. Despite the changes, family as an institution has not metamorphosed itself into something else nor do the changes imply decline in family values and life. Equating the phenomenon of change to decline in value is endemic and results from the comparison that is made between family in this era with a supposedly "golden mythologized family" of former times. Graham Allan aptly captures the idea stated above in the introduction to the well acclaimed "Sociology of the Family". He says: "change there [that is in family life] has most certainly been, but this does not imply there is no stability"[79]. It is thus worthwhile to look at

---

[74] Ibid.

[75] Cf. ibid. p. 49.

[76] Angela de Malherbe made the statement at the IXth International Congress for the Family in Paris, in 1986. The original phrase is "in unseren Familien in Europa ist die Familie 'verletzt'." Cf. XIV. Internationaler Kongress für die Familie, Bonn 1989 e.V. (ed.), Familie ist Zukunft, Bonn 1989, p. 23.

[77] Ibid., p. 25. „Die Familie in Spanien ist sehr tief verwurzelt. Dennoch leiden wir – wie alle anderen Länder in der Welt – unter dem Einfluß von Strömungen, die seit vielen Jahren entstanden sind."

[78] Cf. J. Grand' Maison, The Modern Family, 1979, p. 47.

[79] G. Allan, Introduction, 1999, p. 5.

some of the elements of family that have prevailed till today and that make it recognisable as a universal lived-reality.

1.3 Some Constants of Family Life in Society

As already seen above, whereas some people think that the family has changed completely and has, therefore, lost its importance, since most of the functions that it hitherto performed are now taken over by other institutions, various conferences and writings on family seem to want to give back to the family its somewhat lost importance by trying to underline its role as the bedrock of society. In her foreword to *Familie ist Zukunft*, Gabriele Plettenberg sees the family as being located today in high course; it is for the large majority, in particular for young people, a source of personal happiness[80]. The echoes of the statement from G. Plettenberg are that even in the so-called fragmented, paradoxically programmed city, the family remains one of the few *loci* of total integration of the human individual. The family still functions here as a place where people can be at home to talk about their work, leisure activities, love-affairs etc. They are in search for a multi-dimensional solidarity[81], and the family seems to be a good response to satisfy the longing for integration. The word <u>seems</u> is used here because not all people may long for family relation or desire integration into a group. It has been observed that one person out of a hundred wishes that he or she lives without a family[82]. That does not erase the fact that family stands out as a better option than the other comparable places of resort, which are mostly without the permanency associated with family[83].

An equally undeniable and enduring element of family, that transcends all levels of technology, modernisation and all forms of support systems that a society provides for its members, is the ability of the family to remain that essential unit in the social structure of the society in which norms and values, beliefs and knowledge, and practical living skills are passed on to the young members in the society. This makes the family play and maintain its pivotal role as the school of the socialisation of the young. In this regard, it provides the setting necessary for much of the learning that takes place and accompanies the transformation of a helpless and completely self-centred infant to a responsible and socially useful adult for the benefit of society. As already discussed above,

---

[80] XIV. Internationaler Kongress für die Familie, Bonn 1989 e.V. (ed.), Familie ist Zukunft, 1989, p. 11. The original text is as follows: „Familie steht zwar heute hoch im Kurs und ist für die große Mehrheit, insbesondere auch für junge Leute, eine Quelle persönlichen Glücks."

[81] J. Grand'Maison, The Modern Family, 1979, p. 53.

[82] Cf. XIV. Internationaler Kongress für die Familie, Bonn 1989 e.V. (ed.), Familie ist Zukunft, 1989, p. 11.

[83] J. Grand'Maison, The Modern Family, 1979, p. 50. Friedrich Bechina supports this view of the family being the locus of social integration by describing the family as the original form of every human community characterised by vertical relationships (between parents and children) and horizontal relationships (among the siblings). See Friedrich Bechina, Die Kirche als "Familie Gottes". Die Stellung dieses theologischen Konzepts im Zweiten Vatikanischen Konzil und in den Bischofssynoden von 1974-1994 im Hinblick auf eine „*Familia-Dei*-Ekklesiologie", Rome 1998, p. 464f.

the family is a school of life where an exchange takes place between the younger and the older generation in the form of an unwritten generational contract: the young learn from the old and the latter in turn transmits to the former skills and knowledge, as those involved in language and writing and in the perpetuation of social organisation. In this school, one learns to receive and hand-over the "baton".

Another functional component of the family that has not changed and cannot be overlooked is its role as ultimate security for most people, be it economic, social – for personal identity and career or emotional. For some people, family represents life and its non-existence would mean the collapse of a whole world order or a loss of reference point. In other words, a disturbance in this unit or social institution called family could mean a disaster for the affected members. Karl Olav Standnes reports of an anthropological study by Stephen A. Grunlan and Marvin K. Mayers, who have demonstrated extensively what it means to belong to a family in a group-oriented community. A reported statement from an old Pomo Indian in North America is worth quoting here:

> What is a man? A man is nothing. Without his family he is of less importance than that bug crossing the trail, of less importance than the sputum or the exuviae. At least they can be used to help poison a man. A man must be with his family to amount anything with us. If he had nobody else to help him, the first trouble he got into he would be killed by his enemies, because there would be no relatives to help him fight the poison of the other group[84].

Jakobus Wössner explains this phenomenon in another form by portraying the family as the most important life centre for the individual in almost every society[85]. This life centre is the primary group serving as the contact point for the individual at birth and caters for orientation for the future. In this group called family the individual experiences warmth, love and finds his or her identity. It remains, therefore, the surest source of economic and emotional security at least at childhood and youth.

A question worth asking is whether the family has changed completely or has only adapted itself to the changed societal situation? From the discussion done so far it can be said that the family has not changed in terms of its relational quality but rather in terms of its functional necessity. It has taken different forms precipitated by exogenous factors such as the industrial revolution, capitalism, urbanisation, modernisation, female emancipation, globalisation etc. The family institution has neither disappeared nor has it given up its role as the place where life begins and where people learn to relate[86]. In the former "patriarchal nuclear family" the family head – the man – determined

---

[84] K. O. Sandnes, A new Family, 1994, p. 55.

[85] The original text can be found in Jakobus Wössner, Soziologie. Einführung und Grundlegung, Köln ^{9}1986, p. 183 and it reads: „In beinahe jeder Gesellschaft ist die Familie das wichtigste Lebenszentrum für das Individuum."

[86] Cf. ibid., p. 50-53.

everything and that means he made all decisions and was at the centre of affairs. In the past there was too great an adherence to a traditional model quite out of phase with new patterns of life, and the family institution had to adapt to this new form of society's demand. The present form is where all participate in the life of the family. The important role of women as home-makers and their invaluable contributions to the budget of the family even in the traditional set-up are well known. Considering the fact that some men desert their families, thereby leaving the sole responsibility of family care on the shoulders of the women, calls for a change in world view and a modification of role play within the family. It is thus no more uncommon in modern times to see women gain reputable positions in society that make them earn equally good money as their male counterparts. This contribution of resources for the upkeep of the family has a positive effect on decision-making in the household or family. Men were seen traditionally as the main breadwinners and made all major decisions in the family. "With more women in the labour force or engaging in more viable income-generating activities, the myth of the men being the sole decision-makers is being challenged"[87]. The functional necessity of the family strongly depends on the societal situation at a time and the needs thereof.

Regardless of where the family is located – in Asia, Africa, America or Europe, internal relations become all the richer because of the multiplicity of ways in which it is open to the external world. At the same time those relations provide a unique kind of experience that is otherwise unobtainable in present-day wider society. It is an undeniable fact that

> the family continues to provide the mutual framework for the emotional, financial and material support essential to the growth and development of its members, particularly infants and children, and for the care of other dependents. It can, and often does, educate, train, motivate and support its individual members thereby investing in their future growth and acting as vital resources for development[88].

The amount of openness to the outside world and the intensity of adaptation depend to a large extent on whether the family in a traditional rural environment or the family in the city is considered.

Concerning change or changes in the family institution, it is neither about a total disorganisation of the institution nor an oversight of the resilience of the family institution. It is rather the adaptation of the institution to the changing world system and how the family as social institution re-forms its structure to correspond to the situation.

---

[87]George Benneh, Family and Development in Ghana. An Overview, in: Elisabeth Ardayfio-Schandorf, Family and Development in Ghana, Accra 1994, p. 10.

[88] This quotation is taken from Aderanti Adepoju and Wariara. Mbugua, The African Family: An Overview of Changing Forms, In: Aderanti Adepoju (ed.), Family, Population and Development in Africa, London 1997, p. 47.

1.4 Religion and Family

A vital cohesive force in kinship relations is religion, thereby depicting interplay of some kind between the social institutions of religion and family. Evans-Pritchard is an example of a social anthropologist who has undertaken an intensive study of the inter-relational character of religion with other aspects of social life. In his opinion, the duty of the social anthropologist is not to explain religion but rather to find out how religion relates to other aspects of social life[89]. In this case one is asking the question "how religion functions and what is it in social structures that makes appeals to supernatural forces contingent?"[90] It must be added, however, that not all sociologists and/or anthropologists support this position of Evans-Pritchard. E. B. Taylor and J.G. Frazer, who undertook earlier systematic studies in the area of religion, sharply differ from Evans-Pritchard. Their interest lies in the question of origins and causes of religion and not the functions and inter-relationship that religion has to social life[91]. The researcher of this study is neither a sociologist nor an anthropologist, and the aim of this work is neither a sociological nor an anthropological analysis of religion, but rather a look at the place of religion in the family and how both are interrelated. In the Mediterranean world, for instance, religion was not seen as an isolated institution but was rather perceived as an integral part of the very core of daily life[92]. The family on its part is considered by many scholars as the field of play of religious life and the transmission of values. Halvor Moxnes even talks about the family being the "centre of religious life"[93]. John M. G. Barclay replaces the concept family with the hearth, which he claims was the centre of life of the whole family. He says that "it was a rare family that did not feel the need to respect the powers which, for good or ill, influenced their welfare"[94]. Be it family, clan or state cult, people come together around a deity or common ancestral tombs, thus showing their common belief as well as their relatedness to one another. In cultures where ancestors are honoured or venerated, the gathering around the "shrine" of the particular ancestor binds the

---

89 Cf. Edward Evan Evans-Pritchard, Nuer Religion, Oxford 1956, p. 6.

90 Max Assimeng, Religion and Social Change in West Africa. An Introduction to the Sociology of Religion, Accra 1989, p. 9.

91 Cf. ibid.

92 Cf. J. H. Hellerman, The Ancient Church, 2001, p. 7.

93 H. Moxnes, What is Family?, 1997, pp. 23f.

94 John M. G. Barclay, The Family as the Bearer of Religion in Judaism and early Christianity, in: Halvor Moxnes (ed.), Constructing early Christian Families. Family as Social Reality and Metaphor, London, New York 1997, p. 67. A similar situation is seen among many other cultures in our times. For example the Bulsa of Northern Ghana: „Die Abstammungsgruppen (Klans, Lineages) bilden in erster Linie Kultgemeinschaften. Sie haben gemeisame ‚Totems', d.h., sie respektieren bestimmte Arten von Affen, Chamäleons, Krokodilen usw. aus dem Glauben heraus, dass die zur Abstammungsgruppe gehörenden Menschen in einem besonderen Verhältnis zu der betreffenden Tierspezies stehen [….] Die Mitglieder einer Verwandtschaftsgruppe bilden mithin unter der Leitung ihres Ältesten eine Kultgemeinschaft". Rüdiger Schott, Ehe und Familie in einer Gesellschaft Westafrikanischer Bodenbauer (Bulsa in Nordghana), in: Mensen, Bernhard (ed.), Ehe und Familie in verschiedenen Kulturen. Vortragsreihe 1981/82, Sankt Augustin 1982, pp. 56f).

family, household or clan together. In the same way the adherence to a common religion could help a family stay together, thereby confirming a certain commonality between family and religion. Three outstanding features here are community spirit, the promotion of cohesion in a community and the regularisation of the network of social and kin relationships. Adherence to a common religion or confession has made some communities to rediscover their common bond and unity, thus serving as the force of social integration and unity[95]. As it were "ethnic religion reinforces all levels of family loyalty as sacred"[96]. It would be a contradiction in terms to talk about religion without mentioning community. For religion is mostly lived out communally.

In the functions mentioned above, the correlation of religion to family is sharply noticeable. It is said that "a common religion can be very useful in holding together a group of people who would otherwise be competing economically and/or politically"[97]. This observation was made by Margaret Peil in 1977, based on the data available on Nigeria at the time and before the *Maitatsine* religious uprising in that country which took place under the motto "the true faith in Allah". Hundreds of lives were claimed under this uprising in the Hausa and other Moslem-dominated parts of Nigeria[98]. This raises the question whether religion does not have the potential of exclusion and disintegration. A survey of the continent of Africa and especially that of the West African region shows religion as a double-edged sword. Families have been torn apart and at other times they have been held together by it. In respect of the advent of Christianity in Ghana Max Assimeng cites L. J. Lewis[99] as saying:

> The Church from its earliest days has exercised a dual influence on society; on the one hand it has been a differentiating influence separating men and women from old ways, and on the other it has been an integrating influence bringing men and women together and providing power for unifying society by giving that inner core of unity to life which makes men and women proof against the stresses and changes in human society[100].

The unifying force is caused by the good news of the gospels which emphasises that every human being is made in the image and likeness of God. The converts also formed a new family of some sort, namely, a "family of God" or "family of believers". This could, however, be a cause of differentiation and alienation in society. From the quotation above, the issue under consideration is the

---

[95] Cf. ibid., p. 95f.

[96] W. V. D'Antonio and J. Aldons, Families and Religions. Conflict and Change in Modern Societies, Beverly Hills 1983, p. 31.

[97] This statement was made by Margaret Peil and quoted in: M. Assimeng, Religion and Social Change, 1989, p. 95.

[98] Cf. ibid., p. 95.

[99] L. J. Lewis was with the Colonial Department of the University of London Institute for Education.

[100] Cf. M. Assimeng, Religion and Social Change, 1989, p. 96.

differentiating influence of religion which separates men and women from their old ways, which is nothing else than uprooting the converts from their cultural roots. The adherence of a family head or even a chief to a certain religion meant the conversion of all his "subjects". Refusal of someone to belong to the same religion meant defiance of authority, with its telling consequences on him or her. Peter Sarpong affirms this point even if cautiously by his introduction of the phrase *unintentional disruption of culture(s)*. According to him the

> missions might have been unintentionally culturally disruptive; the missions remained a structure apart from the local population. Africans who came to profess the doctrines of the missions were adopted, body and soul, into a new way of life and were regarded by their non-Christian kinsmen as outcasts[101].

Such a phenomenon could lead to the feeling of denunciation and alienation from one's own people. This is a situation where religion can be the cause of the disruption in the cohesion and social relationships that hitherto existed in a particular society and culture. Just like every human institution, a religious community also has boundaries. A person thus either belongs to it, for instance through birth and the associated socialisation or through conversion[102] or he does not belong to it. In any case there is a clear-cut dichotomy: I am either a Moslem, a Christian, a traditional believer, a Buddhist etc. or I don't belong to any religious group at all. If I belong to one, I cannot belong to the other[103]. This is the observation we also make about the family. This phenomenon can create tension in a society, although it may also offer the opportunity to tolerance and openness. The individual member gets also some form of identity by the mere fact of belonging to a particular religious denomination, which is further enforced by community prayer and/or sacrifice.

In some societies the family authority system provides order for religious practice. Among the Frafra of Northern Ghana and Southern Burkina Faso, for instance, it is usually the eldest son of the first wife who pours the libation when the family is offering sacrifices. This structure goes through the whole clan. One inherits this responsibility and right to duty from the ancestors, thus affirming the argument that the traditional ruler derives his authority from the sanctity of customs grounded in the family to which he belongs. Since the traditional ruler's authority is derived from the ancestors, who in turn are the intermediaries between the living and the Supreme Being, the religion in this

---

[101] Cf. ibid., p. 85.

[102] Cf. J. G. M. Barclay, The Family as the Bearer of Religion, 1997, p. 69.

[103] This is the observation John G. M. Barclay also made about Judaism. He asserts that "Jewish religious tradition was deeply woven into the fabric of Jewish daily life, with connections as intricate and profound as those we have found in the Gentile world. Although Judaism could embrace Gentile converts (proselytes), it was fundamentally an ethnic tradition: it fostered a conception and practice of religion which was bound up with Jewish ethnic identity, so that to be Jewish and to practise the 'ancestral customs (ta patria ettnê) involved a range of distinctive family practices which were of profound religious significance". Ibid.

case also helps create authority structure in the society just like the family. A somewhat symbiotic relationship exists between religion and family: each is benefiting from and instantiates some elements of the other. The similarities coupled with the complementary roles which they play set the tone for the exploration in this study.

CHAPTER TWO

CONTEXTUAL ANALYSIS OF THE FAMILY IN GHANA

2.0 Introduction

Having considered some aspects of the family, namely in its socio-anthropological dimensions, attention will now be paid to how it is understood within the Ghanaian cultural landscape. The family in Ghana is a crucial part of the society and has gained an incredibly privileged place among the rank and file of the populace. It is for its members the "world", where they are at home. This is usually contrasted with the "outside world", which is mostly regarded not to be friendly to its inhabitants.

In order to understand and appreciate the definition of family particular to a culture, it is necessary to take a quick examination of the society in question. To this end the cultural landscape of Ghana based on the ethnic and language groupings, the religions and religiosity of the people will be looked at. A discussion on the family in Ghana and the nuances inherent therein ensues. Similar to the deliberations undertaken in Chapter One, the membership of the unit called family in Ghana will be examined and the extent to which its boundaries are either closed or opened. The conception of person and personhood is strong base for the Ghanaian perception of human cosmology. The topic will thus be considered under the premise that a good conceptual comprehension of person and personhood in the cultural set-ups in Ghana is necessary for the understanding of the social solidarity and relationships inherent in the various societies. Who is a person in the community and what is the relationship between him as an individual and the community as a "collection" of individuals? Is personhood a given fact or is it acquired with time? The answer to these questions together with the consideration on status and authority in the family in Ghana will aid in a later analysis of the ecclesial structure and authority of the Church in Ghana.

2.1 The Socio-Cultural Background of the Family in Ghana

Although the family is an autonomous social institution, it is closely related to other institutions within the social structure of any given society. This implicates a given level of inter-connectivity among the institutions in this setup. The examination of the socio-cultural context of the family in Ghana is based on the thesis that the environment influences the world view of its members and offers the vocabulary needed to understand the world.

2.1.1 Ghana: One Nation, Many Cultures

A casual look at the geographical divisions of the country reveals a colourful picture of Ghana: savannah, the forest zone and the coastal belt – semi-savannah. The ethnic and cultural compositions are also built along these geographical divisions, all of which can be grouped under the Mole-Dagbane, Akan, Ewe, Guan, and Ga-Adangme[1]. The country is a multi-cultural/ethnic one. The ethnological map of Ghana indicates that it has a total of 65 ethnic groupings[2]. The subdivisions of each group share a common cultural heritage, history, language, and origin. These shared attributes were among the variables that contributed to state formation in the pre-colonial period. Competition to acquire land for cultivation, to control trade routes, or to form alliances for protection also promoted to group solidarity and state formation. There was a feeling of belonging to the same "family". Despite the interrelatedness of many of these groups, each one of them tends to claim some sort of independence and authenticity.

Intrinsic to these ethnic ties is the grouping of the languages. All ethnic groups which have some ties to each other also share a common language heritage. Linguists have placed Ghanaian languages in one or the other of the two major linguistic subfamilies of the Niger-Congo language family[3], one of the large language groups in Africa. The Akan, the Ga-Adangme, and the Ewe ethnic communities live in the South of Ghana and constitute about 44%, 8% and 13%[4] of the total population of Ghana, respectively. The Mole-Dagbane[5] and Guan ethnic communities live in the North and constitute 16% and 4%, respectively. There are several languages under each language group, which are related in one way or the other to one another. For example, under Ga-Adangbe the Ga, the Krobo, and the Adangbe are found. These have many common vocabularies just as the Akan languages including Asante twi (also written Ashanti), Akuapem twi, Fante twi, Akwamu, Ahanta, Nzema, Kwahu, Safwi, Bono etc. do. However, any one group may be distinguished from the others in the same linguistically defined category or subcategory, even when the members are characterised by essentially the same social institutions. Each has a historical tradition of group identity, if nothing else, and, usually, of political autonomy. In some cases, however, what is considered a single unit for census

---

[1] Sometimes the word is also spelt as Adangbe. The two terms refer to the same tribe and/or cultural group.

[2] Cf. Appendix 1.

[3] Cf. John Kuada and Yao Chachah, Ghana: Understanding the People and their Culture, Accra 1999, p. 11. Northern Ghana is predominated by the Gur language branch of the Niger-Congo, and the Akan, the Ewe und Ga-Adangme belong to the Kwa language group of the Niger-Congo. Cf. Steven J. Salm and Toyin Falola, Culture and Customs of Ghana, Westport, Connecticut and London 2002, p. 9.

[4] It must be noted that the statistics are approximations and no absolute figures. This is especially so because Ghana has a large illiterate population (about 25%) with its negative effects on having exact statistical data. This applies to all other statistical data that are given in this study.

[5] Other scholars talk about the Grusi, Gurma and Mole-Dagbani. See S.J. Salm and T. Falola, Culture and Customs, 2002, p. 9. This classification is a more comprehensive and acceptable one. The reason is that the Frafra under which we also find the Talensi and Nabdan belong strictly to the Grusi, even if their languages Gurune, Talensi and Nabd have a relationship with the Mole-Dagbani languages.

and other purposes may have been divided into identifiable separate groups before and during much of the colonial period and, in some manner, may have continued to be separate after the independence of Ghana.

The common spiritual and ancestral roots of the members in these various language branches cannot be denied. This is even seen by some scholars like Max Assimeng to be of great importance for social cohesion. He argues that the provision of a common language by the ethnic communities as well as a spiritual root and common way of life serve to bring people with distant relations into a sociologically wider relationship. The importance of this can be seen in the fact that the tribes and ethnic affiliations tend to provide their members with a "common identity and some temporary release from the strains and anxieties of the daily life"[6].

The summary of the deliberations above is that Ghana is by and large multi-cultural and multi-ethnic, with each cultural and ethnic community having its own history of migration, specific customs, values and rules of behaviour or sharing part of its cultural heritage with one or the other ethnic group. It should be expected that the understanding of family is also influenced by the text of the various languages and secondly by the geographical location of the given people.

2.1.2 Religion and Religious Plurality in Ghana

Ghana does not only possess a multi-ethnic and linguistic landscape but also is religiously pluralistic. In recapturing the content of the novel *The Famished Road* from Ben Okri, Mabiala Justin-Robert Kenzo brings the characters of the novel to also bear on the Ghanaian society. Here the religious ceremonies together with their rites and rituals which occur on a daily basis are being discussed. This practice is not only particular to one religion but rather to all. Kenzo sees religious identity to be a "construct in the state of flux" and asserts that "no one religious tradition emerges as the one established religion"[7]. This presupposes a religious mix or could also be called religious plurality, brought into being through the arrival of Islam and Christianity on the soils of Ghana and later through the introduction of other religions such as Buddhism, Judaism, Rastafarianism, etc. The mix makes itself remarkable through the physical structures of the various religious confessions. It is not uncommon to see mosques and churches in the same locality and that their hours of worship are not very much different from each other. The strength of memberships of the various religions shifted from time to time. Currently Christianity has the

---

[6] Max Assimeng, Social Structure of Ghana, Accra 1981, p. 74.

[7] Mabiala Justin-Robert Kenzo, Religion, Hybridity, and the Construction of Reality in Postcolonial Africa, in: Exchange 33/3 (2004), 261. Mabiala Justin-Robert Kenzo is a Professor of systematic theology at the Canadian Theological Seminary of the Alliance University College in Calgary. His areas of research and interests comprise postmodernity/postcoloniality, philosophical hermeneutics, contemporary theology, African religions and theology.

largest following in the country. Therefore, the traditional religion[8] which had the monopoly of providing the religious "haven" for its adherents and shaped their perception of the Supreme Being, honour of ancestors and respect of the spirit world, is being challenged by others. This happening has brought in new perspectives and flavour to the religious landscape of Ghana and could be seen as a means of helping religion respond to the demands of modern life. It is the reason why the mix is synonymous to plurality of religions and not to religious pluralism. For, whereas the former denotes either the existence or the possibility of many religions coexisting in a given society and/or context, and has a neutral value in itself, the latter is usually associated with amalgamation of units and antagonism. To determine whether religious plurality is a blessing or a curse an examination of the interactions among the various actors is required.

Even though the advent of Islam and Christianity in Ghana, which began in the fifteenth century, brought about a dramatic change in the social institution of religion, the so-called African Traditional Religion in Ghana has maintained its own internal plurality. An important factor in the above statement is the expression "dramatic change". It won't be absolutely correct to say that the African Traditional Religion never underwent change. The aspect and trend of change therein have received, however, little attention. One of the few scholars, who have given some thought to it is Max Assimeng, who observes that "in the course of intertribal warfare, geographical mobility, and societal evolution, new gods, fetishes and charms were incorporated into the structure of existing arrangements"[9]. These 'foreign' gods brought about new forms of taboos, which surely affected the people's way of life. Incorporation of gods also meant in the same manner abandonment of some originally potent ones. This might either be due to the fact that the efficacy of these gods was doubtful or that there was a general disappointment of the aspirations of the men and women of the given society.

The major factor of change was brought about by the missionary endeavours of Islam and Christianity. Such changes can be seen in the composition of the various religious groupings in Ghana. In 1900, traditional African religion comprised 90.3% of the population, Christianity 4.7% and Islam 5%. The ratios in 1949 stood at 66% traditional religion, 30% Christianity and 4% Islam, respectively. There were drastic changes in 1960. The statistics

---

[8] It must be said that some scholars talk about traditional religions. Gabriel Maduka Okafor is one of those who use the concept African religions. Cf. Gabriel Maduka Okafor, Christianity and Islam in West Africa. The Ghana Experience, Würzburg 1997, p. 80. Even though he does not explain what he means by the plural form of the noun, one could correctly guess what he means. The African Traditional Religion (ATR) is expressed in different forms depending on the cultural and family or clan background. The form of worship among the Ewe is for sure different from that of the Frafra. Borrowing from Christian literature, one could talk about the availability of various "*spiritualities*". There are different movements and spiritualities in Christianity and Islam. One does not, however, talk about the Christian religions or the Islamic religions. Rather everything is kept in singular. In the same way, one has to keep the noun in singular when referring to the traditional African belief system.

[9] Sabih A. Kamali, Religion in a Pluralistic Society, in: John S. Pobee, Religion in a Pluralistic Society, Leiden 1976, p. 77.

show that 38.2%, 42.8% and 12% of the population adhered to the traditional religion, Christianity and Islam, respectively.[10] The Asempa Diary of 1978[11] had the following statistics on Ghanaians in respect of their religiosity:

African Traditional Religion	21.61%
Christianity	52.65%
Islam	13.92%
No Religion or other Religions	11.82%[12]

Just two years later, in 1980, the ratios stood at 21.4% traditional, 62.6% Christian, and 15.7% Islamic[13]. These data show, first of all, that religion as a whole is a prominent feature of the social life in Ghana. Secondly, Christianity over the period has become the largest single religious institution and its rate of growth is evidence of a significant vitality of this institution. In summary, it can be said with a reasonable degree of certainty that Ghana is religiously pluralistic and that a significant part of the population, based on the statistics above, sees religion as important. Religion and the Spirit World inextricably bind most of the communal activities of the Ghanaian as well as his or her other interactions. Max Assimeng observes that "in traditional societies [...] religion buttressed almost every aspect of social life, and provided definitions of the universe and man's place in it"[14].

The question is whether there is any relationship between the traditional religion and the "imported" religions. At the beginning[15] the relationship was one of tension with the so-called foreign religions, especially with Christianity, which considered anything traditional as fetish and devilish. This tension resulted in divisions within the Ghanaian society. Christianity and Islam came with Western and Arabian cultures, respectively. There was thus not only a clash of religions but more so of cultures. The strain, however, was more pronounced between the traditional religion and Christianity than between the traditional religion and Islam. Islam got implanted in Ghana through the interaction of the Moslem traders with the given Ghanaian communities. There was not much metamorphosing of the converts, unlike Christianity, which

---

[10] http://www.law.emory.edu/EILR/volumes/spring96/pobee.html (visited on 10th April, 2011).

[11] Asempa Diary is a publication of the Christian Council of Ghana.

[12] The Christian Council of Ghana, Asempa Diary 1978, quoted in : John S. Pobee, Religion and Politics in Ghana. A case Study of the Acheampong's Era 1972-1978, Accra 1992, p. 1.

[13] These ratios must be consumed with caution. Ghana still has about 25% illiteracy rate and not many places in the country are easily accessible. There is also the fear among many traditional people that the information resulting from statistics could be used against them. In that way, it might be impossible to have specific figures as given above. Nevertheless, the trends are useful for the analysis of this study.

[14] M. Assimeng, Religion and Social Change, 1989, p. 68.

[15] The arrival of Christianity on the Coast of Ghana dates back to the fifteenth century. Islam also arrived in Ghana about the same time. Both religions came into Ghana through commercial activities. Christianity started around the coastal regions, while Islam started in the North and middle belt of Ghana respectively.The Dagbon and the Ashanti kingdoms felt the effects of the impact of the trading activities of the Arabs who exchanged cola nuts for salt with the Ashantis. The Ya-Na (the king of Dagbon kingdom) at the time got converted to Islam. Today the Dagbomba culture has been influenced a lot by Islam. All this happened in the sixteenth century.

demanded abandonment of the given Ghanaian cultures. In the present time there exists a relatively cordial relationship among the religions because of inter-religious dialogue, which is lived more in communities and families than it is preached. This topic will be looked at into detail later in this study.

To sum up it can be said that Ghana would be described as a pluri-religious society. Each of these religions is independent. However, they have coexisted for almost five hundred years with successes and failures, with tensions and strife, and with compromises and adaptations. An analysis of how the Church, which represents the Christian religion in Ghana, functions as a family would be reflected among other things in the context of this pluri-religious society. For, as it were, the reality of the Ghanaian family is closely associated with the supernatural reality understood as the visible and invisible environment, the ancestors and God, the Creator.

2.1.3 The Religiosity of the Ghanaian Society

Some scholars such as John Pobee, Busia and Mends describe the Ghanaian[16] as "*homo religiosus,* because of his religious ontology and epistemology"[17]. Although this assumption may be too much of a generalisation, it demonstrates a world-view of the given society. The consequence of the assertion already made, namely that the traditional communities are dominated by the purview of the sacred, is the difficulty to delineate religious activities from secular ones. To the traditional Ghanaian religion is part and parcel of his life. This might have been the reason that led the noted anthropologist R. R. Marett to say that in such communities religion is "danced out rather than thought out"[18]. According to John Mbiti, being an authentic African implies "to be truly religious"[19]. He understands religion to be an ontological phenomenon for the African embracing his whole system of existence. Mention is also made of the religious universe of the African, by which he means that the African is caught up in a religious drama and virtually all his activities are experienced and coloured by religious understanding and meaning[20]. This assertion is also supported by John S. Pobee, who describes the African or Ghanaian as "a *homo radicaliter religiosus* (a radically religious man – religious at the core of his being)"[21].

---

[16] In examining the literature discussing this topic the concentration is on the religiosity of the African rather than of the Ghanaian. Since every Ghanaian is African, the issues applying to Africa (or Africans) also apply to Ghana and its citizens, unless otherwise stated.

[17] J. S. Pobee, Religion and Politics in Ghana, 1992, p. 1.

[18] The quotation can be found in: M. Assimeng, Religion and Social Change, 1989, p. 13.

[19] Cf. M. Kenzo, Religion, Hybridity, 2004, p. 244. Some scholars quote Mbiti as saying that Africans are "incurably religious". No one knows the first time this concept was used and why. It is, however, known that Willy E. Abraham, a professor of Philosophy in the University of Ghana, published a book 1962, *The African Mind*, in which he advocates the perception that "traditional African societies are through-and-through religious". See Jan Plavoet and Henk Rinsum, Is Africa Incurably Religious? Confessing and Contesting an invention, in: Exchange 32/2 (2003) 123f.

[20] John Samuel Mbiti, African Religions and Philosophy, London 1969, p. 15.

[21] J. S. Pobee, Religion and Politics in Ghana, 1992, p. 1. On his part, Mbiti speaks actually from the pervasive religiosity of the African and says that he is notoriously religious. His claim is based

Mabiala Justin-Robert Kenzo contends, however, that this assertion does not hold water and argues that the statement suggests to the post-modern mind a determinism peculiar to a culture proper to another epoch. His argument is that the idea of the incurably religious African has a print of the West and as such belongs to what he terms as "colonial library"[22]. M. J.-R. Kenzo is proposing that the African is neither incurably religious nor incurably irreligious. Leaning on the line of thought of the Nigerian novelist Ben Okri, Kenzo supports the notion that religion in Africa is "a hybrid product" and is a construct of the skills and creativity of the African[23]. Religion is part and parcel of culture and not a finished product from heaven. So it is not absolutely out of place to talk of "religion" as a construct of the human persons: in fact religion is a construct of man inspired by his desire to be in tune with the Transcendent. Nevertheless, to say that the Ghanaian or African is incurably religious is to highlight the role of religion in his day-to-day life and his daily relationship with the Supreme Being. In *Ecclesia in Africa,* Pope John Paul II aptly captures the thoughts of this view by stating that:

> Africans have a profound religious sense, a sense of the sacred, of the existence of God, the Creator and of the spiritual world. The reality of sin in its individual and social forms is very much present in the consciousness of these peoples, as is also the need for rites of purification and expiation[24].

This statement from Pope John Paul II confirms what was already said above, namely that the Ghanaian is a *homo religiosus* and a *homo radicaliter religiosus.* The average Ghanaian is conscious of the presence of the Supreme Being, of the ancestors and spirits. His or her actions are to a great extent connected to them. It has to be borne in mind, however, that every religion operates within a social frame of reference and finds its expression in varied ways in society. This makes the impact of religion to be felt variedly in different corners of society. Max Assimeng observes that

> there appears to be no enduring social network in which the religious connotation does not find expression and impact of some kind. Failure to grasp this has often led to several conceptual confusions, especially in the sociological study of religious change[25].

In examining the literature discussing this topic, the following observation can be made: most writers talk about the religiosity of the African rather than that of

---

on the observation that the various faculties of life of African societies are permeated by religion in such a way that it is difficult if not impossible to isolate it. In his view « religion is the strongest element in traditional background and exerts probably the greatest influence upon the thinking and living of the people concerned ». See J. S. Mbiti, ibid., p. 1.

[22] M. J.-R. Kenzo, Religion, Hybridity, 2004, pp. 244f.

[23] Cf. ibid., p. 267.

[24] Cf. *Ecclesia in Africa*, 42. OR, 20th September 1995, V.

[25] Cf. M. Assimeng, Religion and Social Change, 1989, p. 69.

the Ghanaian. Since every Ghanaian is African, the issues applying to Africa or Africans could also apply to Ghana. Unless otherwise stated, this assumption is valid in the whole of this research. Having made this point, it is worth remarking that it would be a mistake to attempt undertaking a comparative study of the religiosity of mankind, or to begin with one small group and then make a generalisation. This is what Platvoet, Van Rinsum, Kenzo and p'Bitek have done[26] in their write-ups. A comparative study in this regard usually results in "we-they" mentality with their associated emotions and prejudices. In view of the many indigenous religious cults in Africa Kehinde Olabimtan wonders "whether one can speak of a common tradition or recognize them as mutually exclusive phenomena. The issue here is, to what extent can we take a part for the whole, and vice-versa, in this continent-wide mosaic of religious cults?"[27] For example, Okot p'Bitek made a scientific study of the Acholi and Lango in Kenya. From this study he came to the conclusion that the Central Luo has no concept of the "high god ... to whom all knees were bended [sic]"[28], and the expected consequence is his view of the *Luo* and *Acholi* being a group of people in "Africa" with an atheistic outlook[29] that did not require a reference to a Supreme Being. For him, this exception makes it inappropriate to say that the African is notoriously religious.

The existence of many indigenous religious cults is not foreign to the different societies in Africa thus making the claim of p'Bitek not unproblematic to accept. He further asserts that the Luo do not have the Western concept of God at the top in a hierarchic structure. They, however, have the notion of transcendence of a Supreme Being, which p'Bitek rightly identifies as *jok*[30]. From this point of view, it is possible that in a "case like the Central Luo, he [God] has been thus over-spatially conceived to oblivion" at the point in time that he, p'Bitek, "studied and perceived them to be irreligious"[31]. It is interesting to note that the missionaries did not show signs of misgivings about assuming the names of God found among the Luo. It is also with the various concepts of God in Ghana. The *Ewe* call God *Mawu*, the *Dagbomba nawuni*, and the *Krobo Mau*. These are concepts used in daily life and in the liturgical celebrations of the Church.

Without refuting the indifference and irreligious attitude of the *Lango* and *Acholi* group of people in Kenya characterised by the lack "of prominence of the Supreme Being in the traditional cults"[32], one must also admit that the incidence is not only particular to them but rather prevails in many other societies on the African continent. This phenomenon touches on the manner in

[26] Cf. M. J.-R Kenzo, Religion, Hybridity, 2004, pp. 245-268 and J. Platvoet & H. Van Rinsum, Is Africa Incurably Religious?, 2003, pp. 123-153.
[27] Kehinde Olabimtan, 'Is Africa Incurably Religious' II: A Response to Jan Platvoet and Henk Rinsum, in: Exchange 32/4 (2003) 323.
[28] J. Platvoet and H. van Rinsum, Is Africa Incurably Religious?, 2003, p. 137.
[29] Okot p'Biket, African Religions in Western Scholarship, Nairobi 1971, pp. 99-100.
[30] Ibid., pp. 70-73.
[31] Ibid., p. 330.
[32] K. Olabimtan, 'Is Africa Incurably Religious' II, 2003, p. 329.

which the transcendence of the Supreme Being in the traditional societies is perceived. He is to their minds more spatial than personal, even though he is present in the social intercourse of the folk, especially in respect of ethics and morality. The Krobo see *Mau* as the master and Lord over life and death, and he has no interest in the death of humans. He is also known not to be responsible for the evil in the world. He is the one who sends people to live on earth. The fate of the individual, however, is in his own hands and his destiny is determined by the "parting-world" – *sesee* – when he was leaving the other world. The general notion, however, is that *Mau* is far away[33] and does not relate to humans as a personal God. The *Frafra* of Northern Ghana and Southern Burkina Faso call God "*Nawine*" or *Nayine*, depending on where one comes from. The prefix "*na*" has two meanings: it is derived from two sources, namely, *Naba* – chief or king – and *naam* – create or to create. In this case, God is seen as a king, chief or lord. He is also the creator God. The *Akan* on their part describe God at one time as ɔbɔ *adeɛ Nyankopɔn* – God as creator. They even sometimes add *bore bore bɔɔ adeɛ* – the ancient creator God. At other times he is called simply *Nyame*, which connotes dependency of humans on him for fulfilment or satisfaction in life. By having him as God, people get all they need and so they are satisfied. This mentality influences the attitude of the people towards *Nawine* or *Nyame*: he is in everything and has created everything. Kehinde Olabimtam understands the pervasiveness of the African religiosity as follows:

> African peoples' conscious and sub-conscious awareness of and preponderant recourse to the transcendent in virtually all they do, irrespective of whether those activities are formal or informal, social or personal, political or economic, didactic or recreational. The religious components in any of these may be overt or covert; but however they are present, they undergird human existence[34].

Coming back to Ghana, the point of reference of this study, it will be observed that religion and religiosity are intrinsically interwoven into the very structure of society from birth to death, from appeasement of the ancestors in times of disorder which threatens human existence to praise and dance in terms of good harvest. Even at political functions religion plays a role. It is not uncommon to see a traditional priest pouring libation at state gatherings alongside with prayers from a Muslim and Christian leader, respectively. Religion also influences ethics and morality in no small way.

Leaning on the line of thought of Kehinde Olabimtan and Edward Wilmot Blyden the researcher suggests that attention be shifted from the argument as to whether or not the Ghanaian or African is notoriously religious to reflecting on the contribution of religiosity to human civilisation[35]. A

---

[33] Cf. Hugo Huber, The Krobo. Traditional Social and Religious Life of a West African People, Reprint Fribourg 1973 [St. Augustin 1963], p. 235.
[34] Ibid., p. 324.
[35] Ibid., p. 337.

development from its somewhat romantic and aesthetic value blemished with the need for material success and protection against evil spirits which leads to a deeper personal relationship with God, could bring about the development of a profound theology for the good of mankind, thereby revealing the quality of religiosity at the time as being good. If, on the other hand, "the quality is poor, we shall see distortion, confusion, uncertainty and, almost certainly, hypocrisy on a large scale"[36]. The specific contribution will help sustain and nurture "human religious consciousness"[37], and that includes fostering the relationship of the believer with the Supreme Being – God – and/or the deities in a community of the same faith. In this sense religion and religiosity are an opportunity for togetherness, which entails "all the social and psychological questions of interaction, leadership, organization, reward structure, conflict and infighting, and so on"[38]. This cluster of symbolically shared life that is meaningful to the members of the society in question can sometimes serve as a cushion in times of difficulties. The import of the above discussion is that religion is part of the daily life of the average Ghanaian. In leading his life there is no clear-cut delineation of religious activities from secular ones. This is the context in which one can safely talk about the notorious religiosity of the Ghanaian.

2.2 The Ghanaian Family Typography

As already stated, the sense of belonging to a family finds an enviable position among the characteristic elements of the Ghanaian tradition, and the average member of the society wants to be identified with it. Provisions are made for the inclusion of all who by right belong to a kin group. It is the reason for the premises that in the traditional setting there is hardly an illegitimate child or an orphan. For, even upon the death of both parents, a child would still have "parents" who serve as cushion against the odds, at least theoretically. This system is based on the principle of "social rather than biological paternity and parentage"[39]. The siblings of the deceased are expected to take up the responsibility of caring for, in this case, the "orphaned" child. It does not mean that the orphan has it easy with these new parents. However, the social network is supposed to work in such a way that no one is left unattended. David B. Kronenfeld's research on the *Fanti*[40] in Ghana supports this argument. He

[36] Andrew Walls, Christian Scholarship in Africa in the Twentieth Century, in: Journal of African Christian Thought, 4/2 (December 2001), p. 46.
[37] K. Olabimtan, 'Is Africa Incurably Religious' II, 2003, p. 339.
[38] M. Assimeng, Religion and Social Change, 1989, p. 10.
[39] Albert K. Awedoba, Culture and Development in Africa, Legon 2002, p. 92.
[40] David B. Kronenfeld, Fanti and the Analysis of Kinship Terminologies, Urbana and Chicago 2009, pp. 32-34: The Fanti belong to the Akan tribal group of somewhat over 1,000,000 people. They are located in the central part of southern Ghana and have a close relation to the Ashanti. "Prior to the colonial period, they comprised a number of independent political units; these units retain their 'stools' (i.e., thrones) and chiefs and are now spoken of as traditional states. The *Fanti* have matrilineages (*ebusuas*)" that are grouped together into a small set of names clans. The *Fanti* matrilineage controls inheritance. When a member dies, the lineage elders meet and decide on the

writes that among the *Fanti* upon the death of a child's father, the brother of the child's mother or the father's brother "is equally likely to act as his effective foster father, while his father's sister's son (who can be his father's formal heir) is most unlikely to do that" [41]. The general norm in respect to raising the child, disciplining and training him, the people he lives with "function effectively as his parents [...]. Thus, while a child's true parents are most likely to raise him (and his true siblings are most likely to be his effective social siblings) almost any adult in town can fill the parental role"[42]. One could talk about the availability of many fathers, mothers, brothers and sisters of a given person, who may not have any direct generational connection or kin relation with the individual in question. Kronenfeld reports on the response of informants which shows them differentiating between real father "*egya*" – due to the fact that this "figure" was the biological father of the informant or has "fathered" him in some form – and other male persons who also bear this title *egya*. These people are also tagged with the same title either because they are the father's brother or "of father's age or for some other reason that connected the person to or compared him with father"[43]. The same applies to other kin term categories. This observation among the *Fanti* is not a singular phenomenon in Ghana. All other cultures and ethnic groups also have a similar observable fact.

In defining the Ghanaian family, therefore, one has to consider among other things the set of behaviour patterns that bring people to stand in relation to one another. This is based on the assertion that family is not just a biological phenomenon, determined through birth. More than that, it embraces social interactions and relationships which bring people to perform certain duties and to take up certain positions qualifying them to be called father, mother, sister or brother[44]. In fact, the idea of bringing a child up was seen as the responsibility of all and not just that of the nuclear or extended family.

Family is what gives identity and security – economic and psychological – to the person. Through the family he or she gets a sense of belonging to a community, of love and tenderness, a place and time for rest, just to mention a few. Life as a whole begins with relationships but first within the

---

disposition of property of the deceased [...]. The major part of property that the deceased earned or created himself passes to his lineage heirs, but a portion of it may be left to his wives and children (i.e., alienated from his matrilineage). The lineage elders may give the man's property to any person they choose (male or female, old or young, lineage member or not). However, there is a hierarchy of succession among the potential heirs that is expected to be followed unless the next in line is deemed inappropriate. Such a judgement could be based on incompetence, youth, nonlocal residence, or any other factor that could prevent him from effectively utilizing the inheritance. Potential inheritance is the 'social fact' relevant to the kinship terminology because one of the things a nephew potentially can inherit is the family – i.e., wife (or wives) and children – of his maternal uncle. This extended form of the levirate seems to be a kind of old-age insurance for the woman, a kind which is (at present, at least) rarely used, though often talked about, by my informants".

[41] Cf. Ibid., p. 20.

[42] Cf. Ibid.

[43] Ibid., p. 22. See also S. J. Salm and T. Falola, Culture and Customs, 2002, p. 137.

[44] Cf. R. Hettlage, Familienreport, 1992, p. 21. See also D. B. Kronenfeld, Fanti, 2009, p.22.

family: husband-wife, parent-child, and brother-sister. By belonging to it the Ghanaian gets his or her place and identity in society. This renders the relatedness to others in a kin group or in a family-like atmosphere a special quality.

2.2.1 The Family Defined with Reference to House

It could be said with a greater percent of certainty that the family in Ghana is rather lived than defined. Its notion is not easy to conceptualise in exact terms, though its acceptance as the basic social institution to which every individual belongs cannot be challenged. A look at the vocabulary of many ethnic groups in Ghana reveals that some of them do not even have a single word that concretely defines family in the Western sense of the word. Leaning on the materialists' claim that linguistic categories are only weak reflections of the organisations of the things in the real world and that they often do not have relationship to the real world in any way[45], one could see the above factor as irrelevant. The mentalists on their part, however, argue that the human perceptions of the world are structured by linguistic categories. This theory is drawn from the "proposition that we can only think about or perceive the world in the categories that our language gives us"[46]. According to this school of thought, text and linguistic categories are central to the understanding of things and for that matter for a better perception of our world[47]. It is, however, also true that the things in themselves could be such that one does not need a word to describe them, since their meanings are well known and lived out by the members in question. A given social system may even be so complex that one does not get the direct equivalent in other modern and ancient languages. This is based on the assumption that our environment and cultural background also influence our perception of the world. In talking about the *Dagaara*[48] family system, Eugene Suom-Dery says that a close assessment of it discloses a very complex family system which does not offer "straight forward and distinct categorisations with the established anthropological and sociological paradigms"[49] such that the vocabulary of the researcher gets exhausted without the acquisition of an exact semantic and conceptual equivalent which illustrates the given reality. In their relentless search for equivalence in the Western languages, researchers come to a seemingly disappointing realisation that the Dagaare language does not have a specific word synonymous to the English term "family"[50].

---

[45] D. B. Kronenfeld, Fanti, 2009, p. 15.
[46] Ibid., p. 23.
[47] K. Barber, The Anthropology of Texts, Persons and Publics, 2007, p. 103.
[48] The Dagaara are found in the north-west of Ghana and the south-west of Burkina Faso. They are also sometimes called Dagaaba. The language is dagaare.
[49] Eugene Suom-Dery, Family as Subject, of Moral Education in the African Context. Incarnating Christian Ethics among the Dagara of North-western Ghana, Hamburg 2000, p. 164.
[50] Cf. ibid., p. 167.

Edward Tengan drastically demonstrates that the *Dagaara* have no term which has a literal meaning corresponding to the term family[51]. He goes on to explain what it means when one talks about family among the *Dagaara*. His assertion is that the term generally used is *yir*, which is nothing else than a house. In his view "the primary meaning of house is the social house. That is the social web of relationships established by paternity and filiation"[52]. This *yir* denotes even the total patrilineage. So we are not just talking about the physical house, but also the composition of this house which comprises the living and deceased members of the family. *Yir* comes closer to his view about family because of the horizontal component that it translates.

Does it mean that the *Dagaara* do not have the concept of family? They do, however, it is one and the same word that expresses the house as a habitat and as a social system. It means that there are hardly different words that distinguish between nuclear family, extended family, house, household or clan. It is *yir,* which has the literal meaning of "house or habitat (*yir*) and the social house (*yir*)"[53]. The response from an informant illustrates this point vividly, which Edward Tengan recaptures in his book *House of God. Church-as-Family from an African Perspective*:

> I cannot marry any girl from among my patrikin (*yir*) no matter how distant we are in space and no matter the degree of consanguinity. Our grandfathers said that house is more important than anything else. If I go somewhere to visit a friend and I die there, he must search for a house of my patrikin which is also my house in that locality. It is in that house that my funeral rites have to be performed. If he does not belong to my patri-clan (yir) he cannot take care of my funeral simply because he is a friend. Similarly, if I come as a stranger to a village, I ask for a house belonging to my patrikin. Once I find one and I go in to meet them feasting or having a discussion, I am expected to join in freely. I have come to my house, it is my house (*yir*)[54].

The above quotation demonstrates the very meaning of *yir* among the *Dagaara*, namely a social unit made up of the network of social relationships formed through paternity and filiations. This unit promotes the sense of belonging and participation.

The other meaning of *yir* among the *Dagaara* is one involving all those who still do things in common regardless of whether they stay together in one house or are distant from each other in terms of physical space. A uniting factor in the person of a forbearer, whether already dead or still alive, stands as the origin of a particular *yir*, its ritual founder. It is also possible that a house is made up of segments containing members of different generations with their

---

[51] E.Tengan, House of God, 1997, p. 45.

[52] Ibid., p. 48.

[53] E. Suom-Dery, Family as Subject, 2000, p. 167. Cf. also E. Tengan, ibid., p. 47. He gives a report on an informant who sees the definition of *yir* in terms of the horizontal relationships that a house characterises.

[54] E. Tengan, ibid., p. 48.

own families under the headship of the most senior male member of this house or section. "Such a section is referred to as a *logr* (side or section) prefixed with the name of the family head. The symbol of unity of the segment is the main granary which is the symbol of community of life"[55]. Sharing a common granary in this case means belonging to the same segment, working and eating together. The *Dagaara* notion of a house is a dynamic one denoting a physical space where life is generated, and where relationships are nurtured. When one speaks of building a house "*yir*" among the *Dagaara*, these two connotations come into place – the physical house and the giving of life which widens the social relations. Important in the above-mentioned worldview is the functionality of house and family as basic units in society where relationships and life begin. This view will influence the subsequent discussions on this topic. Suffice it to say that most languages in Ghana describe the family in terms of locus and membership. Demographic features, structural characteristics, cultural qualities and the social environment within which people live determine the understanding of family. Among the *Frafra* of Northern Ghana, for instance, one talks about *yire-doma* - inhabitants of a house – when referring to family. An empty house is called *yire*-vɔɔre. It has no special value, since no human beings live in it. In other words the fact that the *yire*-vɔɔre is not inhabited by human beings signifies the non-availability of life. The same unit *yire* is accorded the quality of an organic system through the addition of the word "*doma*" only if people live in it. In this case *yire* acquires the connotation of a family. It can be deduced that even people who do not necessarily share the same descent with the family members but have lived there for some time are also included in *yire-doma*. Apart from these two examples, the ensuing analysis of the understanding of family in Ghana will show that the concept with its treasured values and symbols among the many cultural and/or ethnic groups in Ghana does not always mean exactly the same[56]. The emotional attachment to family, however, does seem to be the same. In other words, the idea of family is anything but not static and it responds to changes in the various societies and the innovation therein. However, no two families are the same in terms of the inner dynamics and the comparison is more complicated when applied to a larger society with different cultural and/or ethnic backgrounds. It is the most basic unit in Ghanaian societies. "It plays an active role in daily activities and provides for the maintenance of social security"[57]. Due to the different geographical zones and ethnic background in Ghana, the structure of the family differs.

---

[55] Ibid., p. 49. The Frafra talk about *yire*, which means house or household. To refer to this house as unit, one adds the name of founder of this *yire*. A similar situation is found among the Frafra. When referring to the members of a family, one talks about Yir-doma – these include all those living in that house and not necessarily only those related by blood. In short, there is no single word in Gurune (one of the languages spoken by the Frafra) that defines family as found in English or German.

[56] Symposium of Episcopal Conferences of Africa and Madagascar, The Church as Family of God. Instrumentum Laboris. Pastoral Letter, Accra (no year), p. 14.

[57] S. J. Salm and T. Falola, Culture and Customs, 2002, pp. 135f.

2.2.2 The Ghanaian Family is Community

From the discussion above, it is worth asking whether it is possible to talk about the Ghanaian family. What is its composition? Steven J. Salm and Toyin Falola in their book *Culture and Customs of Ghana* use the phrase "Ghanaian families" and not "Ghanaian family"[58]. Even though they apply the term to denote the family units and not the family as a social institution in Ghana, it may not be wrong to talk about the Ghanaian families to imply the various connotations of family in the many cultures and languages of the country.

In dealing with the understanding of family among the *Frafra* and *Dagaara* the general notion was considered, namely, that family comprises the living and the dead. One other element that needs to be introduced here is that unborn babies also form part of this social unit called family[59]. The premise ensuing from the discussion above is that the traditional Ghanaian family is different from the European-American meaning of family, which does not go beyond the boundaries of the nuclear family. It embraces a wider spectrum – comprising wider kinship groups – and is not only limited to the living but extends to include even the dead and the unborn. The surviving family members have the names of the "living dead" engraved on their memories. Their names are unforgettable and they are thought to remain interested in the family's affairs. The unborn members are the signs of hope that life will go on and the family name will not fall into oblivion in the cause of time. So what can be said here is that the Ghanaian concept of family embeds in itself the thought of nuclear family but engulfs a lot more.

What is the family in Ghana? The definition offered by Albert K. Awedoba comes very near to the general view of what the family in Ghana may be. According to him it is "a group of related people. The relationship binding them may be expressed in terms of blood or consanguineal ties or kinship ties on the one hand and on the other in terms of marriage or affinal ties"[60]. This definition portrays a view of a family that has wider boundaries. An *Akan* proverb says that *"ebusua ye dom"* which is translated by S. J. Salm and T. Falola to mean "the family is a crowd" since it "can include extended families spanning three and four generations"[61]. As much as one appreciates the effort of Salm and Falola in their attempt to translate the proverb *ebusua ye dom* to mean the family is a crowd, the translation does not meet the intention of the *Akan* speaker. *Dom* in this context should be rendered as community to give family its dynamic character. For, crowd connotes a gathering, which in turn may also mean a collection of people. But that is not what the proverb wants to get across. Rather it is the community of people who are related to each other. This is the element that the proverb carries with itself. It helps the individual member

[58] Ibid. p. 125.
[59] Cf. A. B. C. Ocholla-Ayayo, The African Family, 1997, p. 60.
[60] A. K. Awedoba, Culture and Development in Africa, 2002, p. 88.
[61] S. J. Salm and T. Falola, Culture and Customs, 2002, p. 125.

to be conscious of his behaviour towards other people. The "stranger" may after all be a relative.

The family in Ghana is also described as a community, because in contrast to a crowd or mere association of people, a community is a product of a time. It has a real past and the hopeful future. It draws its strength from history and is supported by the consciousness of memory[62]. Although a person might not have personally participated in the founding of the community or family he accepts it as part of his history. In the same way, he presumes and assumes personal responsibility for the future of it. The same cannot be said about a crowd, mob or other gatherings. It is thus more correct to say the Ghanaian family is a community than to say that it is a crowd.

The description of family considered above is more appealing to the average Ghanaian regardless of his culture and language than the notion of family as "two adults living together in a household with their own children"[63], which assumes that all families are monogamous, but polygyny is practised in Ghana among the non-Christians. There are also other forms of the Ghanaian family: first of all we have two parents living together in one household with children, either biological or adopted. Secondly, there is the reality of the parents living in different households with each child living with one parent at a time. This situation is prevalent in both polygamous and monogamous families.

The third scenario is the single parent family, where the parent takes care of the children single-handedly[64]. This third form is not admired in the Ghanaian society and is a product of the exogenous factors – for instance modernisation – which has a telling effect on the family institution in Ghana today.

There is no consensus among many scholars as to which form the Ghanaian or African family really is: nuclear or extended. John Mbiti posits that the family was in African traditional society an extended one which included children, parents, grandparents, uncles, aunts, brothers and sisters who may have had their own children, and other immediate relatives. Depending on the number of wives that one had, the size of a family could range from a few persons to even a hundred[65]. Florence Abena Dolphene supports this view and argues further that "in African Societies, a man, his wife and his children do not constitute a family. The nuclear family as understood in Western societies is a new concept in African societies. Family in the African sense is the extended family"[66]. Dominic K. Agyemang refutes this position of Dolphene describing it as "wrong and sociologically unscientific". He argues that "the nuclear family is not unique to western societies; neither is it a monopoly of any particular

---

[62] John J. Markey, Creating Communion. The Theology of the Constitutions of the Church, New York 2003, p. 131.

[63] See G. Benneh, Family and Development in Ghana, 1994, p. 5.

[64] Cf. ibid.

[65] Cf. J. S. Mbiti, African Religions, pp. 106f. See also G. Benneh, ibid., p. 5.

[66] Florence Abena Dolphene, The Emancipation of Women. An African Perspective, Accra 1991, p. 3.

society or culture"[67]. His view seems to be burdened with the thought that the extended family system is inferior to the nuclear one. None of the scholars who favour the African or Ghanaian understanding of family to be the extended one has purported in any way to rank one system higher than the other. The position in this study is that it is neither wholly true nor factual to say that the nuclear family system is characteristic of the European and North American societies and had little or no footing in Ghana or Africa. It is in the same way not wholly correct to assume that the extended family, which embraces more members than those of the nuclear family, is the only appropriate system for Ghana or Africa. Mary Getui offers an opinion worth considering. She says that

> With regard to membership, it can therefore be said that in Africa today the family is leaning more towards the nuclear. There are loose ties of the extended family where people come together in times of need such as funerals, but the trend is also more towards individualism mainly because of economic constraints[68].

This goes in line with the thoughts of Eugene Suom-Dery who observes that even before the advent of the European on the Ghanaian soil, the social systems there "including those of the *Dagaaba* knew of both forms of family, nuclear and extended, but the nuclear family is so interwoven into the extended family that it is not easy nor necessary to separate one from the other"[69]. The question is: how do the individuals live out their understanding of family? The experience of the average Ghanaian is that the family is bigger than the nuclear and even sometimes bigger than the extended family. K. E. de Graft Johnson brings in the lineage as an important factor to describe family. He contends that when people speak of the Akan *ebusua* or Ga *weku*, they stress the lineage[70] thereby emphasising kinship ties or lineage. In his opinion, what is usually called family

> is rather the lineage consisting of direct descendants of a putative ancestor or ancestress through the male or female line that is accorded recognition for land ownership, succession to traditional office or inheritance of property. In many ethnic groups there is not even a single word for the nuclear family[71].

---

[67] Agyemang Dominic K., Continuity and Change in Africa. The Paradox of Development, Accra 1996. pp. 10-13.

[68] Cf. Mary Getui, The Evolution of the Family in Africa, in: Theology of the Church as Family of God. Tangaza Occasional Papers/ No 3, Nairobi (no year), p. 41.

[69] E. Suom-Dery, Family as Subject, 1992, pp. 17-19.

[70] See A. K. Awedoba, Culture and Development in Africa, 2002, p. 99. Awedoba sees the lineage as a term occasionally synonymous in meaning to the extended family, and lineage "is a group of people who are usually related consistently and exclusively through either mother or father". In addition to the Ga and Akan use of the terms *we* or *weku* and *abusua* respectively, he makes mention of the *fome* or *hlo* as known by the Ewe and the *dug* by the Tallensi.

[71] K. E. de Graft Johnson, Family Research: The Ghanaian Situation, in: Elizabeth Ardayfio-Schandorf (ed.), Family and Development in Ghana, Accra 1994, p. 13. See also Jean-Pierre Dozon, "Africa: the Family at the Crossroads" quoted in: André Burguière, Christiane Klapisch-

His proposition is the understanding of the family in Ghana as the extended family, which bears the elements of a lineage. That is where the customary authority resides. His position buttresses the fact that a family, even the one nuclear in nature, finds its bearings within the lineage group. It is the reason why he describes the extended family as "a lineage group with affinal attachments, or to look at it another way, it is a nuclear family with part of the lineage of either partner attached to it"[72]. His emphasis is on kinship ties, where father, mother, brothers, sisters, grandparents, uncles, aunts, nephews, nieces and grandchildren are important. No mention is made of spatial arrangements. His understanding of the extended family is that it entails social arrangements in which the individual has extensive reciprocal duties, obligations and responsibilities to relations outside the nuclear family.

But there is also a second understanding of the extended family where cohabitation plays an important role. In this usage, "it is a residential group comprising a series of close relatives built around either patrilineal or matrilineal lines, usually not along both"[73]. G. P. Murdock, W. J. Goode, W. Litwak support this second definition where residence plays a role, although in Litwak's so-called modified extended family, the issue of geographical propinquity does not play a significant role[74].

In summary, it can be said that the general understanding of family in Ghana has two components, namely residence and relatedness, whereas no much emphasis is placed on the spatial arrangement. Importance is rather laid on the different social benefits and obligations, which bind lineage members together. The members have the "right to receive help [...]. Obligations to the lineage keep members in good standing and permit them to draw on the membership benefits"[75]. In this way, family has the element of a mutual aid society.

2.3 The Boundaries of Solidarity within Family System in Ghana

The Ghanaian society is characterised by relating and being related to. The highest form of this relation is that found among members of a kin group as described above. It is, therefore, no wonder that the terms brother and sister are

---

Zuber, Martine Segalen and Francoise Zonabend, A History of the Family Vol. 2. The Impact of Modernity, (transl. into English by Sarah Hanbury Tenison, Polity Press 1996), p. 311. According to him "African familial systems are characterized by the diversity of their modes of filiation, which are patrilineal, matrilineal or bilineal as the case may be, so that every individual is included within a framework which links him to others via genealogical connections; he belongs either to his father's group or to his mother's (or to both according to different modalities). Such lines of descent derive from the collective group and produce what we call lineages (patrilineage, matrilineage), meaning collections of men and women descended either through the agnatic or the uterine line, from one ancestor or ancestress".

[72] K. E. de Graft Johnson, Family Research, pp. 13f.

[73] Cf. G. K. Nukunya, Tradition and Change, 1992, p. 47.

[74] Cf. G. K. Nukunya, Tradition and Change: The case of the Family, Accra 1992, p. 10.

[75] S. J. Salm and T. Falola, Culture and Customs, 2002, p. 127.

preferred to cousins, since the latter connotes a certain amount of emotional distance. Considering the importance of blood relationships in such a society, one would ask who is the brother or sister. In his book *Peoples Differ. An Approach to Inculturation in Evangelisation*, Peter K. Sarpong gives an example of a Catholic nun in a Catholic Girls' Secondary School. One day a Monsignor, who was at that time a deacon, went to the said girls' school to visit his sister. Fortunately or unfortunately he did not bear the same surname as his sister, even though they were from the same parents. After realising that they did not bear the same surname, the nun sent the deacon away and branded him a liar[76]. In the opinion of the nun, siblings should bear the same surname but this was not the case. The aim of Sarpong is to demonstrate how important it is to know the cultural settings in which one works and to respect the elements therein accordingly. This is because peoples differ. The story, however, also demonstrates the complexity of defining the boundaries of the Ghanaian family. Even if both of the siblings were not from the same parents, it would not have been wrong in the Ghanaian context for the deacon to call the girl his sister. In Ghana people must not have the same parents to be able to call each other brothers and sisters. The intention of this section of the research is to find out how inclusive or exclusive is the term family in Ghana. Who is my brother or sister, father or mother?

As already mentioned previously, in Ghana the term family brings to mind "not only blood communal membership of the few living members but also the themes of clan, tribe, affinity, maternity, [...] ancestors"[77]. This evokes a certain amount of solidarity among the patrikin and cannot be sacrificed for any other relationship. In some cases a precise differentiation is made between blood relation and conjugal ones. The *Dagaara* say that "one can never wash away *siblingship*". That is what makes them believe that "a bad brother is better than a good wife"[78]. The general maxim is that a person must always be on the side of his brother against a stranger. It should be noted that someone who is at present a stranger may at another time be referred to as brother or sister. Within the same homestead a stranger may be anyone who does not belong to the clan or village. Outside of the homestead, however, brothers and/or sisters may refer to all those coming from the same village or town or region. It means that a member of the same ethnic group can be called a stranger, because he or she does not belong to the clan or village in question. Outside of this village or ethnic region, however, all those originating from the same locality are called brothers and sisters. Elderly non-kinsmen and women are also called by kin-terms of the nuclear family: fathers or mothers[79]. This throws somewhat overboard the strict term brother or sister which refers to either one's full blood brother or sister, or the half-brother or half-sister. Therefore, a cousin is also my

[76] Peter K. Sarpong, Peoples Differ. An Approach to Inculturation in Evangalisation, Legon 2002, p. 45.
[77] F. A. Oborji, Building Relations, 2003, pp.160f.
[78] E. Suom-Dery, Family as Subject, 2000, p. 56.
[79] D. B. Kronenfeld, Fanti, 2009, p. 19.

brother or sister and this even extends to the clan and lineage. In writing about the Fanti, David Kronenfeld comments on the sibling category *nua*, which "while focused on genuine full siblings, includes half-siblings [...] and is extended broadly both within and outside ego's matrilineage"[80]. If one intends to get exact information on kin ties through the everyday use of kin terms in Ghana, there is the need to ask specific questions that will bring out the desired facts. Then non-lineage members also are commonly "honoured" with such kin terms.

There are, however, ways of differentiating between blood brothers or sisters and other members of the extended family, clan, village or ethnic group who are also accorded with similar title(s). The emotional intensity makes a difference. For instance, the *Frafra* use the category *sɔɔ* to show that a person has a kin relationship with the other or belongs to the particular lineage – maternal or paternal. If a *Frafra* thus says *a dela fo sɔɔ,* it means more than just saying the person being spoken of is a brother or sister to the addressee. It implies that the two persons are blood related but they do not have the same parents. Otherwise the terms *yibga* – younger brother or *kɛɛma* – elder brother will be used. In respect to women, the older male person will address a younger female as *ntã* = my sister; a lady of one's age may either be referred to as *nseba* = my girlfriend or *npoɤa* = my wife, even though they both may not have anything to do with each other sexually; an elderly woman is addressed as *ndɛɛma* = my mother-in-law. These terms help balance relational inequality and create room for rapport.

As a matter of fact the boundaries of the family become thinner and thinner the further a person gets away from the nuclear or extended family, the clan or lineage and homestead. The fact remains that an individual either belongs to a particular family or not. The boundaries are well defined but the doors are open to admit new members especially through marriage. Room is also created for others to identify themselves with the social unit. The problem arises when it comes to social solidarity. People who occupy responsible positions in society often experience the situation whereby the so-called brothers and sisters, either from the clan or homestead, come to seek favours from them. These somewhat special treatments may not have any connection with nepotism or favouritism but rather with real-life situations. For example, a young man who lives in Bongo goes to another man, who hails from the same town but now lives in Kumasi, with the explanation that he wants to stay with the latter whilst he, the former, looks for work. Even if both are not really related to each other in kin terms, the native of Bongo, who is now settled in Kumasi, may feel obliged to help his "brother" against all odds. This does not deny the fact that the situation may entail that strains are put on the host's own family or personal life. Another scenario is when difficulties erupt between two tribes within the Church or mosque setting. The tendency is that many people will begin to ignore the bond of the baptismal water and opt for the blood relation, because "blood is thicker than water". The implication of this

[80] Ibid., p. 302.

phenomenon for the actual ecclesial life in Ghana will be examined in chapters six and seven of this study.

To conclude, it is easy to understand when someone is called sister or brother. It is, however, difficult for the outsider to calculate the amount of emotional attachment and commitment that prevails when a person calls someone from his clan or homestead a brother or sister, or when he begins to use these familial terminologies outside of the family setting, for example, to members of a surrogate family such as Church or voluntary association.

2.4 The Person in Community

The understanding of family is strongly anchored in the sense of community or communality. This illustrates how the individual is perceived in the society: he or she is one who stands in relation to others in the community, the smallest fount of which is the family. Be it in politics, religion or social life, the individual person is seen as one being in a community or as one belonging to it. The element of community was already looked at in 2.2.2. In this section the basic prevailing principle in the Ghanaian cultures, namely the relationship of the individual to God and other human beings will be investigated.

2.4.1 The Concept of Personhood in Ghana

In the Jewish-Christian thought a person is seen as a being made in the image and likeness of God. The dignity and origin of the human person find their concrete description and place in their relation to him. In the Ghanaian thought system the relatedness of an individual to God is a foregone conclusion: God is the creator and principle of life and a person cannot talk about life without making reference to his creator. In that case a difference is made between looking for the origin of this world as reflected in many myths about creation and appropriating the origin of life as such to its original source – God[81]. The Creator-creature relationship is thus not based on the fact that the human being is made in the likeness of God and therefore stands in a special relation to him. The human person is rather part of the great human cosmos called community which is actualised in the family, clan, tribe etc but God created them all. Being made as a community person, however, the human being finds his place and ascription therein. Even in religious practice except in the Christian religion, the person is seen as one who belongs to the worshiping community and not just as one who relates to God as an individual. He is regarded as a concrete being with the dignity accorded to him, who comes to God in company with others: the elders, ancestors and other members of the family or clan. A comparison is often made in this regard. Whereas René Descartes posited: "I think, therefore, I am" – *cogito ergo sum,* representing the Western way of thought, the Ghanaian

---

[81] Cf. Ferdinand Nwaigbo, Church as a Communion. An African Christian Perspective. Theology of the Local Church in the Light of the Second Vatican Council, Frankfurt a. M. 1996, p. 212.

will rather say: "I am related, therefore, I am"[82], thereby showing him as a typical community person or a person in relation to others.

The family has been described in this study as the smallest form of community in Ghana, which comprises the living, the yet-to-be-born and the living dead. These three groups are related to each other through blood or ancestral line and have a link to God, the creator. They were all once in the "mind" of God, came into this world through human parents and will one day return to the kingdom of the ancestors, who are thought to be with God. A person lives with this cosmological awareness and is supposed to lead his life bearing in mind that he is carrying the name of the family, clan and village and should do everything to bring honour to it. Anything that has the possibility of bringing disrepute to the family or clan name can bring repercussions on the individual.

Not only that, the sense of belonging to community creates the awareness of solidarity and participation in the life of others. What is a human person, if he cannot participate in the communal life of the society in which he lives? The traditional society survived on this sense of participation, be it in religious sacrifices; work on the farm; the building of a new house; marriage or child-naming ceremony. Participation in this sense served as the pivot of community life where the person brought his potential to bear and was available to his family and/or community members. In other words, the Ghanaian thought of a person based on participation is that "the very being of a man [or woman] in a society is derived through participation"[83]. This is because every individual person and his community, which is the embodiment of the individuals, is ontologically interlocked.

Participation and solidarity in the life of the community stress the functional component of belonging to such a unit. There is also the emotional element characterised by blood relations, which determine the network of communications, the relation to family, kin group and to the world outside of the individual. This mentality of the person as not being alone but rather connected to others ontologically reflects also in the relation of a family to other family units. A community is made up of individual families, which are related to each other in one way or the other. Francis Anekwe Oborji points out that

> African spirituality and life is [sic] based on the centrality of human beings and the relationships of communities living in the concrete circumstances of life [....] The overall aim is to make their life [....] In other words, one is judged or accepted into the life hereafter, into the

[82] John S. Pobee is quoted by F. A. Oborji, Building Relationships, 2003, p.161. See also John S. Pobee, Grundlinien einer afrikanischen Theologie, Göttingen 1981, p. 43. He wrote in respect of the Akans but this trait has resonance in the whole of Ghana. "Während Descartes für den Menschen des Westens sprach, wenn er sagte *cogito ergo sum* – ich denke, darum existiere ich – gilt für den Akan-Menschen (Ghanaer) cognatus ergo sum – ich bin blutverbunden, deshalb lebe ich, oder: ich lebe, weil ich zu einer Familie gehöre."

[83] Ferdinand Nwaigbo, Church as a Communion, Frankfurt a. M. 1996, p. 214.

communion of ancestors because of his participation in the life of relationship while on earth[84].

Francis Oborji leans on the thoughts of Patrick Kalilombe, who is of the view that the humankind in the African traditional thought pattern is first and foremost the community[85].

The place of the ancestors in the family or community has already been seen as important: they are perceived to be closer to God, intercede on behalf of the living and grant them protection. The life in the community is, however, also greatly influenced by the relationship with the ancestors. Albert Kuuire, who undertook a study of the *Dagaara* family and tribal solidarity, expresses fears that a system in which kinship ties are tremendously sanctioned by the place given to the ancestor, the individual person is in danger of losing self-identity or "any powers of self-determination; and that he is lost in a group in which any attempts at self-assertion would be futile and repressed by the mechanism inherent in his system itself"[86]. These fears could be allayed by the concept of personhood in Ghana as a whole. Its understanding is based on the premises that although a person is a social being, he is also autonomous and is not dissolvably meshed into a social cosmos.

It is precious to be born but it does not end there. The individual has to develop himself to a personhood through multidimensional relationships and social integration[87]. This hints to a dynamic process inherent in the notion of the concept. The fulfilment of this stage is measured through social integration in terms of the conscious participation in the welfare of the community – the fulfilment of one's obligation towards kinsmen and the wider society. Some scholars are of the view that reaching full personhood is not understood as something that is received at birth. Rather it is attained after someone is well advanced in life and in the society, and "indicates straight away that the older an individual gets, the more a person he becomes"[88]. This underpins the existence of an ontological progression between childhood and adulthood. It is also the reason why the aged or elderly in Ghana enjoy enviable respect among the masses. They are perceived as pedigree of "family tradition and knowledge in the cultural, social, and practical domains. Within a traditional household, elders provide advice and counselling rather than great amount of physical labor"[89]. They are mostly in charge of ceremonial rites related to birth and death, since they are thought to be closer to God than the younger ones. In turn, "they are to be accorded honor and respect by the younger people because of their age and life experiences, and they are greeted, seated, and served first in

---

84 See F. A. Oborji, Building Relationships, 2003, p. 161.

85 Ibid.

86 Albert A. Kuuire, The Christian Faith in the Dagarti Culture, unpublished Licentiate Thesis, Institut, "Lumen Vitae", Université Catholique de Louvain 1996, p. 165.

87 Cf. E. Suom-Dery, Family as Subject, 2000, p. 73.

88 R. K. Aboagye-Mensah, Mission and Democracy in Africa. The Role of the Church, Accra 1993, p. 79.

89 S. J. Salm and T. Falola, Culture and Customs, 2002, p. 138.

social gatherings"[90]. Rather than considered a burden old age is seen as a grace within the rank and file of the Ghanaian populace.

This raises the issue of the place of children. The child is conceived as a full member of the community and possesses an individual personality. This is symbolised through the naming ceremony in many cultures. Every name either has something to do with a particular event, with the day of birth, with the life situation of the family or the way the family perceives its destiny at that particular point in history etc. In any case the new born baby takes part in the construction of the history of the family. Through the incorporation into the community the baby also affirms the state of the family or community as an organic unit. The individual is encouraged to build a character for a virtuous living in the family or society. This mentality has prominence in the concept of personhood in Ghana. Time is needed in order to build a character for one's life. Personhood can thus be depicted as "emergent and processual: persons are not given but made, often by a process of strategic and situational improvisation"[91]. It is difficult to say that one has attained personhood as a finished product. It is "webbed in and precipitated out of social relationships"[92]; its development remains, however, a work-in-progress.

2.4.2 We-feeling Versus Individuality in Ghana

If the person is seen as one in a community and if his personality can only be found and developed through it, there is the danger of this individual getting melted up in the collective WE. In every culture there is the thought and feeling of community, expressed in the form appropriate to the given society. John S. Mbiti, for instance, contends that the individual in the African cultural setup identifies his personality only in the interplay of "I and We". In other words, the individual cannot assume his existence as such, if the community were not to exist as a social unit and construct. His view finds place in the saying that "I am, because we are; and since we are, therefore I am". Robert K. Aboagye-Mensah on his part emphasises that "a person is part of, and not apart from others"[93] in his community. He reacts to the views of Ifeanyi A. Menkiti, who describes the African view of community as "a thoroughly fused collective we"[94]. Aboagye-Mensah observes argues that the position of Menkiti is exaggerated. For as much as the community and the relationships within it are very important in the African or Ghanaian society for that matter, the individual still has the opportunity to express himself as such. It could be that unlike his Western counterpart the average traditional African or Ghanaian needs much more courage to transcend societal norms and values of his society in order to reach self-expression and identity. Limiting the individual person as one in a

---

[90] Ibid.
[91] K. Barber, The Anthropology of Texts, Persons and Public, 2007, p. 104.
[92] Ibid., p. 107.
[93] Robert K. Aboagye-Mensah, Mission and Democracy, 1993, p. 76.
[94] Ibid.

"fused collective we", however, would mean to deny him his dignity and responsibility as a person.

Generally, moral obligations among Ghanaians are hailed as cherished values in the society. Great efforts are made to uphold the moral standards, so much so that the members of the society are made to understand that the misconduct of one or the other member in the community could lead to the ancestors getting angry with the whole community. Despite this situation, the individuals concerned would be called to book for their misdemeanour and are rewarded for good deeds. This further explains the theory that the individual in the Ghanaian societies is part of others but not absorbed into the anonymity of the whole.

How does one establish the relationship between characterised "We-feeling" and "individuality" in the Ghanaian society? A community is referred to as a communion of persons. The individual is related to other members in the communion but he retains his individuality. He does not get lost in the collective WE but is accorded his status as a person through living out his character as a human being. Among the *Akan* one hears the saying: "*Asimasi ye nnipa paa*"[95] – translated loosely as: this person is a real human person/being. It means that he has a human heart. This statement stresses the warmness of heart of this individual which qualifies him to be called a human person. However, the discovery of one's own humanness is done in relation and association with others and not apart of them, depicting individuality and the thought of interdependence which typify life in a community in the traditional Ghanaian setting. This notion takes precedence over individualism, just as cooperation has more value in these societies than competition[96]. The idea of interdependence and cooperation and for that matter the essence of community lies in the fact that the individual's consciousness of his being, privileges, his responsibility and duties towards himself and others take place in the context of relation to others[97]. The human person is neither monadic nor atomistic, even though he is a self-existing rational entity or unit. It can be argued, therefore, that the community needs the individual to legitimize its existence. The individual on his part needs the community for cooperation and actualisation of group identity and his personality. Not everybody accepts this position. Some scholars advocate that taking the individual person as the starting point and "building up from this towards a structured aggregate – society"[98], one should begin with the whole and allow the individuals to find their appropriate places in it. It is thus claimed that "it is only through being rooted in a corporate organism of solidarity, co-existence and co-responsibility that the existence of each individual and that of the group can be guaranteed and realised"[99]. This is not the true perception of the individual in the Ghanaian societies. The cultures

---

[95] Cf. Ibid., p. 75.
[96] Cf. F. A. Oborji, Building Relationships., 2003, p. 162.
[97] Cf. R. K. Aboagye-Mensah, Mission and Democracy, 1994, p. 75.
[98] K. Barber, The Anthropology of Texts, 2007, p. 104.
[99] E. Suom-Dery, Family as Subject, 2000, p. 195.

there recognise the individuality, personal will and identity[100] of the individual. Failure to do that would mean to rob him of his rights and obligation as a moral person in society. The individual human being, however, also needs the societies for healthy relationships and living.

2.4.3 Excursus: The Stranger and Ghanaian Hospitality

The stranger or visitor finds himself in this network of behavioural expectations. He or she brings in that component of the individuality that characterises his person. The host on his part creates the enabling environment for his comfort within the family set-up. This is a central thought and norm and falls under the rubric of Ghanaian hospitality.

Even though most of the languages have about the same terminology that means both stranger and visitor, the two categories of persons are perceived differently. Anyone who comes just for a short stay may be described as a visitor. That holds true also for children who die early: they came on visit. All others are strangers, who have the potential of becoming part of the family. Here again there are two groups: babies/children and adults.

Under 2.4.1 the place of the child as a person and full member of the family was discussed. It is generally accepted in the Ghanaian traditional society that the child needs time to learn and take up responsibility in society. The baby or child sees a lot but does not understand much of what is going on. Through socialisation and initiation into the various phases of life, he or she assumes the place in the family or society. Hospitality in this sense would be the accompaniment of the youngster to adulthood. This is a normal phenomenon in all cultures and societies in the world. The importance of this point lies, however, in the way adult strangers are treated.

They are also treated like children or babies. They need time to get to know their environment, to learn the language of the family or people, to understand the culture. Before this takes place the host has the obligation to take care of the needs of the stranger: he gives him water and food – the basic elements for living. It is only after this that the host may ask about the reason for the visit. The visitor is mostly seen as bringer of news – mostly good news. It is, therefore, not surprising that in the greeting rituals nothing negative is said. It is only after the formal greetings have been performed that one may reveal that he has bad news – death or sicknesses etc.

It is also important that the host should exercise patience with the stranger: only the latter can determine when he or she wants to say what. They stand in reciprocal attitude towards each other. It is part of the reason why it is said that "the visitor may come unannounced but he may not leave without the permission of the host". To leave without the permission of the host could mean that the latter is not hospitable enough. The desire to see a visitor or stranger go may imply that one sees him or her as a nuisance. That would be a clear sign of

[100] Kwame Gyekye, African Cultural Values: An Introduction, Philadelphia and Accra 1996, pp. 49f and 63.

non-hospitability. The host may be termed a non-person – inhuman. The family in Ghana is thus seen to be open and welcoming to all members in the society. This enables the individuals therein to participate in its life.

2.5 Authority and Decision-Making within the Family Social Framework in Ghana

The analysis of religion and family in the social setting of Ghana led to the finding that the structure and order of religious practice at a shrine, for instance, can give information about the authority structure within the family or clan. Usually it is the head of a family or clan who leads a religious worship such as the pouring of libation. He offers the sacrifice on behalf of the other family or clan members. As authority figure he also assumes the responsibility of taking care of their needs including the religious ones. This point illustrates the importance of authority and its purpose in the Ghanaian societies: it ensures social order, guarantees unity and coordinates ideas through the so-called African Palaver for the building of consensus.

It is true to say that the communal life in Ghana has its essence and vibrancy in the principle of participation. But it is not done without the involvement of the authority figure. The head of a family, as a symbol of authority, is to direct affairs with love and an attitude of service, remembering that his family is part of a bigger whole, which also belongs to a clan and so on. In short, family and community life revolves around the pivot of authority, understood not in terms of lordship but instead in terms of service and leadership. The person in authority gives orientation to the activities of those led and ensures fairness not only in the sharing of wealth but also in the performance of duty or sharing of ideas. He is to ensure that no one is neglected nor discriminated against in this arrangement.

Beyond the family or clan level, it can also be said that in social interaction authority is based on office and /or seniority referring in its core sense to relative age[101]. This evokes the idea of phases in human development from childhood to adulthood, which gives birth to the term seniority – "where seniority can refer to the age and genealogical criteria of inheritance […]. It also can refer to a subtle interaction of power, respect, precedence, and putative authority. [It] is treated as important by *Fanti* speakers, and importantly affects day-to-day interactions and kinterm usage"[102]. A seemingly clear mode of relationship between juniors and elders is observable: younger persons maintain a lower profile before elderly people. When quarrels ensue, the elder is right at least in public. Max Assimeng writes: "almost invariably when children quarrelled with elders, children were adjudged guilty, not so much because of the substantive nature of the case"[103]. Any behaviour contrary to this norm will

[101] Cf. D. B. Kronenfeld, Fanti, 2009, p. 303.
[102] Ibid., p. 304.
[103] M. Assimeng, Social Structure of Ghana, 1981, p. 74.

be looked at with scorn since it is impudent and uncustomary to challenge persons of older age in public.

As can be seen from the foregone discussion gender has not been mentioned. The authority in most societies in Ghana is often invested in males than females. However, it is not uncommon to see women hold significant offices in some setups.

> The queen mother in Asante and *Ga* society, for example, wields influence over the affairs of the community. The queen mother is usually the sister of the chief and, as the mother of his heir, she is seen as the most important mother in Asante society. With advice from elders, she helps to nominate the candidate for the stool and gives advice to the chief, especially in matters related to women's affairs such as birth, initiation, and marriage. She is also seen as the guardian of the moral education of the younger generation. The Ga stool mother, who holds a similar position at the lineage level, has an important role in rituals dealing with lineage descent[104].

The above-mentioned scenario vivifies the assertion that old or elderly people on a whole have an honorary status in the house, family or clan. For example, one finds among the Krobo that an aged man generally gets the title *nɔkɔtɔma*, which means senior, elder. It is especially so if this aged person is the head of a kinship section. A junior fellow, that means a younger person, respectfully addresses an older man by using the customary term *nomo ɔ* which may be translated with "my senior, my lord". The place of the old woman is not much inferior to that of her male counterparts.

> An aged lady is called *yokɔtɔma* or *yomoyo*, both expressing her old age and her senior status within her kinship section. Similarly to her male counterpart she may expect to be addressed by the young people by her honorary title *yomo ɔ* (my senior lady) or *Yo-Dede-Nyɛ* (first-born lady and mother of a first born) if she is the oldest daughter of a renowned 'house'[105].

It is important to note that despite the authority that some people possess – either through descent or age – the society or family members, as the case may be, expect them to humbly submit themselves to their fore-fathers or ancestors, bearing the old adage in mind: Before the old people were born, there have been people of old.

Apart from the issues mentioned above there are other authority structures in Ghana. On the one hand there is the ascent to traditional political office, such as stool or skin for chiefs and kings, or the headship of a family or clan, ascription to which is based on descent and/or age. On the other hand there are offices, such as that of a priest, bishop, pastor and imam, the ascent to which

[104] S. J. Salm and T. Falola, Culture and Customs, 2002, p. 142.
[105] H. Huber, The Krobo, 1963, p. 91.

is by means of ordination. Other non-traditional offices also exist, the acquisition of which is by means of qualification or of democratic election process. The holders of these offices also receive the needed respect regardless of the age or cultural background of the individuals in question. The basic principle remains service to mankind. A leader who oppresses his people and lords it over them loses as a matter of cause the respect of the masses.

In terms of decision-making various methods are used. The two most popular methods are worth mentioning here: the African palaver method and the consultation among the council of elders. If an issue is of general interest, all members of the family are invited. The views of the adult male members are sought. The women also meet separately to discuss the same issue. Their views are then collated by the oldest woman amongst them who relays their views later to the most senior male figure or authority figure. This method ensures that all sides are heard and that the decision that will finally be made will be to the satisfaction of all. The procedure corresponds to an old adage that says that wisdom is not brewed in one man's pot. The head of the family or clan does not consider himself to be the wisest. He works, therefore, in concert with his elders. There are times when a chief or an elder would say that he wants to consult the old lady. This act buttresses again the point made above that "wisdom is not brewed in one man's pot". It also shows the ideal that is attached to the idea of participation in communal life. Since authority is understood by the average Ghanaian to mean giving and/or protecting life, care is taken to exhaust all channels before a decision is taken. This avoids the creation of wounds.

A Christian Church found in such a society will be well advised to pay attention to this structure. The community of Jesus and the early Christian Church found themselves within particular cultural contexts. The structures and dynamics in these socio-cultural forms also influenced their life. One of such is the family life style or pattern of the Mediterranean world, the subject of the next chapter.

CHAPTER THREE

ROOTS OF EARLY CHRISTIAN IDEA OF CHURCH AS FAMILY

3.0 Introduction

Christianity traces its origin to the Jewish religious traditions. According to the Old Testament, it was a common practice in Israel, that a coreligionist will be addressed as brother (*ah*), a compatriot on the other hand merely bore the title neighbor[1]. As will be presented later, the binding force is no more the motherhood of the *polis* but rather the fatherhood of Yahweh, whose salvation plan of eschatological rule of the whole world began with a small group of people called Israel. Gerhard Lohfink even goes further to say it began "with a family (in biblical terms: with Abraham), a clan, a group, a small people"[2]. By using the terminologies father, mother, brother it is assumed that the individuals concerned have a certain understanding of family in this context and the members understand themselves also as such. Against this background, therefore, an analysis will be undertaken to find out how Israel in the Old Testament can be seen as the family of God. How did this image influence their relationship with God and with one another?

3.1 Kin Terms in Hebrew Scriptures

In many theological books, one finds mostly the use of the metaphor "the people of God" to refer to Israel. Even though all human beings are His people and He is the God of all nations, He, God, decides to choose Israel out of his free will and for the sake of his holy name to be his chosen people (cf. Ezek. 36, 20). This image of choosing Israel as his people seems to predominate over all other images employed in the Hebrew Scriptures to describe the relationship between God and Israel such as God as shepherd of his flock; God as faithful husband in times when Israel had sinned or stood on the verge of violating the covenant; God as mother (Is 49,15; 66,13) and God as the tender of the vineyard. Two metaphors are found in Deut 14, 1f, namely Israel as children of God and as a people consecrated to Yahweh.

The biblical texts in the Hebrew Scriptures show Israel as a family with God being the father. For instance, it is stated in Mal 2,10: „Do we not all have one father? Has not one God created us? Why do we deal treacherously each against his brother so as to profane the covenant of our fathers?"[3] The text here

---

[1] Cf. Joseph Ratzinger, The Meaning of Christian Brotherhood, translated into English by Scott Hahn (*Die christliche Brüderlichkeit*), [2]1993 San Francisco, p. 6.

[2] Gerhard Lohfink, Jesus and Community. The Social Dimension of Christian faith. Translated into English by John P. Galvin, (*Wie hat Jesus Gemeinde gewollt? Zur gesellschaftlichen Dimension des christlichen Glaubens)*, London 1985, p. 28.

[3] One could assume that by talking about one father, the writer is referring to Abraham. The second sentence or question, however, hints more to the fatherhood of God than of Abraham. Regardless of whatever option is taken, we come to the conclusion that there is a common

demonstrates a situation where the relationship of the Israelites with God as father is been used as an argument for better interpersonal relationships among themselves and shows the concept to have a *Sitz im Leben* for the Israelites. In other words, the family concept was one of many images employed by the writers of the Hebrew Scriptures to epitomize the relationship between God and his people, Israel, and was also supposed to determine the interpersonal relationship among the Israelites themselves.

3.1.1 God as Father of Israel

From the many images used to refer directly to God in the Hebrew Scriptures the word "father" is applied fifteen times: in Dtn 32,6; Isa 63,16 two times; 64,7; Jer 3,4.13; 31,9; Mal 1,6; 2,10; 2 Sam 7,14; 1Chr 17,13; 22,10; 28,6; Ps 89,27; 68,6[4]. This shows a not so frequent occurrence. Although the word „father" as a term connoting earthly or blood fatherhood – grandfather, adoptive father – or even the fatherhood of a god is frequently used in the Old Testament, notably one thousand one hundred and eighty times[5], the authors of the Old Testament are very reluctant to apply "father" in reference to Yahweh[6]. Why is the concept not employed more frequently than fifteen times to describe the relationship between God and his people in the Old Testament?

The disinclination to apply "father" to create the bond between God and his chosen people has to do with the fact that God is not presented in the Hebrew Scriptures as one who stands in biological relationship with his people nor is he perceived as a mythological parent of some sort. He relates to Israel as a saviour and as the one who has chosen it as a people as in Hosea 11,1; Deut 14,1f. Even in the case of Deut 32,6 where reference is made to God fathering Israel, the fatherhood should be seen in terms of adoption[7] of the whole of Israel but not of the individual. By choosing Israel as a people and nation of his own, God becomes its father. Where a personal relationship between an individual and God is mentioned, the person plays a representative role: he acts on behalf

fatherhood and a common brotherhood. It should be remembered that one cannot talk about the fatherhood of Abraham without considering his faith in God, which made him the father of Israel. Cf. J. Ratzinger, Christian Brotherhood, [2]1993, pp. 6-12. Here Joseph Ratzinger illustrates a special paternity between God and Israel. All human beings, Israelites and Gentiles, make up the great human family. They all owe their existence to the one through the creative act of God. Despite this indubitable fact, "it still remains that God made a special covenant with Abraham as a special family from the great human family of the children of Adam (or, rather, of Noah)". Here p. 10.

[4] Taeseong Roh, Die *Familia Dei* in den Synoptischen Evangelien, Freiburg i. B. 2001, p. 3.

5 Cf. ibid. See also Ernst Jenni, 'ăb Vater, in: Jenni, Ernst/Westermann, Claus (ed.), Theologisches Handwörterbuch zum Alten Testament (THAT), Band 1, [6]2004, 1.

[6] Cf. E. Jenni, ibid., 14.

7 See also Ps 2,7 :"I will proclaim the decree of Yahweh: He said to me, 'You are my son, today I have fathered you'." Here just as in Deut 32,6, God is seen as the giver of life or creator and not as biological father. See T. Roh, Die Familia Dei, 2001, p. 3.

of the whole nation, for instance a king[8]. The oldest text confirming this position of collectivity is Hos 11, 1-3[9]:

> When Israel was a child I loved him, and I called him my son out of Egypt. But the more I called, the further they went away from me; they offered sacrifice to Baal and burnt incense to idols. I myself taught Ephraim to walk, I myself took them by the arm, but they did not know that I was the one caring for them.

Also in times when conversion and repentance are necessary, the whole of Israel is usually addressed. In the final analysis it is the individual person who repents and returns to God. The individual person will, however, not be addressed in isolation but rather together with his compatriots and coreligionists as a family that is in need of God's favour. It is stated in Jer 31,9, therefore, that in tears the Israelites will return and God shall lead them in prayer. He, God, will guide them to streams of water and by a smooth path where they will not stumble. "For I am a father to Israel, and Ephraim is my first-born son", says the Lord. God is prepared to forgive and to take care of them because he loves Israel as a whole family and will want to save them.

The idea of God being the father of Israel is taken up by the Second Temple literature. In predicting the restoration of Israel, the book of Jubilees graphically presents the relationship as that between father and son. After the children of Israel have returned to him with upright hearts, he "shall be a father to them [...] and they will be called 'sons of the living God'. And every angel and spirit will know and acknowledge" (Jub 1,24-25) that they are his children and he is their father. This and several other texts such as Jub 1,28; 2,20, 3 Maccabees 2,21, re-echo the view in the Hebrew Scriptures, such as Deut 32,6; Jes 63,16; 64,7; Mal 1,6; 2,10; Jer 2,31 3,19, which describe God as the father of Israel[10]. The text quoted above also shows another dimension of the relationship between Yahweh and Israel. The individuals were responsible for their actions or inactions, loyalty or disloyalty to him. His fatherhood is, however, with the whole of Israel as a people. He cares for them as a father cares for his children. He has promised them his blessings, namely that they "will become as numerous as the sands of the sea, which cannot be measured or counted. In the very place where they were told, 'you are not my people', they will be told they are 'Children of the living God'" (see Hosea 2,1). He, however, also disciplines them like a father does his son when he goes astray.

---

[8] Cf. T. Roh, Die *Familia Dei*, 2001, p. 4 and E. Jenni, Vater, ^{6}2004, 15. In 2 Sam 7,14, God spoke through the prophet Nathan about the relation of the former with David, the King of Israel. He said: "I will be a father to him and he shall be my son"; in Psalm 89,27 (...); 1 Chr 17,13: "I shall be his father and he will be my son, and I shall not withdraw my favour from him". See also 1 Chr 22,10 and Psalm 2,7.

[9] Dietrich Rusam, Die Gemeinschaft der Kinder Gottes: Das Motiv der Gotteskindschaft und die Gemeinden der johannischen Briefe, BWANT 7/13 (133), Stuttgart 1993, p. 32.

[10] Cf. J. H. Hellerman, The Ancient Church, 2001, p. 63 and T. Roh, Die Familia Dei, 2001, pp. 16f.

The conclusion drawn from the deliberation so far is that God is the father of Israel. This father-child relationship between the two is neither biological nor mystical but rather it took place through adoption, which finds its roots in Abraham, the founder of the Israelite ancestry. In other words, being the children of Abraham was analogous to being called the children of Yahweh.

3.1.2 The Fatherhood of Abraham

The Israelites relate to God and Abraham in the Hebrew Scriptures variedly. God is their creator; he delivered them from the hand of the enemies; and he promised that they will become a great nation. It is He, who has called them through Abraham to be his own. The individual's personal relationship to God is not spoken much of in the Hebrew Scriptures. The situation is different when it comes to his relationship to Abraham, his ancestor and father. An episode in the gospel of John suggests the self-understanding of the nation of Israel and the individuals thereof to be the biological children of Abraham. As Jesus told the Jews who believed in him that they will be indeed his disciples if they keep his word, so that they will know the truth and it will set them free, they responded "we are the descendants of Abraham" (Joh 8, 30-33). In talking about the purpose of his mission and the justification for going to Zacchaeus' house Jesus said: "today salvation has come to this house, because this man <u>too</u> is a <u>son of Abraham</u>[11]" (Lk 19,9). It must be stated that the biological relationship to Abraham is one element characterising Israel as a chosen people of God. That alone, however, is not enough. Abraham was a man of faith and his loyalty to God was unbroken. The Israelites as children of Abraham are to do the same, namely, be loyal to God. The fatherhood of Abraham should not be taken for granted. John the Baptist told the Jews in Matt 3,9 that they should not presume to tell themselves that they have Abraham as their father, because, "God can raise children for Abraham from these stones". The promise made to Abraham would thus remain unbroken but the membership of the chosen people could change since God is looking for a people, who is true and loyal to him.

Important in this constellation is, namely, that the loyalty to God precedes that of the kin group. As a nation and as individuals Israel always had to make a decision for the Lord, their God. Appeal to one's physical ancestry or consanguinity is secondary to the loyalty to God: one has to make a decision for him. This stance is very important and served to set them apart from all other nations. When the people saw that Moses was taking a long time to come down from the mountain they asked for a god. Aaron could not stand their pressure and agreed that a golden calf be made. Upon reaching the camp and seeing the defection of the people from Yahweh, the God who had brought them out of Egypt, he asked them to make a decision for God. Those who were disloyal to Yahweh were executed (Ex 32,1-29). Commenting on the question, "who is on the Lord's side" (Ex 32,26) Joseph H. Hellerman says that this "question could

---

[11] Underlining is mine.

never again be answered entirely by appeal to one's physical ancestry"[12] but rather to the individual's responsibility to God, namely his loyalty. The incidence in Ex 32 is so important that it found its way into the code of acts in Deut 13, 6-9. The stipulation here is that if a brother, son, daughter, spouse or best friend tries to seduce his fellow man to be disloyal to the Lord, this person should be shown no pity but rather be killed.

From the foregone analysis it can be said that a defection from the ways of the God of the covenant had repercussions for the individuals in question, namely, one could be excluded from the family of God. Now, if the Israelites who descend from Abraham could be excluded from God's family, is there the possibility that people unrelated to Abraham by blood could be clothed with the title children of God or belong to the family (cf. Mt 3,9)? Joseph H. Hellerman, who has made a thorough analysis of this phenomenon in his doctoral thesis, is of the view that "a conceptual door has been left open to the possibility of a people of God without blood ties to Israel's forefathers. For if a descendant of Abraham could be excluded from the people of God, could not the reverse obtain? Could not someone who lacked Israelite ancestry perhaps find a place in God's family?"[13] This vision is embodied in the text of Isaiah and echoed in that of Jeremiah and Zechariah (see Is 60,3; Jer 3,17; Zech 2,11; 8,22f; 14,16). In the eschatological vision Jerusalem is seen as the light of the world and the throne of Yahweh around which all nations will gather. Salvation will not be for her alone but for all nations. She, however, serves as the focus; she is the Lord's throne. Just as God, out of his own free will has chosen Israel to be his special people, in the same way he is the father of the whole of humanity.

3.1.3 Siblinghood amongst the Israelites

Considering themselves as a family the Israelites encounter one another as brothers and sisters. At this level the determining factor is the common blood ancestry (cf. Deut 15:1-3, 7-11). They would rather call themselves children of Abraham or, as the case may be, children of Israel rather than children of God. The blood relation in the common patriarch Abraham enjoins them all to treat each other accordingly as brethren. In Ex 2,11 one does not encounter the word brother but rather fellow kinsman. These are two blood relational categories that underscore their common identity as descendants of Abraham and the importance of standing together to fight the common enemy. In Deut 17, 14-15 the term brother is also used. The purpose here is to avoid infiltration of foreign ideas and rule in the camp of the Israelites. It is the reason for the stipulation that when they reach the Promised Land and should want to appoint a king to rule them, then it should be one of their brothers and not a foreigner[14]. The

[12] J. H. Hellerman, The Ancient Church, 2001, pp. 61f.
[13] Ibid., p. 62.
[14] Cf. Deut 17, 14-15: „'If, having reached the country given by Yahweh your God and having taken possession of it and, while living there, you think, „ I should like to appoint a king to rule me – like all the surrounding nations," the king whom you appoint to rule you must be chosen by

brotherhood in this sense is part of their identity as a chosen people. The foreigner does not know God and may not be able to lead Israel according to the dictates of his law. The use of the concepts brother and kinsman in the texts above is a determining point of departure from that of the Christians. A brother or sister is used in their context to refer even to "persons wholly unrelated by blood or *ethnos*"[15] but whose bond is caused by the one faith in one God.

From this analysis follows that the common or primary meaning attached to the term brother or sister in the Old Testament is blood relations – children from the same father or mother[16] or people with common ancestry. It is a fact without any recourse to the fatherhood of God. With reference to Hosea 2,1-3 where the terms brothers and sisters are used, Taeseong Roh argues in his doctoral thesis entitled *Die familia dei in den synoptischen Evangelien* that brotherhood in this body of text should not be understood to have its origin in a God-Israel relationship. For the concept "children of God" in Hosea 2 has a futuristic or eschatological connotation - „**they will** be told they are children of the living God" - whereas the brotherhood with one another as Israelites has a temporary implication[17] -"**then call** your brothers, 'my people', and your sisters, 'you have been pitied"[18]. This buttresses the point that the Israelites relate to each other as descendants of Abraham and only members of this family are their brothers and sisters. The notion of only considering blood relations as brothers and/or sisters is not shared by all. Ernst Jenni posits that even other people outside of blood relationship such as good friends also bore the title brother, used in this case in a metaphorical sense. This leaves open the option of emotional orientation. It also makes it possible for people without firm family ties to be able to enjoy "substitute" family relations.

In summary it can be said that Israel is a chosen people who has Abraham as its father – one could call it the family of Abraham but also the family of God. This God protects and blesses them. He, however, demands loyalty from them – as individuals and as a nation. The dynamics among themselves is based on common ancestry, which further opens the doors to other non-kin members by the use of the word brother to also mean neighbor, fellow countrymen, colleagues and good friends.

Yahweh your God; the appointment of a king must be made from your own brothers; on no account must you appoint as king some foreigner who is not a brother of yours."

[15] J. H. Hellerman, The Ancient Church, 2001, p. 61.

[16] Cf. Ernst Jenni, 'ah Bruder, in: THAT, Band 1, [6]2004, 99-100.

[17] T. Roh, Die *Familia Dei*, 2001, p. 19.

[18] Roh's argument is contrary to that of W. Günter, who sees in his article Bruder, Nächster, in: TBLNT I, Wuppertal 1967, p. 146-149 (here 147) an example of brothers relating to each other based on God's relationship with his people. He says: „Bei Hosea finden wir die Verwandschaftsbezeichnung Sohn und Bruder im Bilde des Verhältnisses Gottes zu seinem Volk (Hos 2, 1-3). Hier ist der Übergang von Blutverwandtschaft zur geistlichen Bruderschaft zu erkennen."

3.2 The Use of Family and Sibling Terminologies in the Synoptic Gospels

Jesus was born into a human family, into the house of David. In many instances he used family terms in his teachings and even called his apostles brothers. After his death Joseph from Arimathaea asked for the body of Jesus and honoured him with a decent burial. This praiseworthy task was the preserve of a kin member within the Mediterranean family structure[19]. According to the accounts of the evangelists, Joseph from Arimathaea was one of the disciples of Jesus but not a relative. To have given him such a burial portrays the family-like dynamics that existed in the community of Jesus.

At the last Passover which Jesus held with his disciples (see Mk 14,12-25; Mt 26, 17-29; Lk 22, 14-20) he demonstrated that the disciples formed with him a new family. The Jewish Passover meal was a family affair[20]. All of them including Jesus knew this very well. It has been stated nowhere that Jesus held this Passover meal with his disciples as a demonstration against the norm of the time. One could, therefore, argue that the idea of family within the community was a foregone conclusion. After his resurrection Jesus told Mary Magdalen not to cling onto him, since he had not yet returned to his father, their father and to his God, their God. He asked her to go and tell the brothers to meet him in Galilee. Furthermore, after the resurrection of Jesus the apostles put into practice the ideal of fraternity and used kin terms to describe their relationship to each other.

It must be stated that there is no systematic treatment of the family as a social institution in New Testament literature. "It is rather taken for granted as a presupposition which forms the basis for many underlying assumptions"[21]. In other words, the concept was taken as a given reality and the dynamics in the communities took the character thereof. Sociological analysis of the early Church shows, for instance, that conversion to the new religion taking place within households and this began with the so called *pater familias*. After he had embraced the faith, the other household members emulated him. To this end Karl Olav Sandnes says that "the embryo of the community was a family and the household is turned into a congregation. The social matrix of early Christianity was *oikos* and kinship. From the beginning the movement was

[19] J. J. Hellerman, The Ancient Church, 2001, pp. 49-51. This action of Joseph from Arimathaea finds an important place in the tradition of all the four gospel writers: Matthew, Mark, Luke and John.

[20] The Passover meal was a family affair according to the tradition of the Israelites. Ex 12, 3-4. Verse 43 stipulates that no foreigner may partake of it. Verse 48 says however that if a foreigner residing in the same house with them would want to participate in it, then he should be circumcised and should eat the Passover meal according to the regulations laid down.

[21] H. Moxnes, What is Family? Problems in Constructing Early Christian Families, in: Halvor Moxnes (ed.), Constructing Early Christian Families. Family as Social Reality and Metaphor, London & New York 1997, p. 18. In pages 31 and 32 Moxnes explains that the authors were interested in the relationship between husband and wife and the other internal relationships between the family members and not so much the institutional component of the family.

marked by kinship logic and precepts"[22]. Even though the discussion falls outside the scope of this study, it is important to state that the phenomenon of conversion of households was the origin of the theology of the House Church: not only did families embrace the Christian religion but more so the meetings took place in houses and family contexts. Since they came from a particular cultural and religious background, it can be concluded that their views on family and the interactions with each other were influenced to a great extent by them.

A look at the family in Antiquity has shown that through and in it one acquired identity, a sense of belonging and social security. This idea also reflects the cultural background of Jesus and his disciples. They experienced family as a social reality in which relations were lived intensely. Parents were the bedrock of the family unit. Their sacred structure finds its specification in the Scriptures: they were to be honoured. Children who fulfil this noble duty are promised long life. Children are the joy of the parents and the source of their social security for old age. Siblings – brothers and sisters – are members of the family and clan to which one owes loyalty and is accountable. The reciprocity from the brothers and sisters is that they are a source of protection and support in times of difficulties[23]. In describing the Mediterranean family at the time of Jesus, Benito Schneider writes that the Jewish nuclear family should be understood in its relationship to the extended family. An enlightening analogy is Mary visiting her cousin Elizabeth, which can be seen as a pointer to the fact that her child's birth will be a clan affair[24]. This was the family-world of the synoptic gospels and the epistles of Paul, which serves as background to the biblical analysis of the family. The question is, in which way can one understand Jesus' community as family, what role does God play in it and what are the dynamics between the members?

3.2.1 Jesus' Community as Family

A question that has been discussed in many theological circles is whether Jesus intended to found a Church or not? His preaching on the kingdom of God is indisputable. However, the same cannot be said about his teaching on Church except in Mt 16,18 and Mt 18,18 where Jesus uses the word *ekklesia* – Church.

---

[22] Karl Olav Sandnes, Equality within Patriarchal Structures. Some New Testament Perspectives on the Christian Fellowship as a brother- or sisterhood and a family, in: Halvor Moxnes (ed.), Constructing Early Christian Families. Family as Social Reality and Metaphor, London and New York 1997, p. 153.

[23] Cf. G. Lohfink, Jesus and Community, 1985, p. 40f

[24] Cf. Benito Schneider, Kirche als Familie, Schönstatt 1975, p. 16-17. B. Schneider writes: „Im alten Orient des ägyptisch-syrisch-mesopotamischen Halbmondes galt die Kleinfamilie als eine Zelle der Großfamilie im Familienklan der Sippe, des Stammes.... Die jüdische Kleinfamilie muß man sehr im Rahmen und Zusammenhang der Großfamilie des Stammes sehen. Der Stammesvater hat ganz bestimmte Hoheitsrechte. Vielfache Beziehungen gehen nach allen Seiten der Stammesgenossen. Wenn wir im Evangelium lesen, dass Maria über das Gebirge von Judäa eilte und sich mit ihrer Base Elisabeth austauschte, so muss man wissen, dass ihr künftiges Kind auch – anders als im Westen – Angelegenheit und Ereignis der Stammesverwandten war."

Consequently, it can be argued that he did not intend to form a special group of people[25] or institution called Church as we have it today. His teachings and language illustrate to a great extent a perceived identity for his community of followers[26]: a family of God.

At the beginning of his ministry, Jesus called together his apostles in a very radical form and asked them to leave their biological families and all that they had, namely, their source of livelihood. In this study the Semite family has been described as one in which father and mother enjoyed unprecedented reverence from their children and in which loyalty to brothers and sisters had a high value. Against this background one could say that the manner of calling the twelve apostles was a blatant outrage in the ears of his listeners at least at that time. It should be noted here that the requirement of unflinching dedication to matters of the kingdom of God was not an attitude demanded only of the twelve apostles. It was the underlining principle for anyone who wanted to follow him (see Mk 1,16-20). In one narration Jesus is said to have compared following him to putting the hands on the plough. He says: "once the hand is laid on the plough, no one who looks back is fit for the kingdom of God" (Lk 9,62). There is no doubt here that a total commitment is a prerequisite for discipleship of Jesus. Why was this unwavering dedication important to Jesus? What did he want to achieve with it?

The intention of Jesus was to build a community of followers who were dedicated to the spread of the kingdom of God as he himself did. He thus wanted them to share a common life with him as brothers and sisters of the one father, and demanded especially from those in the inner circle a radical turning away from their previous vocations – their economic security – and families. Jesus himself denounced the biological ties and found home in the new family, the composition and character of which he clearly illustrates. It is narrated in Mk 3, 31-35 that his mother and brothers came and asked for him. His answer was "who are my mother and my brothers?" Looking at those sitting around him he said "here are my mother and my brothers! Whoever does the will of God is my brother and sister and mother"[27]. The fact of seeing themselves as children of the Heavenly Father (Matt 5:9.45; 13:38) the community of Jesus experiences a new dimension in God-human relationship and a disruptive effect on the natal unit. They shared one thing in common with their fellow Israelites: God was seen as the father of all of them and only Jesus called God his father

[25] Peter Neuner, Die heilige Kirche der sündigen Christen, Regensburg 2002, pp. 23f. See also G. Lohfink, Jesus and Community, 1985, p. 28. Jesus called concrete people to be his disciples, he ate with sinners and he cured the sick. He built a concrete and visible community, the members therein he called brothers and sisters.

[26] The community of Jesus should be seen to be larger than the twelve apostles. There were disciples who remained in their respective towns and villages and others who wandered with Jesus. Joseph from Arihtmathaea, for instance, was a loyal member of the community of Jesus, even though, he did not move along with him. The same is true of Zacchaeus. The story in Lk 19, 1-9 only indicates that Jesus after the encounter on the road went to his house. Nothing shows that Zacchaeus left his home and followed Jesus. Those who left their homes and moved with Jesus from place to place found brothers and sisters who welcomed and took care of their bodily needs.

[27] See also Mt 12, 46-50 and Luke 8,19-21.

and referred to himself as "the Son of God". The difference between the Jesus community and Israel as families of God is that whereas the Hebrew Scriptures place the ancestry of Abraham as an important factor in determining the membership of the family of Israel, the emphasis in the New Testament is on the act of rebirth (cf. John 1:12-13, 3:3-8). The disciples are socialised into a new family – a recreation of family loyalty of those living under God's reign. So they are in a situation where household and kin-related ties are heavily relativised.

> They are relativized, first, by belief in the breaking of the kingdom of God with the coming of Jesus the Son of God, who establishes the nucleus of a new covenant community open to the Gentiles. This new covenant community is understood as the eschatological family of Jesus constituted, not on the basis of inheritance and blood ties, but on the basis of active obedience to the will of God. They are relativized also by the call to follow Jesus in a life of faith and radical detachment enabling participation in the all-important preaching of the gospel to all nations. Third, they are relativized by the story of Jesus himself, rejected not only by the leaders of his own people, but also by people of his own hometown, and by the members of his own family[28].

If Jesus knew all that but still wanted his followers to forsake everything for the sake of the gospel, then it was because he had the intention of making them free and susceptible of living the ideals of his family image, characterised by an unwavering loyalty to God and the behaviour towards each other was to be one "expressed in generalized reciprocity"[29]. To be able to fit into this new family of God and for impartial dealings with all people in need, "cutting the cord", that is, freeing oneself of family bonds was a necessary ingredient of discipleship, of forming a new family "in which, paradoxically, there are again brothers, sisters, mothers and children"[30].

The idea of Jesus regarding the repudiation of one's family for his sake and for the sake of the Kingdom of God is worrisome to those who value care for parents and children and the loyalty between spouses. The renunciation, however, should not be seen as a virtue in itself but rather for the sake of a greater good called the kingdom of God, presented in its earthly form through the recreation of the family of God. This is because

> loyalty to one's own group and dedication to the status of that group over all others and at the expense of whoever stands in its way are incompatible with a life of mercy, service, and compassion for the neighbor in need or for the social outcasts and the poor existing on the margins of society. Family loyalty certainly conflicts with mercy on

[28] Stephen C. Barton, Discipleship and Family Ties in Mark and Matthew, Cambridge 1994, p. 19.
[29] J. J. Hellerman, The Ancient Church, 2001, p. 67.
[30] G. Lohfink, Jesus and Community, 1985, p. 41.

competitors for prestige or goods with whom one has established longstanding enmity[31].

It is true to say that in the first-century family, faithfulness to familial forms distinguished one from the other in terms of social approbation, status and the structures through which material and social well-being was assured. One could argue that the community of Jesus was a replacement or substitute of their respective biological families, and could only be seen in the light of a surrogate family. It was not only those in the inner circle who were considered as his brethren. Some of the disciples remained in their respective towns and villages and they were also part of the family of Jesus even if they did not move with him from one village or town to the other.

Some scholars see Jesus being iconoclastic in his views on family ties. Taking the texts by their face value, Jesus would seem to be presenting family bonds and discipleship as two incompatible phenomena. Luke 2: 41-50 depicts him disregarding the feelings of his parents, when he remained behind on his family's return from Jerusalem and pursued conversation with religious leaders. It is stated in verse 51 of the same chapter that he returned with his parents and continued to be under their authority[32]. In a second instance, when the uncomprehending relatives of Jesus believed that he was mad and wanted to take him home for his safety and for the sake of the family's honour, he repudiated their responsibility for him and somewhat his kin ties to them[33] by saying: "Whoever does the will of God is brother and sister and mother to me." (Mk 3, 20f. 35; Mt 12, 46-50; Lk 8, 19-21). Karl Olav Sandnes argues that it will be a mistake if one should interpret the text to mean that Jesus is rejecting his biological family. Rather "he is declaring a new familyhood, and his own family will hopefully find their place within the new family"[34]. His family now comprises the fellowship of the disciples, into which his physical family is more than likely included, that is if they also listen to the word of God and do his will. The approach of Jesus to family and family issues can be seen as one meant to establish a new family understanding that fits into his message of the

---

[31] Lisa Sowle Cahill, Family. A Christian Social Perspective, Minneapolis 2000, p. 29.

[32] In a subtle way Jesus' passion for the things of his father, his loyalty to him is being given more weight than the attachment to his earthly parents.

[33] L. S. Cahill, Family, 2000, p. 29.

[34] K. O. Sandnes, A new Family, 1994, p. 71. See also Robert Hamerton-Kelly, God the Father. Theology and Patriarchy in the Teaching of Jesus: Overtures of Biblical Theology, Philadelphia 1979, p. 65. Here R. Hamerton-Kelly posits that the saying of Jesus in Mark 3:35 "would have been understood as a rejection of his family obligations in favor of the kingdom." K. O. Sandnes' argument is then against this assertion. He is proposing that the family is not replaced by the kingdom of God. Rather it is being replaced by the fellowship of believers. None of the parties above is completely correct or completely wrong. In the first place Jesus taught his followers to build a family with emphasis on the fatherhood of God and equality among the brethren, the purpose of which was the actualisation of the kingdom of God. Secondly it is the community of followers who make up the family model that Jesus intended to portray. It is no more blood relationship that plays an important role but rather the faithfulness to God. All those who live according to the will of God belong to the family of Jesus.

Kingdom of God: discipleship was an alternative, a counter-cultural social structure in which the only influence of kinship structure may be in the form of brothers, sisters and mothers of disciples, who obey God.

3.2.2 God as Father in the Teachings of Jesus

Earthly family structures serve as the nurturing grounds for quality human relations and integration. This phenomenon finds expression also in the bible. The gospel of Matthew, for instance, begins with the genealogy of Jesus through Joseph, followed by the virginal conception of Jesus by Mary and Joseph's acknowledgement of Jesus as his legal son – by the giving of a name (Matt 1,25). This brings Jesus into the Davidic ancestry, thus qualifying him to be called the "Son of David" (Matt 1,1-25).[35] This is what the prophets wrote about the Messiah, namely that he would come from the house of David. And "since Matthew apparently does not consider Mary to be of Davidic lineage (*which would be irrelevant anyway to Jews who traced a son's lineage through the legal father*), it is vital that Joseph accepts Jesus as his own child so that the latter will have a Davidic genealogy"[36]. The family tree of Jesus is, however, not to be understood biologically but rather theologically. In other words it does not have to deal with the biological fatherhood of Joseph[37], since Jesus was conceived by the power of the Holy Spirit and God is the Father, rather it has to deal with the insertion of Jesus into human tradition and especially into the Davidic lineage. Commenting on Matt 1,25: "And he did not have sexual relations with her until she bore a son (v 25a); and he called his name Jesus (v 25b)", John Meier sees a difference in the perception of St. Matthew and modern theological considerations. In his opinion, whereas "our modern theological concerns might focus on the first half of the verse, the emphasis for Matthew falls on the second half"[38], namely, that Joseph accomplished his role as a legal father by inserting Jesus into his lineage, thus making it possible for the prophecy to be fulfilled by the son of David who is at the same time son of God, born of a virgin. V 25a, which deals with the virginal conception, is intended to stress the other truth, namely son of David, also captured by the same text[39]. The conclusions to be drawn are that Jesus was born into the human race through virginal conception; he was the son of David and son of Abraham.

---

[35] Cf. John Meier, The Brothers and Sisters of Jesus in Ecumenical Perspective, in: The Catholic Biblical Quarterly (CBQ), 54/1 (1992) 8.

[36] Cf. ibid. The italics are mine.

[37] Eleonore Beck in commenting on Matthew 1:1-25, remarked: „Die Bezeichnung ‚Stammbaum' gilt nicht im biographischen, wohl aber im theologischen Sinn." See Katholische Bibelanstalt, Die Bibel. Einheitsübersetzung mit Kommentar, Stuttgart 2001, p. 1206.

[38] J. Meier, The Brothers and Sisters of Jesus in Ecumenical Perspective, in: CBQ, 54/1 (1992) 9.

[39] Cf. Richard L. Rohrbaugh, Legitimating Sonship – A Test of Honor. A Social-Scientific Study of Luke 4:1-30; in: P. F. Esler (ed.), Modelling Early Christianity: Social-Scientific Studies of the New Testament in its Context, London 1995, pp. 183-197. See also the commentary by Eleonore Beck on Matt 1:1-25, in: Katholische Bibelanstalt, Die Bibel, 2001, p. 1206. „Durch den ‚Stammbaum' wird sichergestellt, dass Jesus die vom Messias gefordete davidische Abstammung nachweisen kann. Doch der Stammbaum sagt nicht die ganze Wahrheit über seine Herkunft."

For his genealogy traces back to him, the father of the Judeo-Christian faith. Jesus needed the human family to be able to gain his legal status as the son of a particular kin group. This underscores the importance of family in his life. He, however, leads his disciples to a new dimension of the term family: he teaches them to pray to their Father in Heaven (Luke 11,2).

The Aramaic form *Abba* used in Mark 14,36 is characteristic of the image of Jesus about God – he is Father. "The open access to God" that the believers have, added to God's care for them is "described by the family term *Abba*, which is an everyday family word"[40]. In talking about what it means to have God as Father, Jesus starts by recalling the concern that earthly fathers have for their children. A classical example is Matt 7:11 – God, the Heavenly Father takes care of His children more than earthly parents do. Based on this conviction, Jesus could call upon his disciples to leave everything behind and follow him (Matt 5-7). God the father will cater for their needs. And so they can and should seek first the kingdom of God, whereupon all other things shall be added onto them. His care for them is so great that even the amount of hair they have is been taken note of by God (Lk 12,7).

A very important element in the family of God idea of Jesus is loyalty to God. This point was mentioned briefly at the beginning of this section. The concept is expressed strongly in Luke 14,26, where Jesus teaches that anyone who wants to be his disciple must be prepared to hate father, mother, wife, children, brothers and sisters, and even his own life[41]. There are difficulties in rendering the real meaning of the word "hate" or hatred in Luke 14, 26. Whereas the Greek form of the word "*μισέω*" can be translated literally to mean "to hate", some scholars are arguing that it should be perceived to have the connotation of "to love less", "to sever one's relationship with the family", "to leave aside or abandon"[42]. Joseph Hellerman suggests that it is only in this sense of understanding the text that a parallelism with the gospel narrative in Mk 3, 31-35; 1, 16-20 can be found. Here, Jesus renounces his own family relations and demands similar behaviour from his disciples. A swap of family ties or

---

40 Ibid., p. 67.

41 Arland Jacobson observes the position of Jesus in Luke 14,26 as not just being radical but rather "it would have been profoundly offensive". Arland D. Jacobson, Divided Families and Christian Origins", in: The Gospel Behind the Gospels: Current Studies in Q, ed. Ronald A. Piper, NovTSup 75, Leiden 1995, p. 363. See also http://books.google.de/books?id=F_KbL5s6h_kC&pg=PA361&lpg=PA361&dq=Arland+Jacobson,,+Divided+Families+and+Christian+Origins&source=bl&ots=VjFMDY24Z3&sig=gO8XLa1eWc4ltSfzPX8NYKkMZNM&hl=de&ei=tArBTZ6vNZCe-QbfhNT5Aw&sa=X&oi=book_result&ct=result&resnum=1&ved=0CCEQ6AEwAA#v=onepage&q=Arland%20Jacobson%2C%2C%20Divided%20Families%20and%20Christian%20Origins&f=false (visited on 4th March, 2011). In the Jewish society in which Jesus grew up, "filial obedience" was the norm and children were to honour father and mother. The punishment for disobeying parents is stoning to death (Deut 21,18-21). Although Jesus knew of this stipulation he still demands this radical behaviour from his disciples. The kingdom of God is clearly placed above blood relations and economic security.

42 J. J. Hellerman, The Ancient Family, 2001, p. 72.

loyalties[43] takes place here with a new family structure, whereby relationship to each other is no more based on blood but rather through faith in the one God. The idea of loyalty to God is the most probable explanation why Jesus can ask his followers to let the dead bury the dead (Matt 8,22) against what is found in Gen 25, 9; 50, 1-26; Lev 10,1-5. Burial was one of the duties of members of a family or clan. Among the Israelites and even in gentile nations, it was impious and insulting to leave a deceased relative and especially a deceased parent unburied. He or she was to be buried the same day and not to be left overnight. This moral duty notwithstanding, Jesus exhorts the potential disciple to follow him and let the dead bury their own dead (Acts 5,6-10; 8, 2). Arland Jacobson commenting on this text argues that "Jesus' call is utterly insensitive, in any context but especially in that of first-century Palestine. It is an insult to the most inviolate of all bonds, those of the family"[44]. If Jesus asked for radical fellowship of him to the neglect of a revered pious familial duty, then it must have been for something greater, namely, the union with God. They are to pray to him so that his kingdom may come and his will be done on earth.

Furthermore, they are to imitate him in the way he loves and forgives. In Lk 6,35 Jesus enjoins his followers to love their enemies and to be generous to all who ask them for help. If they do this without the hope of getting anything in return, they will have a great reward and will be called the children of the Most High, who is kind also to the ungrateful and the wicked. The goal of the members of the family of God is then to be as perfect as their heavenly father (Mt 5, 48).

3.2.3 Jesus' Community of Brothers and Sisters

As described in the previous section, the words father, mother, brother or sister in the vocabulary of Jesus as presented in the gospels are no more confined to the terrains of the natural family but rather have won a new social vigour (see Mk 10, 29-30), in the sense that they refer now not only to blood relations but rather they are also used to address members of a fictive family – called family of God. Since this community seeks to replace the natural kin ties at least in the circle of Jesus and his disciples, it also had to cater for the relational and material needs of its members, which were hitherto provided by the biological kin group.

The narrative in Lk 8, 1-3, especially verse ,3 hints at a probably common purse of Jesus and the followers in the inner circle: "with him went the Twelve, as well as certain women [...] and many others who provided for them out of their own resources". It demonstrates the sharing and solidarity prevalent in a kin group at the time. Going back to the burial of Jesus, it can be argued, on the one hand, that Joseph of Arimathaea offered his new grave for Jesus' burial as an act of piety. On the other hand, one also finds an idea of a "fictive" kinship solidarity including the sharing of material resources. Considering that

---

[43] Cf. Ibid.

[44] A. D. Jacobson, Divided Families, 1995, p. 262.

Jesus and some of his disciples journeyed together and spent time with each other and added to the fact that they left their biological families and formed this new community or family, it would be expected that a certain atmosphere prevailed in which they expressed their "family-like affective intimacy"[45] to one another. Joseph Hellerman is categorical in this respect and contends that Jesus and his followers "related to one another according to the standards of PKG [patrilineal kinship group] solidarity"[46], herein exemplified by the action of Joseph of Arithmathaea.

Important in the discussion under consideration is the word *ἀδελφός* used by the synoptics and the place of human family in the language therein. John Meier proposes that the word means first and foremost blood-brother, either a full or half-brother, that is, with one common biological parent. Apart from that, "every other use of *adelphos* in the NT falls under the general rubric of a figurative or metaphorical sense"[47]. His contention is that the metaphorical meaning of the term includes all those instances where "brother" is used to imply broad relationships "that cannot be equated with the bond forged by direct blood relationship or marriage"[48]. This thesis of John Meier suggests that family means more than blood relations in the language of Jesus. He found domestic life and household management as one of the most useful metaphors in presenting his teachings on the Kingdom of God but widened the boundaries thereof. In other words the composition and roles played in this family of God have taken on a character seemingly contrary to that known in kinship groups.

Peter Neuner in referring to the import of Mt 23,8 for the Church today reiterates the importance of fraternal relations between the members of the community of those who believe in Christ Jesus, without insisting on ranks or hierarchical structures. He is emphatic in his position and says that the internal structure of the community of believers is to be characterised by "siblinghood". Since they are children of one father in heaven, they are consequently brothers and sisters. This should be seen in their life and vocation as such[49]. Even though Neuner uses this image to explain the ecclesial intention of the author of the Gospel of St. Matthew, namely, to be a non-hierarchical community, his position fits into the schemata under discussion. If the family of God around Jesus is to fulfil its mission as leaven for the whole society, then the members would have to relate to one another in a manner that is worthy of emulation – they have to live as brothers and sisters, as intended by Jesus. This thesis finds support in the occasion of the last supper where Jesus washed the feet of his disciples, reported only in the Gospel of John 13, 1-18. Through this act he showed them to learn to serve and that all of them were brothers. Their greatness could and should only be demonstrated through their service to God and mankind.

---

[45] J. J. Hellerman, The Ancient Church, 2001, p. 92.
[46] Ibid. p. 71.
[47] J. Meier, The Brothers and Sisters of Jesus, 1992, pp. 19-21.
[48] Ibid., p. 21.
[49] Peter Neuner, Die heilige Kirche der sündigen Christen, Regensburg 2002, p. 50.

An additional element worth considering is that not masculine or feminine categories are decisive in the interpersonal relation in this family of God but rather the roles that the individual persons play at a given moment. The answer provided to the apostle Peter in Mk 10, 28-30 assumes an approach devoid of gender discrimination[50]. In this body of text all the disciples are being addressed equally as mother, brothers and sisters. The *community of believers* take up these roles in a replacement form. Karl Olav Sandnes, who refers to the community of believers in Jesus Christ as a redefined family, remarks that it replicates "the biological family not in terms of traditional gender roles, but rather in that the replacement-family refers to people taking up the basic functions of the family"[51]. This family is redefined in the sense that one experiences in it aspects of equality and inclusiveness, of friendliness, joy and a fellowship of sharing, of responsibility, of a hierarchical structure of obedience and "*servantship*"[52]. In comparing the use of family metaphors in the ancient Roman society with that of the early Christians Eva Marie Lassen makes a remarkable observation. She observes similarities in both social circles but also dissimilarities. In her view the Roman family metaphors were intended above all things to portray "hierarchical power relationships" in the aristocratic political system of the state. The kin terms used by the first Christians neither created nor supported earthly hierarchical order. "When in the Gospels, to take the most prominent texts, family metaphors were used to describe inter-human relationships, their function was primarily to create equality and a new sense of belonging"[53]. Robert J. Banks recognises the frequency of appearance of the kin and family terms in the teachings of Jesus and their significance. The rate of recurrence of the family terminologies in the Gospels which he describes as "numerous" leads him to the conclusion that "the comparison of the Christian community with a 'family' must be regarded as the most significant metaphorical usage in all"[54]. By creating the family of God through the categories of the human family, however, Jesus deviates from relationships defined by kin ties to a family type that emphasises the fatherhood of God. Those who call themselves his followers are to show their loyalty to the one true Father in heaven above every other authority in heaven or on earth. On their part, his followers are to relate to one another as mothers, brothers and sisters. The ruling principles are not power and hierarchy but rather equality and fraternal love.

---

[50] Cf. J. J. Hellerman, The Ancient Church, 2001, pp. 66-68.

[51] K. O. Sandnes, A New Family, 1994, p. 72.

[52]Cf. Ibid.

[53] Eva Marie Lassen, The Roman Family: Ideal and Metaphor, in H. Moxnes: Constructing early Christian Families, London and New York 1997, p. 114f.

[54] Robert J. Banks, Paul's Idea of Community. The Early House Churches in their Historical Setting, Grand Rapids 1980, p. 53.

3.3 The Pauline Community as Family

In the communities of St. Paul the principles of fraternity similar to that of Jesus were prevalent. Some scholars term the ecclesial life under the earthly leadership of Paul as Church-as-Community[55] of brothers and sisters, seen in terms of *koinonia*. The above-mentioned phenomenon brings out the vocation of these communities, namely to share communion with God and with one another, which was lived out with an extensive use of family and household vocabularies. In the writings of St. Paul an expansion of the Christian faith exists, and this takes place along "family lines in family-oriented society"[56]. He, St. Paul, knew the importance of the family social system for the spread of the gospel. Conversion began most of the time as a household affair and meetings were held also in houses and/or families. It is, therefore, not surprising that the apostle Paul opted for this social unit as the most favoured social model for his vision of the Christian Church. The frequency of use of such terminologies to describe his communities is considered by Vincent P. Branick to be "striking"[57]. Arguing along the same line of thought, Joseph Hellerman highlights an ubiquitous nature of the Church as family in the Pauline literature. He argues that the idea is "central to Paul's understanding of the manner in which interpersonal relationships are to function in the communities to which he writes"[58]. Three kinship concepts and their frequency of use can be found therein: Sibling terminology – 118 appearances – in terms of adelphē = 5, adelphos = 113; father terminology – 40 appearances – in terms of patēr = 40 and inheritance terminology – 14 appearances – in terms of klēronomeo = 6; klēronomia = 1 and klēronomos = 7[59].

The question is what was and is the meaning behind such an employment of family terminologies? Just as in Jesus' use of kin metaphors, the family in the Pauline literature should not just be seen as a social construct but more so it should be understood as a concept that underscores the importance of interpersonal relationships and the relationship of the individuals to God, the creator of heaven and earth.

Some New Testament scholars claim that Paul's use of family metaphors in his writings is more than a stylistic formality, more than a terminology and conceptual structure. He utilises the imageries as "a strategically crafted attempt to challenge and sometimes shame"[60] his readers to whom he addressed his letters so that they would put up a behaviour that is in consonance with the

[55] Cf. P. Neuner, Die heilige Kirche, 2002, p. 54.
[56] K. O. Sandnes, A New Family, 1994, p. 72.
[57] Cf. Vincent P. Branick, The House Church in the Writings of Paul. Zachaeus Studies: New Testament, Wilmington 1989, p.16.
[58] J. J. Hellerman, The Ancient Church, 2001, p. 92.
[59] These figures are taken from the research findings of Joseph J. Hellerman, ibid. pp. 92 & 246 and are restricted to the letters of Paul to the Romans, 1 and 2 Corinthians, Galatians, 1 Thessalonians, Philemon and Philippians, which are considered by most New Testament scholars as the letters where Paul's authorship is (most) authentic.
[60] Ibid., p. 93.

value system of family ties prevalent at his time, but also to lead a life that corresponded to their call as children of God. It is interplay of two factors. First of all, the family terminologies are used to help uphold moral and norms in the Christian communities. The second usage is ontological, that is, it is to make the Christians know who and what they are: children of God, whose duty it is to bear witness to the love of God. Since they are brothers and sisters there cannot be divisions, greed and dominance amongst them.

3.3.1 The Father Terminology in the Pauline Corpus

In Gal 4,1-7, Paul addresses his converts as children of God and these may also call God *Abba,* father. Drawing from the treasure of kinship language structure at his time, he accentuates this special relationship between God as Father and the Christians who have become his children through Jesus Christ, which took place out of God's own free will and love. That is to say that God sent his Son at his own appointed time

> born of a woman, born a subject of the Law, to redeem the subjects of the Law, so that we could receive adoption as sons. As you are sons, God has sent into our hearts the Spirit of his Son crying, '*Abba*, Father'; so you are no longer a slave, but a son; and if a son, then an heir, by God's own act (Gal 4, 4-7).

The idea that God calls his own creatures, human beings, to be his children is also the concept embedded in 1 Thes 1,4-5. Therein St. Paul adopts two elements to back his argument: human and divine components. He writes that the Gospel came to the addressees of his letter "not only in words [proclaimed through human beings], but also in power and in the Holy Spirit and with great effect". It is this Spirit of God who creates the relationship between the hearers of the Word and God himself. Whereas in Gal 4,4-7 it is easy to see a direct reference to a filial relationship between God and the readers of Paul's epistles, 1Thes 5,5 is an indirect allusion thereto.

Just as it has been observed in the Hebrew Scriptures, in the literature of the Second Temple writers and in the teachings of Jesus, so it is with St. Paul, that obedience to God the father and his commandments is greater than all other things. Not even circumcision or the changing of one's status, such as from that of a slave to a freeman, could par with it. He uses the image of slave in 1 Cor 7, 21-24 to illustrate his stance:

> So, if when you were called, you were a slave, do not think it matters – even if you have a chance of freedom, you should prefer to make full use of your conditions as a slave. You see, anyone who was called in the Lord while a slave, is a freeman of the Lord; and in the same way, the man who, when called, was a freeman, is a slave of Christ. You have been bought at a price; <u>do not be slaves now to any human being</u>[61].

[61] The underlining is mine. Cf. also 1 Thes 4, 1.

The last phrase of the text above could also be translated to mean: *be slaves only to God.* Rendering the text in this form helps illustrate vividly the preparedness to be loyal to God and to work for the realisation of his reign. Since Paul was not part of the inner circle of Jesus during the earthly life of the latter, one could guess that the teachings of Moses and the Prophets had an influence on his position on obedience of the commandments of God.

Another seemingly important aspect of St. Paul's use of kin imageries to appeal to his readers is the desire to create an identity for his communities, which was peculiar to their status as followers of Christ. This was also meant to distinguish them from other groups that existed at the time but were outside their boundaries. Consistent with the teaching of Christ they were to reject the struggle for honour prevalent in the societies and cultures in which they lived. In reminiscence: the Mediterranean society at the time of Paul perceived honour as a precious commodity. The group in which the individual person found himself could accrue to him honour but it was also expected that he would put in his quota to uphold this family or community honor[62]. Bruce J. Malina argues that honour in the Mediterranean world was always presumed to exist within one's own biological family – among all those one called

> blood relatives. Outside that circle all persons are presumed to be dishonorable, guilty, if you will, unless proved otherwise. It is with all these others that one must play the game, engage in the contest, put one's honor and one's family honor on the line[63].

The communities of Paul recognised honour as attribute, especially when it had to do with God. However, they were not to fight for power and glamor, since all of them were servants of the one Lord, Jesus Christ. In his letter to the Romans 12,11 Paul even asked the individual readers to regard others as more important than themselves. The task of the follower of Christ, which is to bring honour to God, is not extricated from meekness expressed in selfless service.

Although St. Paul stresses the fatherhood of the one true God in whom there is no difference between Jews and gentiles, the introduction of another fatherhood typology in the person of Abraham is perceivable in the letter to the Romans. As already observed previously in this work, the assertion to descend from Abraham, the ancestor of Jacob, the father of the twelve tribes of Israel, was the focal point for national identity of the Israelites. Paul uses this figure of Abraham and describes him first of all as "our forefather according to the flesh" (Rom 4,1). He then clothes Abraham with the title of a man who put his faith in God, who promised the former many descendants. Drawing on this premise Paul "makes Abraham the ancestor not only of Jews but also of believing non-

[62] Philip F. Elser, Family Imagery and Christian Identity in Gal 5:13 to 6:10, in: H. Moxnes (ed.), Constructing Early Christian Families. Family as Social Reality and Metaphor, London and New York 1997, pp. 122-124.

[63] Bruce J. Malina, The New Testament World: Insights from Cultural Anthropology, revised edition, Westminister 1993, p. 38.

Jews"[64] with one contradistinction: whereas the Jewish notion of Abraham was associated with ethnic identity, Paul reforms and gives it a new connotation. According to him, since Jesus Christ was or is a progeny of Abraham, the person who has faith in Jesus is also a descendant of Abraham – without distinction between Jews and Gentiles (Galatians 3: 15-29).

Unlike Jesus, however, St. Paul makes a diversion in the use of the father figure: at one and the same time he accrues to himself the title of father to the communities he founded[65] and of a brother to all the believers. He calls the faithful in Corinth (1 Cor 4, 14-17) his children. In the pastoral letter to Titus, written in the name of St. Paul, the latter is purported to have written the following: "greetings to you, Titus, my true son in the faith we share" (Titus 1:4a). K. O. Sandnes claims that the use of the metaphor father in Titus 1:4a is connected to Paul's "role as a mediator of salvation and the Spirit. The metaphor thus refers to his role of bringing his converts to life; he is their begetter"[66]. The basis for his fatherhood is, therefore, Jesus, whose gospel he proclaimed. St. Paul wanted the members of his communities to imitate him in his steadfastness in the Lord[67]. The concept "father" when applied to St. Paul himself is thus not meant to create a hierarchy or make him acquire certain favors from his communities but rather to help them see their communion with him in Jesus. The author of the pastoral epistle to Titus thus assumed the intention of St. Paul and attributed his write up to the Pauline corpus.

3.3.2 Unity and Fraternal Solidarity within and among the Pauline Communities

It was an important component of the life of the Pauline communities that they would be available to one another in times of need. It was also expected that they be capable of admonishing and encouraging one another in matters of faith (cf. 1 Thes 5, 11-14) while remaining united in mind and humble in spirit (cf. Phil 2, 1-4). A classical case study is the community in Corinth which was beset at one time with separation and disunity. This factional antagonism arose out of the question as to who belonged to Paul, Apollos, Cephas, Christ (cf. 1 Cor 1,11-12). There were also divisions when they met at the Lord's table (cf. 1 Cor 11, 18-33). The meals were held in groups according to social ranks. Paul responded to this situation by emphasising unity of purpose as a hallmark of the community. It was one of the ingredients for authentic proclamation of the gospel and for fostering genuine fraternal love amongst people who called themselves brothers and sisters in Christ (cf. 1 Cor 6:5; Rom 14:15). The

---

64 Cf. Halvor Moxnes, Theology in Conflict, Studies in St. Paul's Understanding of God in Romans, NOVTSup 53, Leiden 1980, p. 241-53. See also H. Moxnes, What is Family?, 1997, p. 29.

65 Christian Mhagama, Pauline Churches as God's Family. A Search from the Roots, in: C. McGarry and P. Ryan, op. cit., 2001, p. 188.

66 K. O. Sandnes, A New Family, 1994, p. 80.

67 See also Gal 4, 12-15; Gal 6,10; 1 Thes 1,6-7.

consideration of one another as children of the one father entailed living together in fraternal love and offering one another support in every form. St. Paul writes: "on the subject of mutual charity you have no need for anyone to write to you, for you yourselves have been taught by God to love one another. Indeed, you do this for all the brothers throughout Macedonia" (cf. 1 Thes 4:9-10). This text depicts a phenomenon of the Pauline communities as being those which shared their earthly possessions with one another. This virtue of sharing could even be described as the trade mark of every Christian community. Poor communities were helped financially by other well-to-do ones. Paul encouraged the Church in Corinth to support the Christian community in Jerusalem (2 Cor 8-9). But the support did not only end in material things. The members of the "Pauline Christian Family" were urged to pray for one another. It is a fact that his communities were autonomous but they were also inter-dependent. Neither a community of Paul nor a member thereof acted or was to act like a monad. Paul even showed an example in this regard: although he stressed the need to earn one's own bread and he did earn his own money, he accepted help from the brethren from Macedonia. This was during the time when he was in Corinth and in need (2 Cor 11, 9). His missionary work was supported by a Church other than the one in Corinth, thereby showing the interdependence and fraternity in the communities.

From the foregone analysis, two factors that catered for unity among the members of the Pauline communities are discernible: their faith in Christ Jesus[68] and their personal pledge to live in mutual harmony and agreement with others through prayer and acts of charity. The question is: who belonged to this family of Christ? It is worth noting that in both the Greco-Roman and Jewish cultures of the first century, a person belonged to a religious community by virtue of the family identity, the traditions of one's kin group and the elders thereof. For the Christian fellowship, kin groups did not serve as a condition for membership. It is also important to add that the members of these communities who shared the common faith in Christ and mutually supported each other were from different ethnic, geographical and cultural backgrounds. One thing that brought them together and cemented their relationship was the sense of a new and common non-biological family as stated in Gal 3: 26-28: "…in Christ you are all children of God through faith….There is no longer Jew or Greek, there is no longer slave or free, there is no longer male or female; for all of you are one in Christ Jesus". St. Paul does not only describe the communities as a family but rather he goes further on to visualise the Christian fellowship as being without internal boundaries based on race, status or gender. The household and family perspective is given a special character with the abolition of the distinction between slaves and free, female and male. "In the Christian fellowship the polarity between sexes, so fundamental to all family life, is of no interest"[69] any more. It is a Family of Christ in which there are no traditional roles of status and gender. The absence of the sex-polarity signals then a renaming of the Pauline

[68] L. S. Cahill, Family, 2000, p. 34.
[69] K. O. Sandnes, A New Family, 1994, p. 79.

family: it is not a natural family created through birth but rather a family created through baptism with its anchor in God. The members are bound together by the faith they profess. They share their property and strong emotional ties with one another. The consideration of family terminologies in the New Testament demonstrates to some extent the significance of the vocabulary in the ecclesiology thereof and plays a replacement role in respect to the natural family – the Christian Church is a family but with a difference: it is a family of God.

From the deliberations so far it has been observed that the term family of God has been used as a synonym for the kingdom of God, without one necessarily naming it as such. It must be noted, however, that the Church as family and the Church as kingdom of God are terminologies that refer to "a basic and significant similarity"[70]. In both situations God's reign prevails and the individuals therein relate to one another with fraternal love, solidarity, respect and warmth. In both the Church as family and the Kingdom of God hierarchical structures do not play any significant role apart from that of service and the doors are open for the inclusion of all humans of good will. When one talks about the Church as family of God, it is done with the consciousness that it is a family among families. Then even the human race itself is a big family of God. In this cosmos the Church finds itself, with its special character as leaven.

3.4 Christian Fraternity in the Early North African Church

The gospel message and the Christian movement spread to different parts of the world without losing its communal character as a family. The believers treated one another as brothers and sisters. The situtation did not only apply to those of the local Church. Rather similar fraternal treatment was given to those of other sister Churches, such that one can talk about "fraternity of the entire Church"[71]. In this section the situation in the Church in North Africa will be examined. The choice is based on two grounds: the life and development in the North African Church had a great impact on the entire Church. The first catechetical school in the world was established here and had Clement around AD 180 as one of its teachers and principals. This school played an important role in the evangelisation and teaching effort of the Church. Personalities such as Tertullian and Cyprian have also contributed immensely to the terminological development of the concept Church-as-family of God. As will be seen in the following subsections it was Tertullian, who for the first time introduced the term Church as mother. Cyprian on his part developed the concept but went further to complicate matters by calling those, who were not baptized in the Catholic Church as children of the step-mother. These factors make it appropriate to examine briefly the Church in North Africa. Special attention will then be paid to the teachings of Tertullian und Cyprian as much as these affect the research under consideration.

---

[70] Ibid., p. 82.
[71] G. Lohfink, Jesus and Community, 1985, pp. 154f.

In dealing with the North African Church it is worth mentioning the Churches in Egypt, which alone had more than 80 bishops around AD 300, Cyrenaica, 'Africa' or Carthage and Numidia, Mauretania, and Tripolitana. This region had experienced Greek and Roman imperialism at various stages in its political development. This episode later had consequences on the life of and development in the Christian Churches of North Africa. They were persecuted by the Roman political authorities and many Christians lost their lives. The founder of the North African Church, John Mark is reported to have been martyred[72]. Apart from the loss of life, many others were also put into prison. A third element worth mentioning is the emotional conflict that some of the new converts went through. An example is Perpetual whose conversion to the new religion was seen not kindly by her father, who most probably was not a Christian[73]. The Christians lived in a society where kinship ties were very much cherished. The conversion to Christianity meant that one was somewhat cut off from the sociological bond of his kin group, if the whole family was not yet Christian. The survival of the persecuted Church depended thus in fraternal solidarity grounded in the one faith in Jesus Christ. The imprisoned Christ followers were (mostly) taken care of by their brothers and sisters – of the faith family and not of the family of origin. They also addressed and treated one another as children of the one father in heaven.

3.4.1 Tertullian and Christian Fraternity

At the end of the second century and the beginning of the third century – circa AD 160- 225 – a young man called Tertullian appeared on the Christian leadership landscape. Before his conversion to Christianity AD 192 he was a lawyer. He later on separated himself from the Catholic Church and led an ascetic life. These two issues notwithstanding, his writings give insight into the brotherhood that existed among the Christians. In the treatise of Tertullian on *Our father* he perceives God not only as father of Jesus but also the father of all Christians. As already stated, the concept of the Church as family got a new flavour in this treatise through the introduction of the term Church as mother. Tertullian is of the view that in the Father and the Son the mother[74], here the Church, is also recognised (cf. *De Oratione 2.5-7*).

At the time of Tertullian the term family did not only have a conceptual significance for the Christians in Carthage and their relationship to the whole family of faith. More so it found practical expression in their daily lives: the Christian brothers and sisters were to live in harmony with one another; they

[72] Cf. Iris Habib Masri, The Story of the Copts, Cairo 1978, p. 14 and Jonathan Hildebrandt, History of the Church in Africa. A Survey, Achimota - Accra [4]1996, p. 8.

[73] This incident is illustrated in *The Passions of Saints Perpetua and Felicitas 3.* See also Geoffrey D. Dunn, The Early Christian Fathers. Tertullian, London and New York 2004, p. 16 and J. H. Hellerman, The Ancient Church, 2001, p. 169. Perpetua's family was a divided one. In the midst of the persecution, she held to her faith and opted for her family of faith and denounced her loyalty to the family of origin.

[74] The concept of Mother Church will be looked at into detail when dealing with Cyprian.

were to show loyalty towards the Christian family; and to support each other with material resources, especially the imprisoned confessors and the needy in their various communities[75]. Tertullian, whose views represent those of his Christian contemporaries, understood Christian brotherhood as a lived-reality and writes:

> Over the fact that we call ourselves brothers, they fall into a rage – for no other reason, I suppose, than because among them every term of kinship is only a hypocritical pretence of affection. But, we are your brothers, too, according to the law of nature [...]. But, with how much more right are they called brothers and considered such who have acknowledged one father, God, who have drunk one spirit of holiness, who in fear and wonder have come forth from one womb of their common ignorance to the one light of truth [...]. So we, who are united in mind and soul have no hesitation about sharing what we have. Everything is in common among us – except our wives (*Apol. 39.8-11*).

It can be read out of this text that Tertullian was defending a point that seemed to have been used by his opponents, namely that Christian fraternity was unrealistic, a utopia and empty of affection[76]. Tertullian held the view that the demonstration of fraternal love and solidarity is the mark of Christianity. He writes in Apol. 39 that through the practice of the special love found in the fellowship with one another, the non-Christians would say "'see how much they love one another'; (for they hate one another), 'and how ready they are to die for each other.' (They themselves would be more ready to kill each other)" (Apol. 39.7). The idea of the community of Jesus as family also finds its continuity here. The difference, however, is the motherhood of the Church in the theology of Tertullian, which was absent in the teachings of Jesus and the apostle Paul. The consequence is that loyalty is not only rendered to God, the father but also to the mother Church and to the members therein. The determining factor for belonging to it remained baptism in the one Lord, Jesus Christ[77].

3.4.2 Cyprian and the One Family of God

The concept of the Church as a community of brothers and sisters gained further colouring under Cyprian. First of all, he names the Church spouse of Christ and mother. According to him, only those who come from the same mother are the true brethren and he gives a restrictive view on the composition of the fraternity in the Church. The reality of persecution necessitated that the Christians held

---

[75] Cf. J. H. Hellerman, The Ancient Church, 2001, pp. 174f.

[76] Cf. G. Lohfink, Jesus and Community, 1985, p.155f. Caecilius observation that "they call one another promiscuously brothers and sisters" supports my opinion that Tertullian's position was apologetic and a reaction of the pagan views on the Christian brotherhood at the time.

[77] This was not only the position of Tertullian but rather the general view in all the Christian communities. Cf. J. Ratzinger, Christian Brotherhood, ^{2}1993, p. 37.

together against the common foe. A clearer identity as children of God was thus necessary. Seeing the Church as family made it possible to draw the boundaries of the Christian community and the non-Christian populace. Faith became thus a mark of identity. Beyond the spheres of membership and identity the Christians of the North African Church, who saw themselves as sons and daughters of one father God, were to imitate him in their daily life. Using God as the model for their daily living Cyprian demanded that kindness and mercy be shown to those lapsed Christians who had repented and wanted to return to the bosom of the mother. By doing so, they, as God's children, would be imitating their father in heaven, who is full of mercy and compassion[78].

Another element worth mentioning is that there was a certain level of connectedness between Cyprian's restrictive perception of membership to the Christian fraternity and his views on Church unity. In his position against the opponents Cyprian argues that it is impossible to contend against the Church and at the same time assume to be in it. He posits that a true child of God is the one who is born of the Church. Only such a person can call God father: "He cannot have God as a father who does not have the Church as a mother" (De Cath. Eccl. 6). This is the deciding point in the theology of Cyprian on the Church as family of God. Common fraternity is only possible because the Christian faithful have one mother called the Church and sibling solidarity and loyalty to this family is an important factor.

His thoughts on the motherhood of the Church and the common fraternity had practical consequences for the faith-family. For, as already examined above, true Christian fraternity takes place only within the one Church. All those outside it, both baptised and non-baptised alike are not considered in the theology of Cyprian. The common human origin is in this sense not enough to allow someone to be called child of God. It is, therefore, no wonder that one does not find the use of the term universal brotherhood or fraternity in the writings of Cyprian: the scenario is the Christian brethren against the others and/or the Christian brethren on the one hand and the non-Christians on the other. He expresses this clearly in his treatise on "Our Father". In chapter ten thereof Cyprian proposes that "we ought not to observe and understand this alone, that we call Him Father who is in heaven, but we join in saying 'Our Father'"[79]. By the term "we" he means those who believe; those sanctified through Jesus Christ: only those "restored to the birth by spiritual grace have begun to be sons of God"[80]. Whereas Tertullian draws the mother figure of the Church from the Lord's Prayer and uses it to show the importance of the brotherhood among the Christians, Cyprian like Firmilian employs it to make denominational differentiation – in order to exclude heretics and schismatics. If this position is taken seriously, the ecumenical movement in the

---

[78] In Epistle 59 he writes that "bearing in mind this kindness and mercy which He shows, we have no right ourselves to be over rigid or harsh and callous in caring for our brothers. Rather we ought to mourn with those who mourn and weep with those who weep".

[79] *Dom. Or.* 10.

[80] Ibid.

Church would have difficulties: there would be no common basis any more. Cyprian's mother terminology has another practical implication: the "non-brethren" did not receive help from the baptised of the Catholic Church.

The consequence of Cyprian's treatise is that true faith can only be found in one Church, and that now forms the basis for the brotherhood. The fatherhood of God seems to be taken for granted or finds its legitimacy only in combination with the motherhood of the Church. So he writes:

> There is only one Church which outspreads itself into a multitude [of Churches], wider and wider in ever increasing fruitfulness; just as the sun has many rays but one only light, and a tree many branches yet one only heart, based in the clinging root; and, while many rills flow off from a single fountain-head, although a multiplicity of waters is seen streaming away in diverse directions from the bounty of its abundant overflow, yet unity is preserved in the head-spring. Pluck a ray away from the sun's body! Unity admits no division of light. Break a bought off a tree! Once broken it will bud no more. Cut a rill off the spring! The rill cut off dries up. So too the Church flooded with the lights of the Lord flings rays over the whole world. Yet it is one light which diffuses itself everywhere; the unity of the body knows no partition. She reaches forth her boughs over the universal earth in richness of her fertility, broadens ever more widely her bounteous flowing rivers, and still there is one head, one source, one mother, rich in ever succeeding births. Of her we are born; her milk our nurture, her breath our life. ... He cannot have God as his father who has not the Church as his mother[81].

The above treatise was his pastoral approach to the issue of the readmission of apostatized Christians – caused presumably by the fact of persecution – and the recognition of the baptism administered by the so-called heretics. These, he claims, are not his brothers and sisters since they are not coming from the same mother. He calls them children from the stepmother. Even though the Church did not accept Cyprian's demand that those baptised by heretics be re-baptised, his position is not without consequences on future generations. How should Catholics relate to their fellow non-Catholic Christians? Are they also their brothers and sisters in Christ? If the answer is yes, then more concrete steps have to be taken in the ecumenical movement in contemporary times. An additional problem associated with Cyprian's view on the Church as mother is the danger of infantilising the faithful rather than promoting the fraternal relationship that should exist in the family of God. Since the Church is the mother, then she or those who represent it will say what the children have to do. The duty of the latter would be to obey faithfully. This observation fits into Cyprian's conception on *Ordo* and episcopate as discussed below.

A study of the commentaries on the works of Cyprian as well as his treatise and letters shows an extensive use of family terms within the Church.

---

[81] Edward White Benson, Cyprian: his Life, his Times, his Work, London and New York 1897, p. 182f.

They also present the Church as a lived Faith-family. In his writings the wording "most beloved brethren" is easy to find. This expression was used whenever he addressed a Christian community or a group of brethren[82]. The usage is so extensive that one could be tempted to assume that it was his greetings or normal address formula. This is what Joseph Ratzinger observes. He quotes a statement cited by Schelkle which states that the phenomenon looks like a formula when Cyprian starts the write-up of his epistles with "*fratres carissimi*" – most beloved brethren. Accusation against Cyprian in this issue is that only individual letters addressed to a bishop or cleric bore the singular "*frater*", otherwise he only called a confessor "frater"[83]. In its face value the observation above is correct. When placed within the social context of the time, the view would have to be revised. A sociological analysis of the Mid-third century indicates the existence of two benches in the social order: one for the commons "*plebes*" and the other for the senators. This division enshrined in the civil constitution was taken over by the Church. The commons became the laity and the *Ordo* assumed the image of the senatorial order. Edward White Benson, an acclaimed commentator on the biography of Cyprian and at one time Archbishop of Canterbury proposes that there is no reason to think that these terms were disputed in Carthage as either arrogant or inadequate. This phenomenon even assumes its structure in the sitting order in the Church and "as the senators in court and in basilica had the common-bench (*consessus*), so had the clergy in the congregation"[84]. Granted the difference created between the *Ordo* and the *Plebes* it can be assumed that personal letters might have also taken on such a character. This does not have to do with the interaction that took place in the faith-family.

As the bishop of Carthage, Cyprian was the preacher in the Church and so to speak the chief instructor, the principal arbitrator in case of disputes *inter alia*. Despite this fact, "Cyprian felt at all times bound to act on the principle which in one of his earliest letters he lays down – 'to do nothing without the information and advice of presbyters, deacons and laymen'"[85]. He had an ardent desire to promote the family atmosphere within his episcopate evidenced by his appeals to the faithful to take care of the needy and poor and those in prison. He also shared with them his personal property as detailed in Epistle 13. The difference in approach is found in the severance made between those Christians who remained in the bosom of the mother Church and the heretics including those baptised by them. In respect of those who remained in the bosom of the mother Church no difference was made in terms of their locality and/or origin. In his second epistle one finds a correspondence with Eucratius, a colleague

[82] In his treatise on the unity of the Church he used the term brotherhood to refer to the community of Christians. "Let no one deceive the brotherhood by lying; let no one corrupt the faith by a perfidious prevarication of the truth" (cf. chapter five on unity of the Church by Cyprian). The translation is taken from Roy J. Dferrari, The Fathers of the Church, volume 36, 1958, p. 99.

[83] J. Ratzinger, Christian Brotherhood, ^{2}1995, p.39.

[84] E. W. Benson, Cyprian, 1897, p.19.

[85] Ibid., p. 32.

bishop in Thena, who wrote to Cyprian to seek his opinion on the case of a former actor who upon conversion to the Christian faith gave up his profession. He, however, taught other Christian brethren a course in acting. The question was how to treat such a brother and how to deal with his material wellbeing. Cyprian wrote *inter alia* thus:

> if such an instructor pleads poverty and straitened circumstances, his needs can be alleviated along with those of others who are supported by the provisions of the Church [...]. But if your church is unable to meet the cost of maintaining those in need, he can transfer himself to us and receive here what is necessary for him in the way of food and clothing[86] (Ep. 2.2.2-3).

Even though Cyprian might not have written a personal letter to him with the address "my beloved brother", since the former theatre instructor was neither a bishop nor cleric nor confessor, he treated him as a brother.

In conclusion, one would say that the concept of the Church as family got a new coloring in the era of Cyprian in respect of terminological expression and (re)interpretation. The dynamism or relationship among the brethren to one another, however, did not change. They were not to be loyal only to the body called family of God but also to each other. The Church, however, gradually assumed certain structures from the civil constitution, which set the pace for future development. As will be shown in chapter four of this study, the ecclesial life gets mixed up with political administration upon the arrival of Constantine. The term brother and sister consequently got confined to monastic life where the ideals of the ancient Church as family were lived intensely.

[86] Quoted in ibid., p. 185.

CHAPTER FOUR

ECCLESIAL MODELS IN VATICAN II

4.0 Introduction

From the discussion in chapter three it can be observed that the Church lived and operated within the cultural and civil frameworks of the particular society in which it found itself, be it in Jerusalem, Corinth, Rome, Ephesus, Antioch, Galatia or Carthage. Some of the cultural elements were reshaped to fit into the life of the Christian communities and the gospel message, without necessarily disregarding the forms they had in the respective societies. The self-understanding of the early Church, that is, the image that it amassed for itself paid attention to the social contexts of the members. These socio-politico factors also affected the image of the Church as a community of faith. The summary of it is that in every stage in history, the Church tried to define and redefine its identity or self-understanding.

In his opening address to the second session of the Second Vatican Council Paul VI acknowledged the pronounced use of images[1] in scripture to illustrate the being of the Church. He described images such as the temple of God, the house of God, the bride of Christ, the mystical body of Christ etc. used in the Holy Scripture to mark out or illustrate the nature of the Church as beautiful[2]. They are, according to Paul VI, rich in meaning and provide the platform upon which the Church can reflect upon its presence in the world as a visible community that is hierarchically ordered but at the same time as a community with inner mysterious strength. Paul VI asserts that the encyclical of Pius XII, *Mystici corporis,* somewhat uttered the wish of the Church to have a description of itself and in what needs to be seen as more than a mere utterance, the Church was prompted by this encyclical to formulate a befitting and satisfying concept of itself[3] that was most appropriate to the thinking and belief system thereof. Even though the Church may be seen in some sense as an

[1] As mentioned earlier on in the general introduction, images and metaphors are by nature ambiguous. This, however, does not make them lose their usefulness or importance. For the ambiguity therein „induces an appreciation for rich layers of meaning and the inexhaustible depth, reach, and even mystery of the poet's subject. This is a quality extraordinarily appropriate when the subject is a mystery such as God or the Church". John W. O'Malley, Trent and Vatican II: Two Styles of Church, in: Raymond F. Bulman and Frederick J. Parrella (eds.), From Trent to Vatican II. Historical and Theological Investigations, Oxford 2006, p. 311. In this article John O'Malley demonstrates the differences and similarities in the language style of both Councils. Whereas metaphors and images were totally absent in the documents of the Council of Trent, in which "all the canons and decrees, […], utilized language that avoided metaphors in order to avoid ambiguity", Vatican II employs images to describe the self-understanding of the Church. Cf. ibid., p. 308.

[2] Cf. Paul VI, Die Aufgabe, in: Yves Congar, Hans Küng und Daniel O'Hanlon (eds.), Konzilsreden. Was sagten sie? Wie wird die Kirche morgen sein? Die authentischen Texte geben Auskunft, Einsiedeln 1964, p. 21.

[3] Cf. ibid.

institution, it is also a mystery and has its roots in God, who sustains it. It is, therefore, within the Church's nature to be always open to ever greater explorations of itself. In the view of Paul VI, it is this nature of the Church that permits it to undertake a deeper reflection on its life and being[4]. He observes, however, that the search for the truth about the Church of Christ is not to be carried out through dogmatic definitions but rather through such declarations by a special office of teaching of the Church that rightly expresses what the Church thinks about itself. Implicit in the above analysis is the consideration that theology cannot remain with the perception of the Church as an eternal objective truth but rather must go on to reflect upon the various ways of transmitting the faith and to take on the responsibility of making its thoughts and identity understandable.

In his encyclical *Ecclesiam Suam*, Paul VI wrote that the mystery of the Church is not a truth to be confined to the realms of speculative theology. It must be lived, so that the faithful may have a kind of experience of it, even before they come to understand it clearly. And the faithful as a community will indeed recognize that they belong to Christ's Mystical Body when they realise that part of the ministry of the Church's hierarchy is to initiate men and women into the Christian way of life, to beget them, teach them, sanctify them, and be their leaders[5]. This statement from Paul VI encourages an active participation of all the members in the Church's life to be able to adequately understand it. The Church is a reality in history – a dynamic reality[6]. It is, therefore, not out of place if it uses many imageries or symbols to articulate its being. For it is not impossible to discover in a musical symphony a *cantus firmus* even with many varied musical components[7]. This assertion is part of the foundation of this chapter and the ensuing ones.

In this portion of the study a historical survey will be examined on how the Church has understood itself in the cause of history and the images it assumed for its ecclesiological development. This will be followed by the ecclesiological models in the documents of Vatican II. It must be said that some of the models are overlapping. That is to say they are found in Vatican I and II, thereby allowing for continuity and innovation.

---

[4] Cf. ibid., p. 22: The German translation is taken Yves Congar, Hans Küng and Daniel O'Hanlon (eds.), Konzilsreden, Was sagten sie? Wie wird die Kirche morgen sein? Die authentischen Texte geben Auskunft, Einsiedeln 1964. "Denn die Kirche ist ein Geheimnis, eine verborgene Wirklichkeit, die von Gottes Gegenwart ganz durchdrungen wird. Ihre Natur ist dargestellt, dass sie immer eine Vertiefung ihres Selbstverständnisses zulässt."

[5] Paul VI, Encyclical Letter *Ecclesiam Suam*, 37. See also http://www.vatican.va/holy_father/paul_vi/encyclicals/documents/hf_p-vi_enc_06081964_ecclesiam_en.html (visited on 14th March, 2011)

[6] A. Dulles, Models of the Church, New York 2002, p. 19.

[7] Cf. Bernd Jochen Hilberath, Zwischen Vision und Wirklichkeit. Fragen nach dem Weg der Kirche, Würzburg 1999, p. 24.

4.1 The Ecclesiology before the Advent of Vatican II

The fact established thus far is that the Church began as a small and almost insignificant group of believers who considered themselves as brothers and sisters. The communal life among the Christians demonstrated a two-dimensional form of union[8]: horizontally through interpersonal bonds and vertically through their relationship to God, the father, who has accepted them into this new family through his Son Jesus Christ and in the Spirit. This image of a community of brothers and sisters in Jesus Christ, who see their offices and charisma as a special gift of grace was personalised and lived out by the individuals even if in the midst of persecutions. The Church understood itself as universal and one in spirit and deed even though diversified.

A dramatic change occurred during the reign of Constantine (AD 306-337). From this time on the Church gained cultural, social and political greatness[9]. It even assumed the structures of the political imperial state so much so that the bishops put on the titles and honour that accrued to the civil servants or administrative officers of the Roman Empire. The Church saw itself as a carbon copy or "mirror" of the imperial power - *imitatio imperii*. Biblical texts on the Kingdom of God were quoted to substantiate this position. It was no more only seen as the Kingdom of God on earth but also as an empress – "*imperatrix*"[10]. The hierarchical structure taken on by the Church later on heavily affected its identity and life. For, with the advent of this epoch the Church moved gradually away from its understanding as a theological subject to a juridical institution. The effort was not the examination of the relationship of the brethren among themselves and the emphasis on the eschatological component of the Church, but rather the struggle for power and titles: who is greater, the pope or the emperor? Beyond this power struggle was the cementation of the worldly, societal, political and institutional structures in the Church. One could even talk about a papal monarchy under the reign of Gregory VII, who per an edict 1073 acclaimed that there is only one pope. E. W. Benson reports that the title Pope or Papa was not only reserved to the Successor of Peter but also to other bishops of distinguished sees, such as Lyon, Rheim, Arles, Vienne, Carthage, Alexandria among others. According to Benson, "the first appearances of the title Papa at Rome are in inscriptions to the honour of Marcellinus A.D. 296 – 304 and Damasus 366 –384"[11]. It is thus surprising that Gregory VII appropriated the title Pope to himself alone,

---

[8] John J. Markey, Creating Communion. The Theology of the Constitutions of the Church, New York 2003, p. 46.

[9] Cf. Siegfried Wiedenhofer, Ekklesiologie, in: Theodor Schneider (ed.), Handbuch der Dogmatik, Düsseldorf [4]2009, p. 75.

[10] Cf. P. Neuner, Die heilige Kirche, 2002, p. 79 and p. 93. See also H. Wagner, Dogmatik (STh), Stuttgart 2003, p. 81. „Jedenfalls tritt mehr und mehr die sichtbar-institutionelle Seite von Kirche, gestaltet nach den Ämtern, Strukturen und Gesetzen des weltlichen Imperiums, hervor. Kirche wird selber ‚Imperatrix et Domina', der Gedanke geistlicher-sakramentaler Communio tritt in den Hintergrund. Im *Hochmittelalter* wird die Kirche vollends zum *Papststaat*".

[11] E. W. Benson, Cyprian, 1897, p. 30.

although it was not the preserve of his See[12]. This step undertaken by Gregory VII had tacit consequences. The universal Church with diversified communities gained more and more the colours of uniformity. Apart from that the pope, the bishops, the clerics and monks became those who dictated the life that the laity had to live. The problem associated with Cyprian's concept of the motherhood of the Church, namely, infantilising the faithful, comes up here in the form of paternalism. In this regard all those not in clerical or religious stand had nothing to say. They were more or less consumers of the products of the hierarchical structure.

No single ecumenical council till Vatican II succeeded per dogmatic constitution to lay out a self-understanding of the Church that was most appropriate to a given time: its existence and identity seemed to have been taken for granted and the hierarchical institution with clear cut roles and authority system were reinforced. It must be remarked that the observation made does not mean that efforts were not made at all in this regard. The coming of reformation and the consequent division in the Church[13] led the Roman Catholic Church to begin thinking about developing an ecclesiology per promulgation of a Council. The Council of Trent took it up, however, without success. This attempt was continued in Vatican I. The products of the deliberations here are *Supremi pastoris* and *Tametsi deus*, none of which became an acclaimed document of the council.

It is generally agreed that the ecclesiology between the Council of Trent and Vatican II maintains the visible structures of the Church as a necessary condition for salvation and the primacy of the powers of the pope as being indispensable for the apostolicity. This partly led to the assumption that the only true Church is the Roman Catholic Church under the auspices of the apostles and their successors[14]. The least description of this type of ecclesiology is that it was apologetic and defensive. As a reaction to the position of the Protestants who "stressed the invisible and inward character of the Church and were therefore seen as ultimately rejecting the whole of the Church's mediatory powers"[15], and aided by the national ideologies of the seventeenth and eighteenth centuries, which questioned the legitimacy of the papal office, the Catholic Theologians emphasised the visible and hierarchical character of the Church. They placed such an emphasis on their outward appearance so much so that other equally important aspects, for instance, the spiritual dimension of the Church, were virtually left unattended. The above ecclesiological standpoint does not only shake the validity of the prayer of Jesus that "they may be one" but also had consequences for the membership of the Church. The apostles proclaimed the Word of God. They baptised those who accepted it and believed

[12] A more detailed discussion can be found in ibid., pp. 29-31 and S. Wiedenhofer, [4]2009, p. 75.
[13] Cf. P. Neuner, Die heilige Kirche, 2002, p. 8.
[14] In Chapter Three of this study we saw this position briefly with Cyprian. In his treatise Cyprian perceived communion with the bishop(s), the successors of the apostles, as a necessary condition for Church unity.
[15] J.J. Markey, Creating Communion, 2003, p. 31.

in God. These formed the Christian communities called Church, the members of which saw themselves as brethren. Since Jesus Christ is the Word-made-flesh and the proclamation of the Word came before the formation of the Church, the principle of unity can and should be Jesus Christ. The above point notwithstanding, Pope Pius XII stipulated in his encyclical *Mystici corporis Christi*, that those who are really (*reapse*) members of the Church of Christ are those who have not withdrawn themselves from the unity of the Church[16]. Church should be interpreted here to mean the Roman Catholic Church. The teaching of Pope Pius XII in *Mystici corporis Christi* does not only have an implication for the unity of the Church but also has the potential of distorting the import and content of the apostle creed. At all times one has to bear in mind the difference between *credo in Deum Patrem ..., in Jesum Christum ... in Spiritum sanctum* from *credo Ecclesiam.* It is a belief in the one true God through Jesus Christ and in the Holy Spirit. This Spirit works through the Church, which is a community of believers in the resurrected Christ and a community of worship. In this context we experience the Church's divine origin and foundation[17]. Since it is also a community of believers its reality as a human construct cannot, however, be denied.

4.1.1 The Church as *Societas Perfecta*

The text of the Schemata of Vatican I, which was, however, not promulgated due to the Franco-Prussian war, illuminates the ecclesiological views that dominated towards the end of the nineteenth century. It states that "we must believe that the Church of Christ is a perfect society" (*Supremi pastoris* 10). Furthermore, "the Church is an assembly of the faithful of Christ, a true society, yet far holier than any human society"[18] (*Tametsi Deus* 2). This institutional and hierarchical conjecture of the Church was repeated in the words of Pope Pius XII who sees it as an error in divine truth, when some people assume the Church to be an invisible, intangible reality or merely something

---

[16] Pius XII, Eycylical letter *Mystici Corporis Christi,* 29th June 1943, 22. (Hereafter MCC).

[17] Peter Neuner illustrates this divine origin by analyzing the word in the Germanic languages. He goes further to also show the human hand that is also at work in this institution called Church. He says: "Dieser Doppelaspekt: Herkunft von Gott und menschlicher Einrichtung und Gemeinschaft, kommt auch in der Etymologie zum Ausdruck. Die in den germanischen Sprachen verwendeten Begriffe: *Kirche*, englisch *church*, niederländisch *kerk* leiten sich her vom griechischen *kyriakón* bzw. dem volkstümlichen griechischen Wort *kyriaké:* Haus Gottes, Herrenhaus. Hier steht im Zentrum der Aspekt der Tat Gottes, seine Berufung". See P. Neuner, Die heilige Kirche, 2002, p. 9. In the above mentioned form, however, the human aspect is expressed. It is a godly establishment without the work of human hands. A closer look at the word in Italian (*chiesa*), French (*église*) and Spanish (*iglesia*) reveals another component of the concept. From Greek *ekklesia*, which has found its way into Latin (*ecclesia*), the element of Church as assembly, a congregation or community comes into play. The religious element seems to have disappeared from here. For ecclesia as such denotes the coming together of the citizens of a state or city, the purpose of which must not be religious in nature.

[18] This text is taken from Patrick Granfield, Patrick Granfield, The Church as *Societas Perfecta* in the Schemata of Vatican I. Church History, 1979/48, pp. 431-446. Here p. 431.

pneumatological, united by an invisible bond[19]. Since it was the teaching of the pontiff, one would categorise it as being part of the official theological position at the time, twenty years before Vatican II.

During Vatican II Karol Wojtyla, the bishop of Krakow and later Pope John Paul II, made the following intervention:

> Although the notion "People of God" is in itself best for explaining the social nature of the Church, it does not seem best for describing the Church in *actu*, because it does not explicitly convey the idea of *societas perfecta*.... The Church is a *societas perfecta* in the supernatural order, i.e., disposing all the means necessary to attain the supernatural end[20].

Commenting on the above statement Patrick Granfield explains that Karol Wojtyla's preference for *societas perfecta* rather than "People of God" was more probably influenced by his personal political experiences in a communist system than his theological principles[21]. The argument of Granfield could be contextualised within the political dispensation in Karol Wojtla's home country at the time of Vatican II: the relationship between Church and State in Poland was seriously strained. It is also important to remark that personal political convictions can influence the theological outlook of a person and vice versa. The validity of one issue does not exclude the other. Therefore, it would not be wrong to assume that both principles influenced his personal theological orientation and viewpoint, namely the theology at the time and his personal experience of communism in his home land Poland. Whatever the case may be the fact remains that the Church has been influenced to a great extent by the cultural and political developments in the world and has hence also borrowed structures and terminologies from socio-political society[22].

The term *societas perfecta* traces its origin to the fifth century during the pontificate of Pope Gelasius whose attempt (496 A.D.) to distinguish temporal from spiritual authority or civil from ecclesiastical authority led to the development of the theories on Church-State relations. The consequence of this action was the birth of a social reality called *res publica christiana*[23]. This new social order, which could be termed as the "Christian commonwealth"[24],

---

[19] MCC 14.

[20] The English translation is cited in Patrick Granfield, The Rise and Fall of *Societas Perfecta*, in: Concilium 157 (7/1982): May Church Ministers be Politicians?, Peter Huizing and Knut Walf (eds.), p. 3. (English language editor Marcus Lefébure).

[21] Ibid.

[22] Bernd J. Hilberath is not surprised at this development. In his view the human institutions are not bad in themselves and could therefore be used as by the Church as building stones. He says: "Ein Blick in die Geschichte zeigt, daß Kirche nie ohne Anleihen bei gesellschaftlichen und staatlichen Organisationsmustern ausgekommen ist. Warum auch? Sind menschliche Organisationen grundsätzlich schlecht, oder sind sie nicht als Teil menschlicher Lebensgestaltung auch Bausteine für eine Kirche?". Bernd Jochen Hilberath, Zwischen Vision und Wirklichkeit,1999, p. 31.

[23] P. Granfield, The Rise and Fall, 1982, p. 3. See also Peter Neuner, Die heilige Kirche, 2002, p. 95.

[24] P. Granfield, The Rise and Fall, 1982, p. 3.

indicated the coexistence of the two powers, i.e. civil and ecclesial, in one reality. Over the centuries the issue of power sharing between these two distinct social units that formed the one existing society remained a point of controversy. In other words the state tried to intervene in ecclesial matters and vice-versa[25]. As long as the "marriage" between the two independent units harmonised, the Church did not need to position or redefine itself. The opposite was also true. In response to the increased disharmony between *imperium* and *sacerdotium* and as an answer to the marginalisation of or assault on the Church by the secular power throughout Europe and as a result of the birth of autonomous states in Europe, the Church redefined itself as "a separate and distinct society existing alongside, but not dependent on or answerable to the local and national societies in which it existed"[26]. This was especially the case in the eighteenth and nineteenth centuries. A perfect society in this sense does not refer primarily to the holiness of such a social unit but rather to its independence and completeness – it "possesses all the means necessary to attain its proposed end"[27]. *Societas perfecta* expresses self-sufficiency and autonomy. It was an inversion from the unitary perception of a society to a more or less dualistic term – the Church as *societas perfecta* and other societies[28]. A political conflict, which finds its root in the struggle for power, leads to a theological discourse with lasting consequences for the Church.

Franciscus Rautenstrauch was probably the first to have used the concept *societas perfecta* 1785 as a theological term. Many a theologian and canonist of the eighteenth century who were enflamed by this concept, however, portrayed both the Church and the state as perfect societies, with the proper power, what one could also term *potestas propria,* belonging necessarily and essentially "to the Church as a perfect society"[29]. They used the term to counter the stance of Protestant theologians and canonists at the time, who preferred seeing the Church as a *collegium* within the state to perceiving it as a perfect society. The Magisterium of the Roman Catholic Church also picked up the idea of *societas perfecta* in the nineteenth century and used it extensively in its writings.

---

[25] Cf. See also P. Neuner, Die heilige Kirche, 2002, p. 94f. He observes that since the time of Constantine the emperors saw themselves as defenders of the faith and for that matter of the Church. This was not without problems, since the civil authorities also wanted to be involved in the appointment of bishops. The apex of this happening can be found in the "*Dictatus papae*" (1075) of Gregory VII (1073-1085). The following excerpts throw more light on the problematic: He (the pope) alone can depose or reinstate bishops. He (the pope) alone may use the Imperial insignia. All princes are to kiss feet of the pope only. The pope may depose emperors. See Texte zur Theologie D 5, Nr. 72.

[26] John J. Markey, Creating Communion, 2003, p. 32f.

[27] P. Granfield, The Rise and Fall, 1982, p. 3.

[28] The concept perfect society was not only used by canonists, the magisterium and theologians to depict how the Church understands itself. Patrick Granfield mentions also the concordats the Church signed with Spain (1953) and the Dominican Republic (1954) in which both states "recognize in the Catholic Church the character of perfect society". See P. Granfield, The Rise and Fall, 1982, p.8.

[29] Ibid., p. 5.

Although the final documents of Vatican I do not contain the term perfect society as such, since the constitution on the Church with its formal title *Schema constitutionis dogmaticae secundae de ecclesia Christi secundum reverendissimorum partum animadversions reformatum*[30] was not formerly promulgated, their content and spirit were deeply influenced by it together with the thoughts of Robert Bellarmin (+ 1621) on what amounts to the true Church. According to Bellarmin, the one true Church is "the community of men [coetus hominum] brought together by the profession of the same Christian faith and conjoined in the communion of the same sacraments, under the government of the legitimate pastors and especially the one vicar of Christ on earth, the Roman pontiff"[31]. Furthermore, he says that the Church is as "visible and palpable as the assembly of the Roman people, the Kingdom of France, or the Republic of Venice"[32]. This view adds weight to the instantiation of the Church as an institution and a society separate and independent of others. This phenomenon brings to focus the following essential features: i.e., a structure of governance, accepted confessional *formulae* and prescribed forms of public worship, a constitution and identifiable members with a specific form of hierarchy or authority. Even though the element of communion is not completely absent in Bellarmin's definition of Church, the institutional component was over-emphasized in the cause of time to the detriment of the former. The institution per se is not bad, since every human organisation, regardless of the divine component inherent in it, would need orientation and authority structure. The dangers of institutionalism or what Yves Congar calls hierarchology[33] cannot, however, be relegated, to the background.

> By institutionalism we mean a system in which the institutional element is treated as primary. [...] Institutionalism is a deformation of the true nature of the Church – a deformation that has unfortunately affected the

---

[30] This document is commonly called *Tametsi Deus*.

[31] Robert Bellarmin, quoted in: Avery Dulles, Models of the Church, New York 2002, p. 8. See also Harald Wagner, (STh) Dogmatik, Stuttgart 2003, p. 82 and Disputationes de controversiis Christianae, adversus huius temporis haereticos, Ingolstadt 1586-93, III, 2: De ecclesia. According to Robert Bellarmin the Church is a "coetus hominum eiusdem christianae fidei professione et eorumdem sacramentorum communione colligatus, sub regimine legitimorum pastorum ac praecipue unius Christi in terris vicarii Romani pontificis". This statement can be found in his work: See also Harald Wagner, (STh) Dogmatik, Stuttgart 2003, p. 82.

[32] The translation is taken from Patrick Granfield, The Church as *Societas Prefecta* in the Schemata of Vatican I, p. 439. It must be observed that this idea was taken over by Pope Pius XII in Mystici corporis Christi 14. He, however, reconstructed it to fit into the spirit of his time and into the intention of his encyclical. As already observed, Pope Pius XII saw neither the bond of unity nor the Church itself to be invisible. That is what Bellarmin terms as "visible and palpable".

[33] Cf. Frederick J. Parrella, Conclusion: A Clash of Ecclesiologies, in: Raymond F. Bulman and Frederick J. Parrella, From Trent to Vatican II. Historical and Theological Investigations, Oxford 2006, p. 322. It must be stated that Congar's ecclesiology does not in any way ignore the hierarchical principle in the life of the Church. In his view, both the communal and hierarchical principles are needed in a balanced form so that the Church can appropriately develop itself. Peter Neuner, Yves Congar. Zwischen « nouvelle thélogie » und II. Vatikanischen Konzil, in : Peter Neuner and Gunter Wenz (eds.), Theologen des 20. Jahrhunderts, Darmstadt 2002, pp. 188f.

> Church at certain periods of its history, and one that remains in every age a real danger to the institutional Church[34].

One important consequence of the definition of Church offered by Bellarmin is the explicit demarcation of the boundaries of membership. These comprise only those who belong to the Roman Catholic Church and exclude the so-called pagans, the Moslems, Jews, Buddhists, heretics and apostates. Also added to this list are the Catechumens, who cannot yet fully participate in the *vinculum liturgicum* due to lack of baptism, the excommunicated persons and schismatics[35]. We could talk about the ecclesiology of "ins and outs". People who are searching for God and not sure of their stand in faith are not considered here. It is a demonstration of Church as a society with visible and clear-cut membership, which makes little room for dialogue.

The model of the Church as "*Societas Perfecta*" finds its realisation in the avowal on the visibility of the true Church of Jesus Christ with the four distinguishing marks of unity, holiness, catholicity and apostolicity of the Church[36]. When these values are over-emphasised it can lead to the suspicion that the Church could exist on its own without having anything to do with other institutions. It would mean the Church presenting itself as a *monad.* This experience of isolation has already been made by the Roman Catholic Church in the past. It was the time when the Church placed itself as the only true Church and in some way antagonised the secular society for more than a century. Vatican II corrects this position in *Gaudium et Spes* by making the encounter of the Church with cultures and other institutions in the world an imperative.

In the documents of Vatican II one also finds the use of the words "institution and society". However, the emphasis is no more on juridical stipulations but rather on hierarchy and governance of a Church that has the Vicar of Christ and successor of Peter as the visible head. He has the task of directing the affairs of the House of God[37]. Coming back to an argument made previously, namely, that the Church is from and of God, it follows that the Church does not need to develop static structures to justify its existence[38]. It

---

[34] A. Dulles, Models of the Church, 2002, p. 27.

[35] Cf. A. Dulles, Models of the Church, 2002, p. 8. See also Peter Neuner, Katholische Identität im religiösen Markt der Möglichkeiten, in: Peter Neuner and Birgitta Kleinschärzer-Meister (eds.), Ökumene zwischen 'postmoderner Beliebigkeit' und 'Rekonfessionalisierung', Berlin 2006, p. 56.

[36] The Council of Constantinople promulgated these four distinguishing marks of the Church and they were seen in a very legalistic form and very much concentrated on the pope, giving birth to a "papal-centred" ecclesiology. The Council of Florence 1442 went further to give the necessary condition for salvation in the visible Church. This standpoint was strengthened by the threat of damnation for all those who thought otherwise.

[37] Cf. Dogmatic Constitution on the Church *Lumen Gentium,* 18 (hereafter LG).

[38] It is stated in *Lumen Gentium*, 3 that „the Church – that is, the kingdom of Christ already present in mystery – grows visibly through the power of God in the world. The origin and growth of the Church are symbolized by the blood and water which flowed from the open side of the crucified Jesus (cf. John 19:34)." This reason is strong enough for the Church and it does not need other reasons to defend her existence.

does not derive its strength and viability from institutional structures but from God. It is founded on Christ and experiences the presence of God, its source and sustainer. Avery Dulles contends that "the innermost reality of the Church – most important constituent of its being – is the divine self-gift"[39]. Even though it cannot be denied that the Church has manifestations of both sacramental and juridical features, the hierarchical and institutional dimensions do not and should not bring about a play-down of the mysterious character of the Church. The term mystery is used to imply that "the Church is not fully intelligible to the finite mind of man, and that the reason for this lack of intelligibility is not the poverty but the richness of the Church itself"[40]. It is the kingdom of Christ which grows visibly through the power of God in the world. All men and women are called to union with Christ, who is the light of the world, from whom we go forth, through whom we live, and towards whom our whole life is directed[41].

To sum up: even though the perfect-society Ecclesiology was not the only known ecclesiology from the Council of Trent to the eve of Vatican II, it was the most pervasive one[42]. It eroded the traditional theology by creating a mechanistic view of grace whereby "active" membership of the ecclesial institution and its formal structure including the participation in its laid-down rituals were necessary conditions for the reception of grace. God's personal revelation thus was reduced to the confines of the doctrines and their interpretation through the Church's teaching authorities[43]. This feature has been described in this study as the play-down or lessening of the Church as a theological subject and the upholding of hierarchology, which negates the purpose and meaning of ecclesial life.

4.1.2 The Church as Body of Christ

Among Roman Catholic Theologians, Johann Adam Möhler (1796-1838) is said to be the one, who brought new vigor into the ecclesiological discussion in the nineteenth century[44]. One could even talk about a paradigm shift in the understanding of the Church. Its proper interpretation would be to perceive it as a rebirth of a theological thought of the first century Christians, especially in the spirit of the Pauline literature. In the year 1825 Adam Möhler brought out his thesis which shifted from understanding the Church through its juridical and structural dimensions to the very principle underlying the life and being of the Church – the Holy Spirit. His reflections placed the Holy Spirit in the center of life and being of the individual Christians, who have been part of the history and tradition of the Church. The principle here is a comparison with the human

[39] Cf. A. Dulles, Models of the Church, 2002, p. 9.
[40] Ibid., p. 10.
[41] LG, 3.
[42] Patrick Granfield, The Church as *Societas Perfecta*, 1979, p. 431.
[43] J. J. Markey, Creating Communion, 2003, p. 34.
[44] Cf. Patrick Granfield, The Church as *Societas Perfecta*, 1979, p. 434.

body. It is made up of various organs which are united and animated by one life principle. In the same way, the Church is made up of different parts "but is united in a single, underlying and transcendent Spirit that [shapes] all of these diverse activities into 'a community of love' that is itself the expression of the divine life"[45]. Möhler is not against the structures in the Church. In his view, these structures which are born out of the historical developments of the Church are necessary and important. He goes beyond the perception of the Church as a static and almost inert institution, to seeing it as an organism living in and through history. By its nature and like all other living things, it changes, grows and develops over time[46].

The theology of the Body of Christ was taken up at Vatican I. The first chapter of the schema *Supremis pastoris* was even named after it, namely, "the Church is the Mystical Body of Christ". The reasons were that

> it is used frequently in the scripture; it expresses the most important aspect of the Church, its divine essence; it is polemically useful against the Protestants who claim that Catholics consider only the external dimensions of the Church; it gives a balanced view of the external and internal elements of the Church; and, finally, it reminds the faithful of an idea that is little known but is important in this materialistic age[47].

Although this innovative ecclesiological treatise found its way into the corridors of Vatican I, it was not accepted as the most appropriate metaphor, owing to the thought that the image Mystical Body of Christ does not contain the exactness and clarity of thought needed at that time to define the Church[48]. The concept appeared only fifteen times in *Supremi pastoris* unlike the term *societas* which appeared fifty-four times. The French bishops at Vatican I even criticised the metaphor as being "too abstract and mystical"[49]. Their explanation was that it finds its proper meaning in mystical theology. One could, therefore, not build a schema on the Church based on this metaphor. Added to that is the fact that conceiving the Church as the body of Christ might mean also seeing it as *Christus prolongatus*[50]. The consequence could be that criticism on or of the Church could imply a critique on the founder – Jesus Christ.

In short, not much attention was paid to the metaphor „Mystical Body of Christ" immediately after Vatican I (1870)[51]. It experienced a renaissance from 1920 onwards and reached its apex with the publication of the papal encyclical "*Mystici Corporis Christi*" in 1943 by Pope Pius XII. According to him, "the Mystical Body of Christ" is the most appropriate image of the Church. He posits that

---

[45] J. J. Markey, Creating Communion, 2003, p. 35f.
[46] Ibid., p. 36.
[47] Patrick Granfield, The Church as *Societas Perfecta*, 1979, p. 434.
[48] Cf. J. J. Markey, Creating Communion, 2003, p. 37 and Patrick Granfield, ibid., p. 434f.
[49] Patrick Granfield, The Church as *Societas Perfecta*, 1979, p. 434.
[50] P. Neuner, Die heilige Kirche, 2002, p. 112.
[51] See J. J. Markey, Creating Communion, 2003, p. 37.

> if we would define and describe the true Church of Jesus Christ – which is the One, Holy, Catholic, Apostolic Roman Church – we shall find nothing more noble, more sublime, or more divine than the expression "the Mystical Body of Jesus Christ" – an expression which springs from and is, as it were, the fair flowering of the repeated teaching of the Sacred Scripture and the holy Fathers[52].

One important positive contribution of this encyclical is that it is one of the documents that have explicitly praised the contribution of the laity even if the Pope describes them as having an "honourable, if often a lowly place in the Christian community"[53]. Some see in the encyclical the advocacy of the individuality and freedom of will and conscience of the lay faithful. The members are not caught up in a congregated whole, rather they give meaning to the existence of the Church. Since the internal principle of the Church is the Holy Spirit, who edifies it with true life, the divine component and source is also ensured[54].

On the question of who the members of this body are, pope Pius XII answers categorically:

> Only those are to be included as members of the Church who have been baptized and profess the true faith, and who have not been so unfortunate as to separate themselves from the unity of the Body, or been excluded by legitimate authority. [...] It follows that those who are divided in faith and government cannot be living in the unity of such a Body, nor can they be living the life of its one Divine Spirit[55].

The theology of the Body of Christ found its way again into the Schemata and discussions of Vatican II. The metaphor of the Church as the Body of Christ helps first of all to explain the ecclesial body as a communion of persons. Seen in its sacramental form it represents Christ in history and gives meaning to the work of the Holy Spirit, "the unifying force at the heart of the Church"[56]. Harald Wagner asserts that by describing the Church as Body of Christ Vatican II personalises an ecclesiological option which has gained grounds in the many past years. According to him, it must be made clear that the Church is a living organism which is vivified by the Holy Spirit. Church is not an apparatus set before the faithful rather they themselves are and make up the Church[57].

---

[52] Ibid., 13.
[53] Ibid., 17.
[54] Cf. ibid., p. 40.
[55] MCC, 22 (see also MCC, 41).
[56] J. J. Markey, Creating Communion, 2003, p. 59.
[57] Harald Wagner, Dogmatik, 2003, p. 84." Mit der Beschreibung der Kirche als 'Leib Christi' (LG I,7) macht sich das Zweite Vatikanische Konzil eine ekklesiologische Option zu eigen, die in den Jahrzehnten zuvor immer mehr an Boden gewonnen hatte. Kirche, so soll deutlich gemacht werden, ist ein lebendiger, vom Hl. Geist belebter Organismus.... Kirche steht den Gläubigen nicht als Apparat gegenüber, sondern sie selber sind die Kirche".

Some theologians argue that it is not accurate to use the terms static for the body of Christ theology and dynamism for that of the People of God. For, as it were, there is life and dynamism in the ecclesiology of the Body of Christ. Wagner is one such person who says that the static label given to the Body of Christ ecclesiology has to do with the Neo-Scholastic movement of the 1950s. According to him neither biblical backgrounds nor the history of theology imbued the image with such an impression. The image signifies unity in and through Christ. The one Body of Christ has different parts characterised by the various ministries, charismas and offices; and especially through the many members thereof[58]. An important feature here is that the model shows identity and development. With the use of this model, the Church is understood in many respects as a Eucharistic community, especially in respect of the individual Church community – parish or diocese[59] (1 Cor. 10 and 11). One can compare these views with those of the Church as family. In its organic form it grows through rebirth and is united through the fatherhood of God, sustained by the power of the Holy Spirit and the members get their strength by being fed at the table of the Lord. The parish could be seen as the nuclear family and the diocese an extended family. In the same way one could look at the diocese as a nuclear family which shares communion with other sisters in the extended family. This thought will accompany the rest of this research.

The problem associated with the concept of the Church as Body of Christ is the exclusivity that comes with it. One is either a member of this body of Christ or not. It stands the risk of reducing the membership and communion to the active participation in the celebration of the Eucharist. The above point notwithstanding the concept serves to give all members of the body their respective places within the whole complex. No one is less important or over-proportionally meaningful than the other(s).

4.2 The Central Ecclesial Images in Vatican II

In the foregone deliberation it has been observed that up to Vatican II no particular ecumenical Council had come up with an ecclesiological constitution that clearly defined the self-understanding of the Church. The Council of Trent was beset with issues resulting from the Reformation. It thus got itself engaged in giving answers to the issues raised by ecclesial Protestantism and to "reforming the structure of Catholic life" [60]. The emphasis was not to present an ecclesiology. Vatican I came close to it but could not promulgate the document on the constitution of the Church because of the incursion of the Franco-Prussian war which caused the abrupt end of the council in 1870. Only *Pastor aeternus* and *Dei Filius* saw the daylight. This dogma brought up heated debates on the place of the bishops in the Church. It was even discussed whether the bishops were then the civil servants of the pope. The ensuing consequence was

[58] H. Wagner, Dogmatik, 2003, p. 84.
[59] Ibid.
[60] Frederick J. Parrella, A Clash of Ecclesiologies, 2006, p. 323.

the question regarding the place of the episcopacy. Some people saw the Church as the papal Church with its juridical construction and asked the question whether the proclamation of the primacy of the Pope then meant the elimination of the episcopacy. To correct this anomaly Vatican II sought to emphasise the importance of the episcopacy and put the stress on collegiality. This was already contained in the first proposal, whereby the office of the bishop was placed quite side by side with that of the pope. Apart from this difference the proposal remained faithful to the text and spirit of Vatican I, namely, hierarchical.

Most of the Fathers of the Council were, however, not in favor of the concept of the Church that permits it to be understood from the point of view of a particular office or function - not even from that of the bishop. The dominating view was thus a Church with a common basis for all its members – the baptism[61], through which all share their bond to Jesus Christ, who is priest, prophet and king. From this commonality it is then easier to talk about their offices or functions within the one Church. It also opens the way for a theology that is open to an ecumenical and multicultural world.

It must be added that the spirit of Trent and Vatican I was not totally absent at the Vatican II. Bernhard Jochen Hilberath observes that the proposal that was handed out to the Fathers of Vatican II dealt with the Church as an antagonist. It found itself in conflict and confrontation and had to assume a clear position against the odds of the time. It was laid out in a hierarchical structure: magisterium, authority and obedience etc. The language and structure of the document experienced therefore the expected resistance. Then, the council's fathers, wanted to do away with triumphalism, juridical language and clericalism. The result was the image of the People of God becoming the leading ecclesiological metaphor of the council. The concept shows that the Church is not to be understood "as an eternal community with unchangeable teachings and rituals but as a historical and dynamic reality with a rich and vibrant theological tradition"[62]. One of the promulgated documents of Vatican II, the Dogmatic Constitution on the Church *Lumen gentium,* incorporates the spiritual component of the Church and reflects upon it as an integral component of its ecclesiology. In other words, the document does not over-spiritualise the metaphors nor does it only see the Church from the point of view of the structures and the juridical aspect. The task here is to seek an equilibrium that allows for life and dynamism.

4.2.1 The Church as Sacrament

Under the models of the Church mentioned above, Church as institution and Church as Body of Christ, certain difficulties were encountered including the mentality of exclusivism that comes with a strict institutional model and the question of membership of the body. Among the many images that are offered in *Lumen gentium*, the document opts also for an ecclesiological typology of the

[61] See P. Neuner, Die heilige Kirche, 2002, p. 110f.
[62] F. J. Parella, A Clash of Ecclesiologies, 2006, p. 321.

Church as sacrament. In it one reads that "the Church in Christ is in the nature of sacrament[63] – a sign and instrument, that is, of communion with God and of unity among all men"[64]. Two elements worth appreciating here are the inner grace characterised by God's self-revelation on the one hand, and the external and visible structure of the Church on the other[65]. They become two inseparable entities and show the divine and human aspects of the Church[66]. The Church is at once "holy and always in need of purification"[67] – holy because it is of God. The Church is always in need of purification because it brings sinners to its bosom. This dual image finds an apt expression in the words of Peter Neuner who talks about the holy Church of sinful Christians[68]. He does not see the two components as being against each other. Human beings are "imperfect" instruments, who find perfection in God, their creator. This falls in line with the definition of sacraments in the Code of Canon Law 840. Sacraments are

> signs and means by which faith is expressed and strengthened, worship is rendered to God and the sanctification of humankind is effected, and they thus contribute in the highest degree to the establishment, strengthening and manifestation of ecclesial communion [69].

The signs referred to in this definition are the rituals or ceremonies of worship celebrated by a community of Christians gathered[70] by the power of the Holy Spirit, the purpose of which is to worship and to be sanctified.

This model has appealed to many Catholic theologians of the twentieth century and has its theological anchor in the Church fathers beginning with Cyprian, Augustine, Aquinas and gained new flavor in the modern times through Karl Rahner, Edward Schillebeeckx and Yves Congar, among others[71]. Henri de Lubac is said to be one of the great proponents of this model. He rejects any attempt that leads to "a merely secular and sociological understanding of the Church as institution"[72]. His proposal is a concept of Church as sacrament which harmoniously combines the divine and human

[63] Underlining is mine.
[64] *Lumen gentium*, 1. See also *Lumen gentium*, 3.
[65] Cf. *Lumen gentium*, 8.
[66] Cf. Second Vatican Council, The Constitution on the Sacred Liturgy *Sacrosanctum Concilium*, 2: "The Church is essentially both human and divine, visible but endowed with invisible realities, present in the world, but as a pilgrim, so constituted that in her the human is directed toward and subordinated to the divine…"
[67] Ibid.
[68] The original title of the book is "Die heilige Kirche der sündigen Christen". In it he describes the life of the Church through the various epochs. He highlights the hand of God that has carried the Church through the test of time and how human dealings have tainted its image. See P. Neuner, Die heilige Kirche der sündigen Christen, Regensburg 2002.
[69] The English translation is cited in Monika K. Hellwig, Sacraments, in: Michael Glazier and Monika K. Hellwig (eds.), The Modern Catholic Encyclopedia, Minnesota 1994, p. 775.
[70] Cf. ibid.
[71] Cf. A. Dulles, Models of the Church, 2002, pp. 55f.
[72] Henri de Lubac is quoted in: Ibid., p. 56.

dimensions in the Church[73]. Just as Jesus is the Sacrament of God, so is the Church in relation to the former. Whoever comes into contact with this visible Church comes into contact with the resurrected Christ and through him with the Triune God. The second Vatican Council thus describes the Church as the "universal sacrament of salvation". Two functional aspects of the Church are brought into focus: it participates in the salvation economy of God. The Church allows itself to be used by God and so becomes his instrument in this world. In this capacity it also serves to lead its faithful and the whole of humanity to their redemption[74] through Jesus Christ. The model calls for the authenticity of the Church based on its apostolicity – which gives it that right of being a sign of salvation in and through the historical Jesus, by the power of the Holy Spirit. Seen as a sacrament, the corollary is the reliance on God's grace, whose workings are beyond the limits of the institutional Church. This is a reminder of the old image of the Church as moon. Jesus is the light of all people including the Church as people and family of God. This makes the Church dependent upon him for the needed light and grace, demonstrating in a unique way that Jesus is in the Church but is at the same time apart from it[75].

Approximately ten years before the advent of Vatican II a Jesuit theologian by the name of Otto Semmelroth called the Church „*Ursakrament*"[76]. In English one would attempt translating the word as the primary sacrament, primeval sacrament, primal sacrament or the fundamental sacrament. This way of expressing the self-understanding of the Church was, however, not wholly taken up by Vatican II. In the opinion of the Council Fathers Jesus is the primary and fundamental sacrament – *Ursakrament*[77]. The Council, therefore, attributed this term to Jesus and described the Church as a sacrament, and this means that it is a sign and instrument for the union with God and of all humanity (LG 1;9; see also LG 48 and 59). It has the character of a "Realsymbol". Since Jesus is the Sacrament of God itself – *Ursakrament*, Harald Wagner argues that the Church can only be seen in an analogous sense. Jesus who unites or reconciles mankind with God lends this quality to the Church to be sign and instrument for the unity in God and with the human race. Wagner further argues that one should always keep the difference between the Church as sacrament and the various sacraments in the Church in mind. The Church is dependent upon Christ and must always see itself as a holy and sinful community[78]. One could say that the Church is a creature of the "Word", *creatura verbi* – in some ways a product thereof and at the same time it is a servant of the "Word", *ministra verbi*, which it has received from the Lord. One perceives in this context the difference between the Church as sacrament on the one hand, and the Church as instrument or vessel of the sacraments on the other.

---

[73] Cf. ibid.

[74] Cf. LG 48 and Pastoral Constitution on the Church in the Modern World *Gaudium et Spes*, 42 (hereafter GS).

[75] Cf. P. Neuner, Die heilige Kirche, 2002, p. 112.

[76] Otto Semmelroth, Die Kirche als Ursakrament, Frankfurt/Main 1953.

[77] H. Wagner, Dogmatik, p. 87.

[78] Ibid.

Important to note is that a sacrament is the outer sign of the inner grace. It may be possible to imagine a sign having no correlate in the real world. However, it is not the same with a sacrament which is a sign of something that actively exists. As Avery Dulles puts it "the conferral of a sacrament is an event; it is the self-accomplishment of a grace-filled dynamism seeking an appropriate bodily expression"[79]. Furthermore, a sacrament "is a socially constituted or communal symbol of the presence of grace coming in fulfilment"[80] and is celebrated not in solitude but rather in a community called Church.

Peter Neuner looks at the sacramental dimension of the Church from the point of view of mystery and points out that by doing so the Church goes back to the tradition of the early Christians and makes it – the tradition – fruitful. His argument is to dismiss the idea of labeling the Church with the image of institution and hierarchy to the detriment of the spiritual dimension[81]. The first article of *Lumen gentium* brings out this point very clearly. In defining the Church as a sacrament, the document emphasises the symbolic character of the Church for an intimate union of God with the whole of humanity, which finds expression in a community – the sociological unit symbolising unity.

4.2.2 The People of God

The concept "the People of God" asserts that all Christians irrespective of their function in the Church have received a permanent apostolic task in and through their baptism. An Appreciation of this position of Vatican II calls for a critical examination of previous views in the Church. An analysis of the history of the Church shows a development which did not at all times favour an ecclesiology based on participation. In the eleventh century Cardinal Humbert from Silva Candida wrote that just as the clerics did not accrue to themselves worldly power, so should the laity not also be involved in spiritual matters[82]. At the beginning of the 20th century, Pope Pius X sharpened the view expressed by Cardinal Humbert from Silva Candida in his encyclical "*Vehementer nos*" of 11th February 1906 by saying that "the Scripture teaches us, and the tradition of the Fathers confirms the teaching, that the Church is the mystical body of Christ, ruled by the *Pastors* and *Doctors* […] - a society of men containing within its own fold chiefs who have full and perfect powers for ruling, teaching and judging"[83]. In his view the Church is

> essentially an *unequal* society, that is, a society comprising two categories of persons, the Pastors and the flock, those who occupy a rank in the

---

[79] A. Dulles, Models of the Church, 2002, p. 59.
[80] Ibid.
[81] P. Neuner, Die heilige Kirche, 2002, p. 111f.
[82] Citated in Sabine Demel, Zur Verantwortung berufen. Nagelproben des Laienapostolats, Freiburg i. Br.-Basel-Wien 2009 p. 21.
[83] Pius X, Vehementer nos (11th February 1906), ASS 29 (1906), 3-16, 8. See also http://www.vatican.va/holy_father/pius_x/encyclicals/documents/hf_p-x_enc_11021906_vehementer-nos_en.html (Visited 15th June 2011).

> different degrees of the hierarchy and the multitude of the faithful. So distinct are these categories that with the pastoral body only rests the necessary right and authority for promoting the end of the society and directing all its members towards that end; the one duty of the multitude is to allow themselves to be led, and, like a docile flock, to follow the Pastors[84].

This illustrates a situation in which the inner structure of the Church was clearly divided: the laity on the one hand and the pastors on the other. Based on this background one could expect an open confrontation and criticism[85], since the thought was out of date with the life situation of the faithful. Adult Christians, who work hard for the development of their respective societies, cannot be expected to become mere recipients of the teachings of the pastors like docile flocks. Such a situation has the potential of creating a two class system in the Church: the leaders and the docile led. The fathers of Vatican II, therefore, wanted to distance themselves from an image of the Church as a society of unequal members and to buttress the common roots of all, namely, Jesus Christ, the resurrected Lord. Hence they opted for the concept "the People of God" to describe the Church's understanding of itself. This concept implies a reorientation for the life of the Church, perceived as sacrament or mystery and characterised concretely in the people of God[86]. It is interesting to note that the initial meaning attached to the concept was that it implied the laity. The current meaning, however, is that the terminology "the People of God" comprises the laity as well as the clerics. *Lumen gentium* in particular stresses the baptism as basis for belonging to the Church, as a means of getting initiated into the people of God. All Christians find their mission and call in this one act of baptism as prophets, teachers and priests.

4.2.2.1 The Context of the People of God

Two important issues are worth considering when dealing with the context of the concept "the People of God": God as creator and the economy of redemption. Just by looking at the wording of the concept one finds the centrality of God and his divine role as the head and creator of the Church that bears the name "the People of God". In addition to that the metaphor emphasises the continuity in the history of salvation, that is, the prevalence of the old and new covenants, Israel and the Church in the one concept.

Taking the bible as the starting point, Israel is conceived as the chosen people of God. It went through the desert with God, who had no special place

---

[84] Ibid. See also http://www.vatican.va/holy_father/pius_x/encyclicals/documents/hf_p-x_enc_11021906_vehementer-nos_en.html (visited 15th June 2011).

[85] Guiseppe Alberigo, A Brief History of Vatican II, trans. By Matthew Sherry, (original *Breve Storia del Concilio Vaticano* II (1959-1962), Maryknoll – New York 2005, p. 71.

[86] Cf. B. J. Hilberath, Zwischen Vision und Wirklichkeit, 1999, p. 26f. This re-orientation was a prophetic move and implied the readiness of the fathers of the Council to read the signs of times – freedom and equality.

than a tent. It was a people on a pilgrimage and serves as an example for the Church, which has joined this enterprise of a people on a journey, whose destiny is God himself. To use another image – it is a congregation that is being gathered by Christ' Spirit. Since its membership increases, since more and more are interested in the message of Christ, they come to this congregation of believers. Through its self-renewal and through its being in time and history, it is also experiencing exodus and is *„ecclesia semper reformanda"*[87]. This shows the dynamic dimension of the Church as a historical organism led by the Holy Spirit.

Not only is Israel a sign for the Church, it also laid down the foundation for the development of the image of the People of God. Israel is People of God – bearer of the old covenant and the Church carries the stamp of the New Testament through Jesus Christ. Both, however, find their origin in God. Then Jesus did not come to abolish the old covenant but to bring it to fulfillment. The validity of God's promise of salvation to Israel was not lost with the coming of Jesus, but rather it found fulfilment in him. It is also important to add that just as it would be wrong to assume that Israel has lost its character as the People of God or that the Church has come to replace Israel as the real People of God, it would also be wrong to assert that the Church has only picked up a concept from the Old Testament and personalised it[88].

As Peter Neuner observes, Jesus came and preached to the people of Israel, whose integrity he wanted to restore. He promised salvation to all, seen as a people and not just as individuals. He came for the people of God but Israel is first in this category. Therefore, there is only one people of God and not two or more, since there is only one God, the creator of heaven and earth. Neuner goes on to explain the biblical origin of the concept. The words *am*, and *laós* in Hebrew and Greek respectively are used in the bible mostly in the singular and mean people. *Gojim* and *ethnoi* are used in their respective languages to represent nations, that is, when one talks about other groups of people other than Israel[89]. The same term in its singular form is used to describe both Israel and the Church. This is one of the reasons why he is against the use of the concept "new people of God" when referring to the Church. For, as he puts it, it is possible to talk about the old and new covenants in the biblical language but one cannot talk about the new people of God, which replaces an old one. The concept is an all-embracing reality which inhabits the members of the old covenant and those of the new[90].

One other sign of commonality of both covenants is the holding of a meal, concretised through the celebration of the Passover meal and the

[87] Cf. P. Neuner, Die heilige Kirche, 2002, p. 116.
[88] Cf. Ibid. See also Bernd Jochen Hilberath, Zwischen Vision und Wirklichkeit. Fragen nach dem Weg der Kirche, Würzburg 1999, pp. 28f.
[89] Cf. P. Neuner, Die heilige Kirche, 2002, p. 29.
[90] Cf. ibid., p. 30. See also Siegfried Wiedenhofer, Ekklesiologie, in: Theodor Schneider (ed.), Handbuch der Dogmatik Vol. 2, Düsseldorf [4]2009, p. 93.

Eucharist, respectively[91]. Whereas belonging to the covenant meant mostly but not necessarily that the individual members traced their biological ancestry to Abraham, the same episode is not true in the Church. Decisive here is the sacrament of baptism, which brings the members into a special communion called the People of God. Irrespective of confessional differences, baptism binds the faithful of the community called Church into the People of God.

4.2.2.2 The Relationship among the Members

The People-of-God ecclesiology raises the question on the relationship between the various members of the community, especially between the clerics or hierarchy and the non-clerical members. To this end, the constitution on the Church, *Lumen gentium,* speaks about the common basis of all Christians: they all share in the priesthood of Christ. This gives birth to the difference made between the term universal priesthood or the common priesthood of all the baptised and the hierarchical or ministerial priesthood, which has the function of serving the whole of the people of God. These two forms of priesthood differ essentially and not just in degree[92]. This point could be seen as an attempt to correct the misconception of the biblical term *laós*, which was used initially to refer to the Christian community but later meant only the laity. A word that was used to differentiate the Christians from non-Christians turned out to be applied only to the laity – those without Holy Orders[93].

According to Otto Hermann Pesch, the original intention of the concept of the People of God was to give a name for all those without ministerial or hierarchical office in the Church[94] – as already mentioned earlier on. This understanding of the concept would have been a sheer continuation of what Pius XII wrote in his encyclical *Mystici Corporis.* This idea did not, however, find its way into the constitution on the Church of Vatican II. It is a new way of looking at Church and living as a community of believers coming from different cultures, countries and continents.

It does not mean that Vatican II abolishes the hierarchical structures or authority in the Church. It puts them in perspective, namely to serve the people of God. This deems to set equilibrium in the life of the Church and to draw the attention of all its members to the core of its being and vocation. In other words, the emphasis on the common priesthood seems to free the Church from the

[91] It is all the more sad that Vatican II makes mention of "the new people" of God. *Lumen Gentium* states that Christ, the Lord, high priest taken from among men (cf. Heb. 15:1-5), made the new people 'a kingdom of priests in God, his Father'. As already said above, we can only talk about an old and new covenant but not of an old and new people of God. We can only have the people of God, made up of members of both covenants.

[92] The translation is taken from Austin Flannery (ed.), Vatican Council II Volume 1. The Conciliar and Post Conciliar Documents, [3]1996.

[93] Cf. P. Neuner, Die heilige Kirche, 2002, p. 78.

[94] Cf. Otto Hermann Pesch, Das Zweite Vatikanische Konzil: Vorgeschichte – Verlauf – Ergebnis – Nachgeschichte, Würzburg 2001, p. 175.

narrow confines of a particular institutional structure. At the same time, it is a community of believers with a concrete and historical character which protects it from becoming a merely intangible and ahistorical conception.

4.2.2.3 The Essential Contribution of the People-of-God-Ecclesiology

Through the concept "the People of God" the Church identifies itself with the rest of the human family and pays special attention to the cultural differences of the various local Churches and the people therein. In reference to Acts 1,35 the fathers of the Council said that "at all times and in every race, anyone who fears God and does what is right has been acceptable to him". They go on to say that "destined to extend to all regions of the earth", the Church "enters into human history, though it transcends at once all times and all racial boundaries"[95]. This brings out the ecclesiological vision invoked by *Lumen gentium,* namely, the anthropological dimension of the Church which makes room for communion to take place.

It is also a revolution in the concept of the people of God that the communion within the body of Christ has a much better possibility of being realised than was the case with earlier councils which condemned in no uncertain terms all those who did not belong to the one Catholic and apostolic Church. The generosity and openness of Vatican II can be seen in the wording of *Lumen gentium* 16, which shows understanding to the situation of "those who, through no fault of their own, do not know the Gospel of Christ or his Church, but who nevertheless seek God with a sincere heart, and, moved by grace, try in their actions to do his will as they know it through the dictates of their conscience". Rather than condemning them, the Church sees this situation as a challenge to look at its evangelisation effort and how it meets the spiritual needs of those who are searching for truth with a sincere heart.

By providing various stages of being in communion with the one catholic and apostolic Church, one sees anew the possibility of giving back to the word „catholic" its real connotation, especially as it is in the creed. The term catholic in the apostolic creed is not a confessional description. Rather it shows the real character of the Church as a whole: it is pointing to the universal dimension of the Church and demonstrates that the sacramental fullness and the message of Christ are ensured in this one Church. The Church is in this case catholic because it lives according to the teaching and in the grace of the Lord[96]. Among the people of God there is no difference between Jews and Gentiles, rather all are called to form one body in Jesus Christ. As an organism the Church enjoys a great deal of variety, which enhances its beauty. If one should fear to promote this richness, which embellishes the unity and gives real meaning to the term catholic – in Greek: kat'holon – whole, totality of the parts, universal, one would be impoverishing the whole human history. It is important to repeat the point made earlier on that even though the Vatican II

---

[95] LG 9.

[96] Cf. P. Neuner, Die heilige Kirche, 2002, p. 86

acknowledges the unity of the People of God it does not lose sight of the fact that they comprise citizens coming from all nations[97]. They are, however, in communion with each other in the Holy Spirit, the principle and source of unity. The principle of universality adorns the People of God as a gift from the Lord himself. This, however, does not dispense the Catholic Church from its ceaseless and efficacious attempts to seek "for the return of all humanity and all its goods under Christ the Head in the unity of his Spirit"[98]. This brings again the divine dimension of the concept "the people of God" into focus. Accepting the fact that the Church is going through human history with trials and tribulations, the document affirms that it is being strengthened by God's grace. "This accentuates God's ongoing presence in history, as well as God's definite choice to reveal himself through a concrete, visible, and historically contingent group of people"[99] called Church, which is in need of self-renewal.

Important in the language of *Lumen gentium* is also the mutual or communion character of the People-of-God ecclesiology. It says: "he [God] has, however, willed to make men holy and save them, not as individuals without any bond or link between them"[100]. This statement shows that it is God who calls – illustrating the humble character of the metaphor. At the same time it arouses the desire to know why God is calling and in which form they are to live their life. The Fathers of Vatican II are categorical in their language: those called to this special community are to live in communion with God and with one another. The People-of-God ecclesiology also acknowledges that the Christians who form this people of God also belong to a bigger community called humanity. Even if they are a chosen people and a royal priesthood in and through Jesus Christ, they share their divine identity with other human beings, who are also created in the image and likeness of God.

4.3 Communion in the Ecclesiology of Vatican II

One of the visions or dreams of Pope John XXIII upon the convocation of Vatican II was the development of a theology of the Church which will enable it to differentiate between „eternal truths" and their proclamation in context. This entails reading the signs of the time and offering the appropriate responses to the needs thereof. Twenty years after the end of the Council, however, the extraordinary Synod of Bishops in Rome declared that „Communion" – in Latin *communio* – was the intended ecclesiology of Vatican II.

Having looked at the Church as "the People of God", it would be important at this stage to ask what moved the Bishops to opt for Communion as the intended vision of Vatican II. Is it a correction or a continuation of the metaphors presented in *Lumen gentium*? For, communion is not explicitly stated in the documents of Vatican II as the intended ecclesiology. Even if it may not

[97] Cf. LG 13.
[98] Cf. Ibid. 13.
[99] J. J. Markey, Creating Communion, 2003, p. 61.
[100] LG 9.

be out of context of the vision of the Fathers of the Council to undertake such an adventure, an important question is whether a hidden or better put an alien idea found its way into the hall of the Extraordinary Synod of Bishops in the year 1985. Examining the Church as a Mystery or Sacrament in *Lumen gentium* 1, Body of Christ in *Lumen gentium* 7 or the People of God in *Lumen gentium* 9 one experiences the presence of a Trinitarian Ecclesiology as the foundation of the Church. This is said regardless of the fact that communion-ecclesiology could also be a way of bringing the debates on the structures of the Church to an end. Under 4.2.2.2 of this study a differentiation has been made between the common priesthood of all the baptised and the ministerial priesthood through the expression "of essence and not merely of degree". Some theologians argue that if all baptised are equal, that is, if they are all brothers and sisters in the one Lord, then one should also create the necessary structures that would do away with ranking of the members[101]. In other words, the metaphors should not be used as ecclesiological cosmetics but should rather be translated into concrete actions. This is where communion plays an essential role.

Although the word communion in itself does not bring in a new spirit into the already existing metaphors, it serves to clarify the way the Church wants itself to be understood: it is a communion, that is, a community of believers, expressed through people of God, Body of Christ and sacrament[102]. The main point here is the element of community characterised by the Greek word *Koinonia,* granted by God, through which the individuals enjoy mutual help, and through which witness is given to the abundance of life that God has intended for all human beings.

4.3.1 Biblio-Theological Tradition of Communion

One of the tasks of the ministerial priesthood, in Latin "*Sacerdos ministerialis*" – the serving priests – is to "assemble the family of God as a brotherhood fired with a single ideal"[103]. The document does not say what this single ideal is. However, one witnesses in it the importance of unity of the people of God which traces its roots to the very beginning of the Church. St. Paul appeals to the community in Corinth to be united and to cater for the needs of all its members. Instead of showing discrepancy in relationship and instead of showing differences in rank and file, they were to build a real "*Koinonia*" translated into their daily dealings with one another. Not only in the Eucharistic communion is a person a brother or a sister but even outside of it. The import of communion here is to place the individual member in the centre of activities. It is this individual who is loved by God and who carries the name Christian. It is this individual member who is to be loved and called brother or sister. This value that he or she carries does not and cannot end in the Eucharistic celebration. B. J. Hilberath goes further to argue that it is inacceptable to only

[101] B. J. Hilberath, Zwischen Vision und Wirklichkeit, 1999, pp. 52f.
[102] Ibid., p. 53.
[103] LG 28. See also Decree on the Ministry of Priests *Presbyterorum ordinis* 6 (hereafter PO).

describe the external structure of the Church as a brotherhood in abstract terms. For him, it is not enough that the office holders only call one another brothers or confreres[104]. It should be the norm that all members of the communion see themselves this way. The words in Gal 3,28 stress that in Christ, "there is neither Jew nor Greek, there is neither slave nor free person, there is neither male nor female". All are one in him, Christ Jesus.

The Church is made up of people. To talk about the relationship between God and the Church also means talking about the relationship between God and his people. This is the basis of creating community and communion. Children grow up in families and Church and experience the integration in these communities. The existence of the building called church is meaningful because it is filled up with people who share the same faith in the one God. Even if the individual Christians do not represent the hierarchy and authority of the Church, they are the concrete instances for most people, including non-Christians. The mention of the word communion thus arouses the notion of community. The mark of a community is the interaction that takes place emanating from mutual interpersonal relations and intimacy among the members. From the biblical and theological standpoint, Jesus is the foundation of every Christian community. The Word became flesh and dwelt amongst us and by this encounter the human race shares fellowship with God the Father, the Son and the Holy Spirit[105] and with one another (I John 1,3).

Inherent in the concept communion – in Latin *communio* – are the elements of plurality and universality, which are characteristic of the human race. Isaiah 26,7b aptly captures this idea: "My house shall be called a house of prayer for all peoples". Although the import of this text is to highlight the purpose of the temple as a house of prayer, which should, therefore, not be disdained or profaned, it also underlines an anthropological presupposition that all humans participate in the one great universal community, which in turn participates in the divine community understood in the Christian tradition as God[106]. Communion in this sense is no more an option but rather an imperative. This is grounded in the fact that "human beings are deeply interconnected and interrelated. Our very individuality is rooted in our communal existence"[107] and the actualisation of one's self takes place in society.

It should be remarked that communion-ecclesiology does not stand in isolation. It relates to and carries with it the spirit inherent in the images of "the People of God" and the "mystical body of Christ"[108] and sacrament. Some Catholic theologians argue that instead of differentiating between the models, one should perceive them as metaphors that talk about the same reality. Their concern is thus a reflection on the sociological concept of community as a

---

[104] B. J. Hilberath, Zwischen Vision und Wirklichkeit, 1999, p. 58.
[105] Cf. Ibid.
[106] Cf. J. J. Markey, Creating Communion, 2003, p. 130f.
[107] Ibid., p. 126. See also GS 12-24.
[108] The images of the "Church as people of God" and "the body of Christ" are presented vividly in Rom 12 and I Cor 12.

principal factor that can propel the Church to renewal[109] – they emphasise the interpersonal dimension of the Church. The supporters of this thesis wish the Church in our time to become a place where one can create rich and satisfying primary relationships. It is one big community with many inter-locking communities woven together into one family of God by the power of the Holy Spirit, who guarantees the unity amongst them. The relation between the models has gone through a period of evolution in the Church, especially with Jérôme Hamer and Emile Mersch. Whereas Hamer illustrates communion in terms of vertical and horizontal relations, Mersch defines communion as "a network of mutual interpersonal relationships of concern and assistance"[110]. He goes further to describe the mystical body of Christ as a communion, which is at once inward and external: an inner communion of spiritual life of faith, hope, and charity signified and engendered by an external communion in profession of the faith, discipline and the sacramental life.

It is the very character of the Church to see itself in terms of a community or communion – demonstrated through diversity, relationship and dialogue. The ecclesiology expresses the organic dimension of the Church and serves as a program of action. An important factor is also the Holy Trinity, who serves as the communion par excellence[111] for all other forms. The unity and communion in the Church is thus an imitation of and participation in the unity existing in the Holy Triune God (LG 4)[112]. According to Walter Kasper, the Church is a Eucharistic communion which is not only a sign of the Trinitarian communion but also its representation[113].

The communion with God which takes place through word and sacrament concentrates itself in the local Church represented by the diocese. The Church in this form is under the authority of a bishop[114]. Some theologians

---

[109] Cf. A. Dulles, Models of the Church, 2002, pp. 48-49.

[110] Emile Mersch is quoted in : A. Dulles, Models of the Church, 2002, p. 42.

[111] P. Neuner, Die heilige Kirche, 2002, pp. 116f.

[112] H. Wagner, Dogmatik, 2003, p. 92. „Dieses Wirken des Hl. Geistes macht es auch verständlich, daß ‚Einheit' und ‚Vielfalt' in der Kirche *gleich-ursprünglich* sind. Der Hl. Geist kann in der Trinität nicht von den beiden anderen Personen (Vater und Sohn) ‚abgeleitet' werden, sondern indem Vater und Geist zueinander in Beziehung stehen, geschieht ‚communio' in Gott. Indem Menschen von Gott zum Glauben befähigt werden, bleiben ihre je eigene Persönlichkeit ganz gewahrt, und zugleich werden sie zur Gemeinschaft im Glauben vereint."

[113] W. Kasper, Communio, 1987, p. 279. See also Wagner, Dogmatik, 2003, p. 90. "Als 'Ikone' (Bild, Gleichnis, Zeichen, Sakrament) dieser dreifaltigen, communio-gewährenden Lebenseinheit Gottes kann Kirche selbst Communio sein und in ihrem Communio-Sein Anteil vermitteln am Leben des dreifaltigen Gottes."

[114] The letter from the Congregation for the Doctrine of the Faith shifts away from the organic structure of Church, which makes room for communion with other confessions, a communion which engulfs many more members than only those of the Catholic Church. It rather focuses on the communion based on the Eucharist. This is expressed strongly in nr. 5 and 11 of the letter. In nr. 11 for instance, one reads: "Unity, or communion, between the particular Churches in the universal Church, is rooted not only in the same faith and in the common Baptism, but above all in the Eucharist and in the Episcopate. It is rooted in the Eucharist because the eucharistic Sacrifice, while always performed in a particular community, is never a celebration of that community alone. In fact, the community, in receiving the eucharistic presence of the Lord, receives the entire gift of salvation and shows, even in its lasting visible particular form, that it is

deduce the development of sacrament-communion as a term emanating from the bosom of a hierarchical communion[115]. This argument is, however, too far-fetched. Hierarchical communion is only mentioned a few times in the documents of Vatican II and only in respect of the relationship between the bishops and their priests.

Undeniable is the fact that in communion-ecclesiology three elements play an important role: God, the individual Christians and the local Church. It also entails participation and responsibility on the part of all members of the Church (see also PO 1; AG 7 und UR 2). Given the danger of individualisation and privatization of the sacramental practice added to the increased pluralism and individualism in modern-day society, one realises the importance of the thought that no one is alone on the path of faith and the one who believes does so together with others.

Notwithstanding the positive sides of the model, there is also the risk of exaggeration and abuse of the community mentality, which could be detrimental to the actualisation of the individual being and personality. One has to be careful not to burden the communion with emotions or sentiments. This is grounded on the fact that different people have different emotional attachment to the concept and identify themselves with the Church at different levels.

Another danger of communion-ecclesiology is when the concept is reduced to Eucharistic-ecclesiology. This runs the risk of reducing the boundaries of the Christian community to include only those who actively participate in its life through the celebration of the sacraments. Since priests and bishops preside over the Eucharistic celebration, an ecclesiology that puts it in focus could lead to hierarchology or institutionalism. The consequence of such an action would be to rob communion-ecclesiology of its beauty and adorn it with clericalism, with the title of a community that only exists to fulfil its own goals. However, the Christian Church which calls itself a communion must not only exist for itself but also be a sacrament, a sign and instrument of God's

---

the image and true presence of the one, holy, catholic and apostolic Church". This statement is made seven years after the Extraordinary Synod of Bishops which described communion as being the intention of the Fathers of Vatican II. The question is what the self-understanding now is: communion-ecclesiology or eurcharistic ecclesiology? Whereas communion ecclesiology is open and emphasizes relationship (with God, among the faithful and with other members of the human family), Eucharistic ecclesiology is hierarchical and limited in some way to itself. One can find the Eucharistic communion in the totality of Communion ecclesiology but not vice versa. Whatever image of the Church we use, care should be taken that unilateral concepts be avoided. Conceiving the Church from the point of view of hierarchy is exactly the same way unilateral just as perceiving it only as a sociological construct. In advocating for the ecclesiology of Communion, Pope John Paul II illustrates what the concept really means. He says: "the ecclesiology of communion cannot be reduced to purely organizational questions or to problems which simply relate to powers. Still, the ecclesiology of communion is also the foundation for order in the Church, and especially for a correct relationship between unity and pluriformity in the Church". See http://www.saint-mike.org/library/synod_bishops/final_report1985.html (visited on 12th April 2011).

[115] H. Wagner, Dogmatik, 2003, p. 89.

desire to commune with his people[116]. But if the Church gives witness to God's communion with humans and the communion of the people among themselves (see LG 1) and if it wants to fulfill this task, then one has to experience it as a community of solidarity. It needs to distance itself from structural and hierarchical thinking which adds no value to its call and mission. Arguing along the lines of the ecclesiology of the Church as family, one would say that authority is for service and the one who serves is a leader but not a Lord. As will be seen later, it is this type of person who is respected and honoured by all in the society – such a person is a lover of life, he is a family person.

4.3.2 Communion and Hierarchy

The thought of communion as seen above could give an impression that hierarchy or authority in the Church has been or should be abolished. As already established the bishop represents the diocese and for that matter the local Church. Through his actions the communion with the universal Church is formed and guaranteed. Priests are seen in this sense as co-operators of the bishops. Together with their bishops they build a sacerdotal college called *Presbyterium.* Through their actions they make "the universal Church visible in their locality and contribute efficaciously towards building up the whole body of Christ"[117]. Associated with the above thought is the use of the concept "hierarchical union" as it is found in the Decree on the Ministry and Life of Priests *Presbyterorum Ordinis.* The document states *inter alia* that "priests are hierarchically united with the bishop in various ways and so make him present in a certain sense in individual assemblies of the faithful"[118]. The text emphasises the unity and cooperation expected of all ordained ministers in the Church: Bishops, priests and deacons. In a sense they build a community which is hierarchical in nature. In other words "the deacons and priest build a *communio hierarchica* with their bishop"[119]. The bishops do so with the pope. Hierarchical union thus serves the purpose of service and does not necessarily show the nature and character of the communion in the Church as a whole.

The intention of the Vatican II is clear: all the faithful form the one true Church of Christ. This position even goes back to Pius XII who emphasised that the

> faithful, more precisely the lay faithful, find themselves on the front lines of the Church's life; for them the Church is the animating principle for human society. Therefore, they in particular ought to have an ever-clearer

---

[116] Cf. B. J. Hilberath, Zwischen Vision und Wirklichkeit, 1999, p. 59. In the opinion of Hilberath, „wenn die Kirche nicht aus sich selbst und nicht für sich selbst lebt, hat sie einerseits transparent zu sein für den Grund, aus dem sie existiert, und andererseits hat sie offen zu sein für die, denen sie ja Zeichen und Werkzeug der Communio Gottes zu sein hat".

[117] LG 28.

[118] PO 5: „ut iam primaevae Ecclesiae temporis testatus est beatus Ignatius Martyr, Presbyteri diversi rationibus cum Episcopo hierarchice colligantur, et sic eum in singulis fidelium congregationibus quodammodo praesentem reddunt".

[119] B. J. Hilberath, Zwischen Vision und Wirklichkeit, 1999, pp. 60f.

> consciousness not only of belonging to the Church, but of being the Church, that is to say, the community of the faithful on earth under the leadership of the Pope, the head of all, and of the bishops in communion with him. These are the Church[120].

To label the Church as a hierarchical communion or union would imply doing disservice to the intention of the fathers of the Council. Even though the various offices in the Church are important, it would do the latter a lot of good not to over-emphasise the hierarchical structure, since the meaning attached to it is usually that of ranks or levels. Communion should, therefore, not be adulterated by combining it with "hierarchy" when referring to the whole Church.

From the discussion above the elements in communion could be summarised as follows: the Church-as-communion is personified in the fine mixture of the relationship between the Holy Triune God and the Church. Through its life and actions the Church functions as a sign and instrument of God's love for and saving act in the human community. John J. Markey contends that the image and language of "community and communion replace that of *societas perfecta* and other more institutional terms for the Church"[121]. He bases his view on the thesis that the option for the communion-ecclesiology is a sign of preference to describe ecclesiology by means of interpersonal over institutional categories through such concepts as discipleship, spirituality and sanctification in social rather than individualistic contexts. As much as community and communion focus on the individuality of the faithful, it cannot be totally accepted that communion-ecclesiology replaces one or the other ecclesiological typology. It is an ecclesiology with a wider communal character which depicts the needs of the time, namely relationship of the individuals with God and among members, and participation of all.

---

[120] Pius XII, Discourse to the new cardinals, Feb. 20, 1946: AAS 38 (1946), 149.

[121] J. J. Markey, Creating Communion, 2003, p. 95f.

CHAPTER FIVE

CHURCH-AS-FAMILY: A CONTEXTUAL ECCLESIAL MODEL

5.0 Introduction

On the African continent the image of the Church as people of God was also accepted as the one depicting the self-understanding of the Church. In fact up till today no one questions its appropriateness for the universal Church. The question remains, however, whether it is also the model that can be translated easily into the various languages and thought patterns on the continent? This question finds its importance when placed within the general ecclesiological landscape. Vatican II took place at a time as most of the Episcopal seats in Africa were occupied by non-Africans. The actual and prominent representative of the continent and also the only black Cardinal at the time, as Klaus Schatz formulates it, was Rugambwa from Bukoba, Tanzania[1]. The question is how much the Church in Africa felt heard at the council, even if it feels bound by the teachings of Vatican II and the self-understanding of the Church therein. Another impetus for the Church on the African continent in its search of an ecclesial model that is contextual in character is the positive outlook of *Gaudium et spes* on human cultures.

A look at the life of the Church immediately after the New Testament era reveals the efforts of many a theologian to develop an ecclesiology that was not only cognisant of the dominant and all-pervasive Hellenistic culture but rather one that also leaned on it. A case in point is Plato who influenced the thoughts of Origen and Augustine as well as those of the neo-Platonists at their time. The deliberations in the previous chapter also show that the whole structure of the post-Constantinian Church mirrored the then known imperial system. Bishops were accorded with honour accruing to members of the imperial court and wore vestments proper of the emperor. They also "presided over imperial political divisions called dioceses [...]. It is also well known that Thomas Aquinas used newly discovered works of Aristotle of the contextuality of medieval theological thinking"[2]. As contemporaries of their times, they developed theologies based on the socio-cultural world view thereof and in a language that was understandable to their respective addressees.

As it were, the Christian faith is and can only be understood in terms of a particular context, which is seen in theological discussions as an imperative and not just an option. In the opinion of Stephen Bevans, „there is no such thing as 'theology'; there is only contextual theology"[3]. He sees this in such

---

[1] Cf. Klaus Schatz, Allgemeine Konzilien – Brennpunkte der Kirchengeschichte, Paderborn, München, Wien and Zürich 1997, p. 290.

[2] Stephen B. Bevans, Models of Contextual Theology. Revised and expanded edition, Maryknoll-New York 2007, p. 8.

[3] S. B. Bevans, Models, 2007, p. 3.

categories as *feminist theology, black theology, liberation theology, Filipino theology, Asian-American theology, African theology, etc.*

The question is how different is contextual theology from classical theology? According to Steven Bevans, classical theology conceptualised theology in the form of objective science of faith, which emanates from reflections in faith based on two theological sources (*loci theologici*) – of scripture and tradition. The substance of this is unchangeable and is placed to be superior to every culture and historically nurtured outlook. Contextual theology, on its part, has another source of theology: "present human experience"[4]. In this case, consideration is given to scripture and Church tradition. Added to that culture, history and contemporary thought forms are accorded validity in theological consideration, thereby bringing the *loci theologici* to number three. This is the framework within which the subjective character of contextual theology should be understood. Subjective here is neither in relation to private nor to relativity. Rather it considers "the fact that the human person or human society, culturally and historically bound as it is, is the source of reality, not a supposed value- and culture-free objectivity 'already out there now real'"[5]. Borrowing the thoughts of Charles Kraft, reality is not just a given fact but rather is mediated by the meaning[6] accorded to it in our cultural and epochal context, "interpreted from our own particular horizon and in our particular thought forms"[7]. Kraft is of the opinion that "neither the absolute God nor the reality created [by him] is perceived absolutely by culture-bound human beings"[8]. Further to this is the view previously illustrated, namely, that what is borrowed would have to be given back one day to the owner. It implies that a theology or ecclesiology, for that matter, that does not pay attention to the cultural images of a particular society will not find its feet therein. This does not rule out the fact that the so-called "non-contextual theology" is also important. It had sense and place at a given time, "but the theology of others can never be our own". As a matter of fact, what is claimed to be non-contextual theology is contextual in respect of the thought patterns of its time and the circumstances thereof. S. B. Bevans posits, therefore, that "a theology that is not somehow reflective of our times, when it is perceived as irrelevant, is in fact irrelevant"[9]. This involves the consideration of the tradition, recorded in scripture and lived out in the life of the Church, and a reflection on the present context that is the daily life-experience of a people at a time[10].

Contextual theology should, therefore, not just be seen as a theology that only considers the contemporary life situation. Rather it encompasses both the past, which is sieved through thorough reflection and the present socio-

---

[4] Ibid., p. 3f.
[5] Ibid.
[6] C. Kraft, Christianity, 1979, p. 296.
[7] S. B. Bevans, Models, 2007, p. 4.
[8] C. Kraft, Christianity, 1979, p. 300.
[9] S. B. Bevans, Models, 2007, p. 4f.
[10] Ibid., p. 5. Cf. also Douglas John Hall, Professing the Faith: Christian Theology in a North American Context, Minneapolis 1993, p. 33.

cultural life experience of the individuals and community. Every theology has always been a contextual one since it was developed within a certain mind-set and epochal dimension. As Stephen Bevans asserts, the Hebrew Scriptures are a collection of theologies: the Yahwist, Elohist, Priestly, Deutronomic and wisdom theologies, respectively. All these theologies reflect different anxieties, times and even cultures of Israel characterising the various stages of its life: from an agrarian society to a monarchy, from an independent state to a vassal of powers such as Assyria, Greece, and Rome[11]. A similar phenomenon is found in the Christian scriptures: each of the Gospels was written under different circumstances and for a particular community. They also addressed the problems of their readers and tell to a great extent the worries they had. In short, the scriptures are also contextual.

5.1 Ecclesial Models Change with Time and Situations

A further look at the history of the Church reveals that some metaphors and images changed in the course of time and that no particular theology was "articulated in an ivory tower"[12] with no orientation to thought patterns and happenings of the place and time in question. In chapter four of this study some ecclesial models were discussed. The aim here is not to repeat such a discussion but rather to highlight changes that take place in ecclesial models to make them suit particular epochal, cultural and socio-political circumstances. The world is made up of different peoples who have their own cultures, languages and ways of life. These things affect their way of perceiving things and their thought patterns. This spirit has or was supposed to have guided the Church from its very beginning. In Acts of the Apostles 15, for instance, the apostle Peter appealed to his brothers not to put an extra burden on the gentiles, since God has purified their hearts by faith. He recognised the work of God in the life of the gentiles too. The trend continued with the apostle James. After quoting from Amos 9, 11-12, he stressed that no obstacles should be put in the way of the non-Jewish Christians, instead the apostles "should send them a letter telling them to merely abstain from anything polluted by idols, from illicit marriages, from the meat of strangled animals and from blood" (Acts 15,20f). The "law" was reframed to suit the socio-cultural particularity of a believing community.

Before the clash of cultures and the restriction on Christian religious freedom in China, the Sacred Congregation of Propaganda Fide issued an instruction in 1659 to inspire and guide the missionaries in non-European territories. It stated that the missionaries should

> not make any attempt nor in any way seek to persuade these peoples to change their practices, their way of life, their dress and customs unless they are openly contrary to religion and morals. There is nothing more absurd than transporting customs or practices from France, Spain, Italy or

[11] S. B. Bevans, Models, 2007, p. 7f.
[12] Ibid., p. 9.

> other parts of Europe to China. Nothing of this should be brought, it is the Faith that is to be brought, a Faith which neither rejects nor offends the way of life or customs of a people unless it is perverse or depraved[13].

The above instruction was written at a time that the Church was turning away from the so-called "pagan mission" to its vision as a world Church. The intention of *Propaganda Fidei* was to prevent the Spaniard and Portuguese from over-burdening the indigenous people in the "missions" with European culture. It thus paved the way for the re-development of the theory of local Churches which pays attention to the socio-cultural circumstances of the faithful. According to Klaus Schatz, such a new orientation or thinking was bound to bring the Church to re-consider its self-image[14]. It was a way of permitting the particular or local Churches to develop a life that suits their cultural situation, and this includes an ecclesiology that would give due consideration to the situation of the Christians in a particular place. It is, however, important that such an ecclesiology does not stand in isolation but rather is compatible with the other models of the universal Church. This will underscore the importance of contextual ecclesial life, which is necessary for effective evangelisation.

In this chapter, the factors that account for the search of a contextual ecclesiological image for the Church in Ghana will be examined. The proposal is that the self-understanding of the Church would be better received if the assumed image is conceivable enough in the language and environment of the particular Church. The deliberation leans on the concept of Church-as-family of God, the proposed image of the Church in Africa. To this end, a historical survey of the re-birth of this concept will be examined. The chapter will be concluded by looking at the various methods of evangelisation and their reception. The search for an ecclesial self-identity is intrinsically linked to evangelisation, since it is the vocation of the Church to proclaim the Gospel message.

---

[13] L'Osservatore Romano, 27th April 1994, p. 19. See also Collectanea S. C. de Prop. Fide, I.42, 135.

[14] Cf. K. Schatz, Allgemeine Konzilien, 1997, p. 269. He says: „Die Entwicklung von der ‚europäischen' zur ‚Weltkirche' kam schließlich in der *Neuorientierung der Mission* zum Ausdruck [...]. Dies geschah zunächst in Fortsetzung spezifisch römisch-zentralistischer Ansätze: nämlich der klassischen Tendenzen der Propaganda-Kongregation seit ihrer Gründung 1622, welche gegen die damalige staatskirchliche Beherrschung der Mission durch das spanische und portugiesische Patronat römische Leitung, einheimische Klerus und Episkopat und Anpassung an nicht-europäische Kulturen wenigstens in äußeren Sitten verfocht. Auf die Dauer musste eine solche Neuorientierung freilich ein zentralistisches Kirchenbild in Frage gestellt und [...] zu einer Neubesinnung auf die Ortskirche als Inkulturation des Evangeliums führen". Even though many non-European cultures were still considered as pagan and fetish in the nineteenth century (this was the reason why St. Arnold Janssen founded the Society of the Divine Word, SVD), the instruction from the Sacred Congregation of Propaganda Fidei was a necessary impulse for theological reflection.

5.1.1 Ecclesial Response to Changes in Society by Local Churches in the 1960s and 70s

An outstanding contribution to the phenomenon of local Churches responding appropriately to the life situation of the Church and its members in society is that of Burkina Faso, formerly Upper Volta. Friedrich Bechina, who has done an extensive study on this topic, makes the observation that as far back as 1962 the Bishops of the country wrote a pastoral letter in which they made mention of the Church being a family of the children of God[15]. The mystery of the Holy Trinity was taken as the basis for the above position. The concept was expounded in the years that followed caused by the immediate socio-political situation in the country, namely, the confrontation of the bishops with the regime at the time in respect of the ownership and running of the Catholic schools between 1964 and 1969[16]. The bishops were surprised to find out that the laity and parents of the children did not have any interest in taking up responsibility in the society on behalf of the Church. The lack of zeal for the matters of the Church in such a situation could trace its roots to the fact that the lay faithful did not identify themselves with the Church. One most appropriate response to this was to adopt a model that is present and real for the average person of the country, namely the family. The bishops observed that every member of their Churches belonged to a family and they participated actively in the life therein. Assuming the extended family as starting point the bishops called into being the *"Organisation de la Communauté Chrétienne"* which aimed at assembling the Christians in the country into an extended family in order to help them relive the values of the early Christian communities. The consequence was the formation of *Communauté Chrétienne de Base*. At the height of this happening, the bishops of the country explicitly acclaimed that the Church in Upper Volta was a family of God. This was contained in their pastoral letter to climax the 75th jubilee celebration of the evangelisation of Upper Volta in the year 1975[17]. The bishops made an appeal at the beginning of 1976 to all the children of the land to dialogue with them. The result of the appeal was that the whole of Upper Volta and not just the Church alone was termed as family. They are children with the same ancestry. Their commonness should thus be the basis for the promotion of fraternal solidarity and unity of purpose.

Remarkably the bishops opted for a Church model that took leave of a clerical Church to one in which the faithful together with the priests and bishops carry the responsibility of evangelisation and the building up of their society. This position goes to answer the question regarding the ecclesiological model which pays attention to the reality of life of the Christian, in order to allow him participate actively and effectively in building the Church of Christ and a humane world. The Church-family – *Église-Famille* – emerged as the most

[15] F. Bechina, Die Kirche als "Familie Gottes", 1998, pp. 384-404.
[16] Cf. ibid., p. 385.
[17] Cf. ibid., pp. 385f.

appropriate option. The concept offers the sense of belonging, unity of purpose, solidarity, reciprocal responsibility for the welfare of all and hospitality. The choice of the ecclesiological image has three pillars: biblical, theological and socio-cultural. It also has two components – divine and human. The divine nature is based on the fact that Church-Family has the Trinity as its likeness[18]. The human aspect is modeled on the perception of the Church as a social unit formed by human beings. According to the bishops, the concept was to take shape in the Basic Christian Communities, considered above as *Communauté Chrétienne de Base*.

Apart from the concrete and explicit description of the image of the Church in today Burkina Faso, there are no records of any other country that also undertook such an ecclesiological endeavor in Africa before the Special Assembly for Africa of the Synod of Bishops 1994[19]. A statement from Bishop Jean-Marie Cissé during the twelfth general congregation of the Synod of Africa 1994 indicates that other Churches on the continent, however, have made efforts to identify models that best suit their situations, even if not much is written on them. In his presentation, Bishop J.-M Cissé mentions first of all the indications of fragility of the Church in Mali. Lamentable, he says, is the dependence of the bishops on external financiers for the implementation of their pastoral projects even though they are the heads of their local Churches. The answer to this situation is the ecclesiological option for "a Church of fraternal communion at the service of the Gospel". By this method small living ecclesial communities are created and promoted. The dioceses in Mali have also developed a common financial policy, which is

> characterized by solidarity within the Diocese and between the Dioceses, solidarity with other Churches and the universal Church. This is expressed by a common fund gathering together the financial resources of our six Dioceses and of missionaries currently working with us. The aim is to achieve a Church that is capable of walking on its two legs, one representing the material and financial means necessary for the People of God to be able to assume their rights and duties, all under the authority of the Head, who is none other than Christ[20].

No name is given to the ecclesiological model in the Church(es) in Mali. Discernible, however, are the principles pertaining to life among family members. Another important factor in the situation in Mali is the desire of the local Churches to gain their own identity through financial independence. Their method resembles the traditional form of having a common silo for a household. The cereals from this common depot are apportioned among the women on a weekly or monthly basis, who then take up the responsibility of cooking for their respective units. It is the

[18] Cf. ibid., pp. 386-93.
[19] Cf. ibid., p. 404.
[20] Bishop Jean-Marie Cissé, A Fraternal Church at the Service of the Gospel, in: OR, 11th May 1994, p. 10.

basic form of solidarity in the traditional savannah family. The method promotes cooperation and life within a bigger household unit. For the bishops of Mali, the exercise of solidarity among the dioceses and missionary congregations is meant to make them be available for the proclamation of the gospel. As will be seen later on in this study the above-mentioned principles – of sharing and solidarity – can only bear fruits if all the members participate in it – the bishops, priests, religious men and women and the lay faithful.

5.1.2 The Church-as-Family: The Cry of the Third World in Vatican II

As already observed in chapter four of this study, the list of ecclesiological models presented in *Lumen gentium* 6 and the articles that follow it is an indication of the inexhaustible options open to the Church to define its identity at a given epoch. Apart from the beauty that they portray, the many images listed especially in *Lumen gentium* 6 show that no single image of the Church can be most appropriate for all people of every culture and at all times. The image of the Church as "the People of God" became the most acclaimed model of Vatican II. It is, however, also known that many bishops of the Third World – Asia, Latin America and Africa – proposed the metaphor "Church-as-Family" of God as the most appropriate model that illustrates vividly the self-understanding of the Church[21]. The adoption of the concept "The People of God" as a compromise was a better one for the bishops from the said Third World. They could live better with a theology that more and more saw the Church as historical reality but is decentralised, even if that meant a loss of some Episcopal power, than a theology that is based on the creation of a system or structure which is closed in to itself with already prepared answers[22]. For them the former theology was a better response to the pastoral situation in their dioceses than the latter.

Going back to history, it can be observed that during the second session of the Council's sitting the concept "family of God" was put at the discussion table by Bishop S. Hoa Nguyen Van Hien. Another supporter, Archbishop G. De Proenca Sigaud from Latin America was of the opinion that the concept Church be defined with the help of *familia Dei* because of its nearness to the everyday life-experience of the faithful. He said that

> the pilgrim catholic Church on Earth is truly the family of God. In this divine family God the good father, [...] Jesus Christ, the saviour, is the invisible head and brother, the first born of all brothers (Rom. 8,29); the faithful – born of God through baptism and fed with the flesh of Christ in the Eucharist – are children of God [...] and brothers to one another[23].

[21] See F. Bechina, Die Kirche als „Familie Gottes", 1997, p. 37f.
[22] Klaus Schatz, Allgemeine Konzilien, 1997, pp. 290f.
[23] Friedrich Bechina has made a detailed examination of this topic in his doctoral thesis. Cf. F. Bechina, Die Kirche als "Familie Gottes", 1998, pp. 37-41. See p. 41 for the qoutation from Archbishop G. De Proenca.

Archbishop De Proenca demonstrates clearly that the call to the Christian faith comes from God himself. The three persons are active in the community that the Christians live in – then all are baptised in the name of God the Father and the Son and the Holy Spirit. At the Eucharistic table the three divine persons are again actively present and giving life to all of creation. Since the Christian faithful are born of God in baptism, it is logical that they are brothers and sisters to one another.

Even though the concept Church-as-family of God was not taken over by Vatican II as the leading ecclesial self-understanding it was not totally ignored in the documents thereof. The frequency with which it is used in the documents demonstrates to a certain extent its importance and compatibility to the other images. In the Dogmatic Constitution on the Church *Lumen gentium* 6 the concept family is mentioned two times. In the first application family life is used together with marriage as one of the images expressing the inner nature of the Church. In its second usage the image is combined with the House of God. It is stated thus:

> often, too, the Church is called the building of God (1 Cor. 3,9) [...]. The edifice has many names to describe it: the house of God in which <u>his family</u> dwells; the household of God in the Spirit (Eph. 2,19.22); the dwelling-place of God among men[24].

The pronoun "his" is used in reference to God. The translation could equally have been rendered as *the house in which the family of God dwells*, to clearly bring out the possessive form therein. In any case *Lumen gentium* 6 gives the first evidence to the use of the image family of God to refer to the Church.

By the application of the concept *Lumen gentium* sends a sign of hope and resurrection to the whole universe, namely that all Christians are brothers and sisters in the one Lord Jesus Christ. The metaphor which portrays unity, solidarity and relationship in our world finds vivid expression in a comparison with the human race which is seeking more and more civil, economic and social unity. The document bestows it on the leadership of the Church at all levels to seek to "eliminate divisions and dissentions in every shape or form, so that all mankind may be led into the unity of the family of God"[25]. In respect of the Christian Church itself the Decree on Ecumenism *Unitatis Redintegration* categorically highlights that "in the confession of one faith, in the common celebration of divine worship, and in the fraternal harmony of the family of God"[26] the Church strives to fulfill the wish of Jesus Christ the Lord, who prayed to his father that all may be one; that we may all live as brothers and sisters of the one Father in heaven – a family of God. On its part *Lumen gentium* further enjoins the bishops and priests to exercise their ministry with the aim of assembling the "family of God as a brotherhood fired with a single idea, and

---

[24] LG 6. The underlining is mine and is meant to bring out the intention of the use of the expression "his family".

[25] LG 28.

[26] Decree on Ecumenism *Unitatis Redintegratio,* 2 (hereafter UR).

through Christ in the Spirit they lead it to God the Father"[27]. The Decree on the Pastoral Office of Bishops in the Church *Christus Dominus* re-emphasises the importance of molding the Church according to the values and structure of family. In it the bishop is encouraged to be "a true father who excels in his love and solicitude for all". This falls in line with his duty to "unite and mold his flock into one family that all, conscious of their duties, may live and act in the communion of charity"[28]. In the spirit of Vatican II the whole of human race, the Christian Church, the Catholic Church as universal Church, the diocese and the parish are all families of God in their own right. In his Post-Synodal Apostolic Exhortation *Christifideles Laici*, Pope John Paul II especially emphasised the structural communion of the universal Church which has the parish as the local Church "living in the midst of the homes of her sons and daughters". He goes further to say that "the parish is not principally a structure, a territory or a building", but rather 'the family of God, a fellowship afire [sic] with a unifying spirit'"[29]. The validity of the image Church-as-family of God finds its place in the promotion of unity and communion. It is in this context that the bishops of the Third World wanted "the Church-as-family" of God to be the model for the universal Church.

5.1.3 In Search of Self-Identity of the Church in Africa

Guiseppe Alberigo is of the view that "some of the most significant and lasting decisions of the [Second Vatican] Council [...] could hardly have had such evangelical inspiration and theological richness without the African contribution"[30]. Yet many have wondered for a long time what the self-understanding of the Church in Africa is. It can be observed in this study that the expression Churches in Africa has been more often used than the Church in Africa. The aim is first of all to express the plurality and colorfulness on the continent. Secondly it is to illustrate the variedness in thought and cultural patterns which makes it possible to talk about the local Churches in Africa, which seek a common principle of operation. Based on the similarities in the various cultures and societies, however, it is not an exaggeration to also talk about the Church in Africa. It has been, therefore, the wish of many an African

---

[27] LG 28. A similar formulation is found in Decreee on the Ministry and Life of Priests *Presbyterorum Ordinis*, 6: „Priests exercise the function of Christ as Pastor and Head in proportion to their share of authority. In the name of the bishop they gather the family of God as a brotherhood endowed with the spirit of unity and lead it in Christ through the Spirit to God the Father".

[28] Decree on the Pastoral Office of Bishops in the Church *Christus Dominus* 16. The Decree on the Training of Priests *Optatam Totius* 5 goes further to describe the seminary as a family which should live according to the prayer of Jesus "that all may be one" (John 17,11). Family could be seen here as the *Sinnbild* for oneness in the Church.

[29] John Paul II, Post-Synodal Apostolic Exhortation *Christi fideles Laici* The Vocation and Mission of the Lay Faithful in the Church and the World 1988, 26.

[30] Guiseppe Alberigo, Conclusion: A Historic Occasion or Bureaucratization? in: Guiseppe Alberigo and Alphonse Ngindu Mushete (ed), Towards the African Synod, Concilium 1992/1, p. 149.

that a council be held on and for the continent so that a common identity and theology could be worked out for the Church. What would be the nature of an African Church? Rose Zoé-Obianga, one of the outstanding ecumenical theologians on the African continent, proposes the nature of a true African Church to be a participating and sharing community[31]. The satisfaction of the hunger for such a Church was achieved at the Special Assembly for Africa of the Synod of Bishops 1994, as already mentioned earlier on.

5.2 The Historical Development of the African Synod 1994

The birth of the Special Assembly for Africa of the Synod of Bishops under the motto: "The Church in Africa and Her Evangelizing Mission towards the Year 2000: 'You shall be my witnesses' (Acts 1:8)" traces its conception to the 1960s especially through the activities of the Society of African Culture (SAC). The wish of the society was the holding of an African Council. The dream gathered momentum at a colloquy held in Abidjan organised by SAC in September 1977 under the theme "Black Civilisation and Catholic Church"[32]. The resolution passed here was again the call for an African Council. The Ecumenical Union of African Theologians (EAAT) founded in Accra in December 1977, also identified itself with the wish for an African council and incorporated this among its major study projects in the year 1980[33]. The deliberations of the said union in Yaoundé, Cameroon 1984 and in Kinsahsa, Congo formerly Zaire 1986 also centred on the need for an African Council.

During the visit of Pope John Paul II to Kinshasa in May 1980, the Episcopate of Zaire added its voice to those already mentioned above expressing the desire of its members for an African Council. This wish was reiterated by Cardinal Malula in the name of the said bishops of Zaire to the then Pontiff in April 1983, emphasising that the holding of an African council "would allow our churches to take stock of the present situation of Christianity and to establish in consultation an adequate basis for the integral evangelisation of our continent in the future"[34].

This project called "African council" gathered flavour among many African intellectuals, theologians and a large part of the episcopate on the continent. It received a universal ecclesial quality when Pope John Paul II on April 23, 1983 in Rome agreed in principle the wish of the African Christians. This led to an increased enthusiasm and hopefulness on the part of the

---

[31] Cf. Rose Zoé-Obianga, When will the Church in Africa become African?, in: Guiseppe Alberigo and Alphonse Ngindu Mushete (eds.), Towards the African Synod, Concilium 1992/1, p. 90.

[32] Engelbert Mveng, The Historical Background of the African Synod, in: Africa Faith and Justice Network (ed.), African Synod. Documents, Reflections, Perspectives, Maryknoll-New York 1996, p. 21.

[33] See ibid., and Ferdinand Nwaibgo, Church as a Communion: An African Christian Perspective. Theology of the Local Church in the Light of the Second Vatican Council, Frankfurt a. M. 1996, p. 356.

[34] Quoted in E. Mveng, The Historical Background, 1996, p. 21.

"homeland" theologians to work towards the conceived African Council. Preparations were then on the way towards the possible holding of the much yeaned great event. To this end SECAM set up a theological committee called "COMITHEOL" to provide materials for reflections on the possible preparation of the Council. Furthermore, two consultations were also organised by the Catholic members of EAAT at Yaoundé in Cameroon and Kinshasa in Zaire.

What the Church in Africa was looking for in their call for an African Council was to build upon a tradition which at the time was dormant[35]. A study of the history of the Church indicates some precedents in the holding of regional councils in 18th century way down to the middle of the 20th century. Between 1791 and 1884 twelve plenary or provincial councils were held in Baltimore (USA). Plenary councils were also held in Australia in the years 1844, 1869 and 1887. China and Japan had their councils 1924, Indochina (Hanoi) 1934 and India (Bangalore) 1950. The African theologians meeting in Yaounde in April 1984 thus elaborated on and explained the concept of the desired Council. What the theologians did not rope into their huddle of issues were the potential difficulties and obstacles that could encumber the holding of an African Council of bishops at this time. Prior to the above mentioned meeting was the coming into force of the *Codex Iuris Canonici* in January 1983. The possibility of holding a Council was clearly stated there. Canon 439 § 1 states that

> a plenary council, that is, one which is held for all the particular churches belonging to the same conference of bishops, is to be celebrated as often as it seems necessary or advantageous to the conference of bishops, with the approval of the Apostolic See[36].

The canon stipulates clearly that a Council can or may be organised by a bishops' conference. It goes without saying that SECAM – Symposium for Episcopal Conference of Africa and Madagascar – which is not a bishops' conference but rather an assembly of regional bishops' conferences, could not apply this otherwise favourable canon to itself without first of all working on its status. The most quoted obstacle to holding an African Council is thus the coming into force of CIC 1983. A lead way out of the blind alley would have been to change the statutes, thereby enabling SECAM to have the needed canonical authority to organise a plenary council. Otherwise it is unimaginable with the present legal dispensation to do such a thing at a continental level.

Though some voices see the provisions of these canons as those determining the holding of a synod instead of a council, some scholars are of the view that factors of divisiveness among the African bishops or the lack of consensus on their part regarding the holding of an African council led to the decision of Pope John Paul II to convoke an African synod. In the Words of E. Mveng, "this legal void was not the result of ignorance or negligence on the part

---

[35] René Luneau, The Expectations of the Catholic Church, in: Guiseppe Alberigo and Alphonse Ngindu Mushete (eds.), Towards the African Synod, Concilium 1992/1, p. 83.
[36] CIC 1983, Can. 439§1.

of the members of SECAM. It stemmed directly from the lack of consensus that divided them"[37]. The differences ranged from role, function and significance of the body SECAM itself to opportunities, programme content and powers of an African council. This lack of consensus led to the lack of the appropriate canonical status of SECAM to convene a plenary council on the continental level. It was somewhat a struggle between the English-speaking Churches and the French-speaking ones. The argument of the former is that they were not consulted. In their view, they were embarking on an adventure without knowing what it really entailed. The result of divisiveness was the lack of majority vote for an African council. The personal decision was thus needed to tilt the balance. The announcement by Pope John Paul II on the 6th of January 1989 regarding the holding of a Special Assembly for Africa of the Synod of bishops brought to a temporary halt on the discussions on the conceived council and rather gave way to the birth of a synod. To some people in Africa, it was a blow in the face but others saw and still see it as a major development in the growth of the ecclesia on the continent[38].

5.2.1 The *Lineamenta*: The Road to Synod of Hope and Resurrection

Upon the announcement by Pope John Paul II to convene the African Synod, the *Lineamenta* was promulgated in Lomé on 25th July 1990. The document begins with a brief history of evangelisation in Africa. The intention of such an act was to reappraise the life of the Church on the continent and its evangelisation methods. This step was made under the premise that a good analysis of the once buoyant Church in Africa which later on declined in vigour is necessary to help chart the way for the future. The document has a self-critical character and pays attention to issues which will enable it get a clearer view for its future course. It states, therefore, that

> the history of the extinction of the Ancient Churches in North Africa and the disappearance of the Churches founded in Sub-Saharan Africa in the 15th and 16th centuries must be seriously considered at this time... For it may be that some of the causes which explain the extinction of those Churches still subsist in some form today[39].

Indeed, some of the causes do still exist and the Church needed at the threshold of the 21st Century an image which touches the heart of the African cultures and that portrays optimism and hope. In reminiscence it can be observed that the North African Church took on Latin as the official language and did not bother to translate the Bible and liturgy into the Berber and/or the Phoenician languages[40]. In the said *Lineamenta* it is stated clearly that

---

[37] Ibid., p. 28.

[38] Cf. René Luneau, The Expectations of the Catholic Church, 1992, p. 83.

[39] *Lineamenta,* no. 7.

[40] Edward White Benson is one such person who has offered a comprehensive analysis of the life and work of St. Cyprian. He talks about the place of Latin in the life of the Church. In Carthage

> historically, the Church in North Africa was a Church which used Latin to the exclusion of all other languages [...]. In Egypt and Ethiopia the Christian Faith was very soon expressed (Bible, Liturgy, etc.) in the Coptic and Ethiopian languages [for instance Ge'ez]. If the Bible and the Liturgy had been translated into the Berber language, it is quite possible that Christianity would have survived in North Africa, in spite of Islam, as it did in Egypt and the Middle East[41].

In other words, the translation of the Bible into and the celebration of the liturgy in the indigenous languages could have made it possible to use the elements of the native culture to create a North African Church, capable of surviving the domination of Islam. The *Lineamenta* goes on to observe that the inhabitants seemed to have eagerly accepted the Latin provincial culture at the apex of the Christian mission. Latin served two purposes: as a Lingua franca and as ecclesial language. When Latin later disappeared, Berber became the only surviving language[42]. In connection with the analysis above Charles Pelham Groves observes that "once again the use of language is found linked with Christian survival under stress of stormy times"[43]. The issue at hand is the use of a non-indigenous language. A foreign language may have a touch of imperialism and may not also gain roots among the people. It must be remarked that language is not the only determining factor for the growth or decline of the Church in a particular area. Other factors such as pastoral care of the individual members, unity of purpose and fraternal solidarity among the members, and the living of exemplary lives of the community of believers in the world are equally important.

Notwithstanding the remark above, a repetition of the scenario finds echo in the history of the Church(es) of Sub-Saharan Africa. The Churches founded in the 15th and 16th centuries in this region of Africa also disappeared.

---

the use of Punic as an official language was discontinued and Latin gained the upper hand. This situation, however, was not in all the Church provinces in North Africa. In Tripolis Punic was still spoken. In the town of Fussala (forty miles from Hippo), it was necessary to appoint a Punic-speaking bishop in the fourth century. This was quite an exception. On a whole, however, Latin had dominance over all other languages. It is reported that Valerius appointed Augustine as his coadjutor since he himself could not teach effectively as a Greek. See E. W. Benson, Cyprian, 1897, xxxv.

[41] See Special Assembly of the Synod of Bishops for Africa, The Church in Africa and her Evangelising Mission towards the Year 2000: "You shall be my Witness"" (Acts 1,8). *Lineamenta*, Vat. City 1990, no. 4. See also http://www.ewtn.com/new_evangelization/africa/synod/lineamenta.htm (visited on 26th February, 2011)

[42] Ge'ez was the language used by the people of Axum, where Frumentuius became bishop in the year AD 356. See J. Hildebrandt, History of the Church, [4]1996, p. 22. It must, however, be stated that it would not be fair to attribute the survival of the Coptic Church only to the use of indigenous language(s). At the time of the invasion from the Arabs, there is displeasure of Copts with the rulers from Constantinople. They thus thought that it would not be worse with the Arabs than with the Byzantines. The leader of the Arab army, 'Amr ibn al, who invaded North Africa, signed a treaty with the Copts. They were to pay him regular taxes. In return he allowed them to practise their Christian religion. Ibid., p. 27.

[43] Cf. Charles Pelham Groves, The Planting of Christianity in Africa, vol. 1, London 1948, p. 110.

Some of the factors accounting for this lamentable situation were the disinterest of the Portuguese at the time to open up the region to missionaries from other parts of Europe and the failure to create an ecclesial body that considered the cultures and contexts of the people as two important components necessary for a deep-rooted evangelisation and Christian life.

In respect of the analysis made so far, one can conclude that not everything went well in the enterprise of the proclamation of the message of the Gospel on the African continent. Though success stories can be told of the missionary work, there were also mishaps and these need to be reappraised. Times have also changed and one cannot continue to use the old methods of evangelisation in our times. An option is to look for a way of improving the current method. Another way could also be to throw everything overboard and begin from the scratch. The *Lineamenta* took the first option but characterises the decline and disappearance of the hitherto flourishing Church in North Africa as a sad fact of history. The episode is summarised as follows:

> The Arab Muslim invasion of North Africa, which began around 643, was completed by the capture of Carthage (698) and Ceuta (709). The Moslems gradually brought about the extinction of Christianity, reducing the number of bishoprics to three for all Africa by the time of Pope Gregory VII (1073-1085). Even these three bishoprics disappeared entirely by the 13th Century[44].

Some African scholars including Justin S. Ukpong[45] see, for instance, the historical illustration of the Church in Africa in the *Lineamenta,* especially with reference to the North African Church, as conveying "a deep impression of the defeat of Christianity and the triumph of Islam"[46]. Ukpong admits that the underlying principle of historical presentation is that history is a teacher of life (*magistra vitae*). This has the purpose of helping the present generation to learn from the past. In his view, however, "history is the story of the victors"[47]. He, thus, would have liked the Church being given such an image in the document. He further contends that since the synod's theme dealt with the future of evangelising missions in Africa, the history of the Church in North Africa should have been told in such a manner that one gets a vision, inspiration, and the commitment needed for the creation of a new history for the Church in Africa in the third millennium[48]. He is, however, quick to add that

> we should not interpret the defeat of the North African Church as a defeat of Christianity, but rather perceive it as the story of the victims seen as

[44] *Lineamenta,* no. 4.

[45] Prof. Justin Samson Ukpong is Vice Chancellor of Veritas University, Nigeria is a renowned Biblical Scholar. See Justin S. Ukpong, A Critical Review of the *Lineamenta*, in: Africa Faith and Justice Network, The African Synod. Documents, Reflections, Perspectives, Maryknoll, New York 1996, p. 33.

[46] Ibid.

[47] Ibid.

[48] Cf. ibid.

> possible real heroes. This is indeed the paradigm of the historical meaning of the passion-resurrection event whereby Jesus, the 'victim' of death in human eyes, was in fact the victor-hero. What should be highlighted is the struggle of North African Christians to maintain the faith[49].

As much as the critique of Ukpong cannot be disregarded, it must be remarked that a critical evaluation of life demands a holistic view of things and that includes accepting one's mistakes and/or failures as part of history, rather than looking at only the good side of the story. Instead of painting a victim-hero picture it would also do the Church a lot of good to accept its past failure in order to be able to create the right conditions for its evangelising mission in our times. Indeed the ability to be self-critical permits the past to be looked at as a phenomenon with positive and negative components. This can make it possible to live with caution in the present time and to learn how to properly chart the way forward. History is not just about dead facts but more than that it tells about the life of a people at a time. It shows where they are coming from and helps them to build a society in the present time with a future orientation. It is laudable that Ukpong goes further to propose that one should

> see a connection between the North African story and today's sub-Saharan stories. We should look at the Church in North Africa as having accomplished a mission, and we should see its 'demise' as a symbol of the seed of Christianity sown in African soil that still sprouts and flourishes today in sub-Saharan Africa[50].

The *Lineamenta* does not disregard in any way the importance of the Church's past history on the continent with regard to its life today. Rather it highlighted its history so that the same mistakes will not repeat themselves. Based on such reflections, the Church in Africa could identify the model that reflects the cultural values and sentiments of the people and are most appropriate for its evangelization mission.

After critically examining the historical past of the North African Church, the *Lineamenta* was divided into two parts: part one examines the general theme of evangelisation including its missionary dimension, the challenges associated with it and the needs at present. Part two of the document dealt with the five sub-themes of the synod, which were described as the tasks facing the Church in Africa in the coming 21st century. The topics included Proclamation of the Good News, Inculturation, Dialogue, Justice and Peace and the Means of Social Communication. Relevant portions of these two parts will be handled accordingly in the rest of this study. This method will enhance a systematic presentation of the work.

The *Lineamenta* concluded with a set of questions to the five tasks mentioned above and these served as guidelines for discussions and prayerful reflection at the grassroots.

---

[49] Ibid.
[50] Ibid.

5.2.2 Reactions to the *Lineamenta*

In the responses collated, a certain amount of dissatisfaction was felt on the part of many African Christians and their leaders. The criticism ranged from the venue of the synod down to the formulation of the "tasks" facing the Church in Africa. One of such outstanding discontents, which is relevant to this study, was a letter from the Zimbabwean bishops. They lamented the absence of the element that characterises the very core of African societies and cultures, namely the family. Quoting Pope John Paul II, who spoke to the Catholic laity in Harare, Zimbabwe, on September 11, 1988, they pointed out the central role of the family within the African traditional cultural set-up: Africa cannot flourish unless its families survive the present social upheavals. The African family must thus find new strength, reaffirm the positive values contained in tradition and assimilate a more personal dimension of understanding, commitment and love[51].

Taking the position of Pope John Paul II as the starting point, the bishops claimed that it is impossible to talk about cultural values in Africa without bringing in the concept of family, because the "African traditional culture is centered on the family". They thus opted for the inclusion of this topic on the agenda of the synod. Conspicuously missing in their proposal is an explicit illustration of the positive values of the African family in the life of the people. They only mentioned some factors which are possibly endangering the traditional family, thus limiting its ability to live out its positive values: "the migrant labor system, social and geographical mobility, unemployment, housing shortages, the corrosive influence of the Western neo-pagan culture"[52]. The "disturbing factors" must be dealt with in order that the African can re-live his cultural values, which, they said, must be fostered through catechesis in preparation for marriage, starting with the youth, and it must be celebrated within the community for all to see. In the view of the bishops, it would be foreign to the African cultural context to deny this new inner and personal reality its corresponding outward and social expression[53]. Cardinal Jozef Tomko's speech on the topic, "The Situation of the Church in Africa and Madagascar – Some Aspects and Observations" throws more light on the issue. He posits that the African family is a place where life is given and protected. By giving the family a special attention in the Church of the continent, he hopes that the thought could enrich the other cultures[54].

The Zimbabwean bishops' proposal, namely, to use the Gospel message to create a family form that has the strength to live out its values as such, with the aim of helping its members and leaders "to recover those lost intellectual,

---

[51] Inter-regional Meeting of the Bishops of South Africa (IMBISA), Our Bishops Want Family on Synod Agenda, in: Africa Faith and Justice Network (ed.), African Synod, Documents, Reflections and Perspectives, Maryknoll-New York, 1996, p. 46.

[52] Ibid.

[53] Ibid., pp. 46f.

[54] Cf. OR, 27th April 1994, p. 18.

spiritual and moral values to build the society upon them"[55], fails to demonstrate clearly what their intention was. Did they want that a pastoral strategy should be developed to save the African family or did they want to give the Church an identity, an impetus for growth by using the family as a model? It seems that they were in for both goals. The second option can, however, only be implied from the outcome of the synod. By taking the family as an ecclesiological model, the Church would try to mould its life according to the good values in the traditional African family. In doing so more dynamism could be gained. At the same time, the importance of the family would be brought to the fore, thereby saving the African family also from losing its much treasured values of solidarity, love and communion.

5.2.3 *Instrumentum Laboris* and some Reactions thereof

The collated views from the Churches in Africa showed vividly a hunger for a self-identity of the African Church, demonstrating a phenomenon whereby a topic which did not find a place in the *Lineamenta* began to win an enviable place in the discussions. Since actions speak louder than words, the African Christians wanted to be clear in their mind who they are as a Church before going out to proclaim what they have. One of the aims of evangelisation is that the hearers of the Word of God will get converted and be baptized. It is thus imperative that the neophytes should know where they belong and what the character of their "new community" is.

The *Instrumentum Laboris* begins almost every section with a theological foundation. Under the rubric signs of the time it states in paragraph 25 that the biblical image particularly relevant to Africa is "that of the Church as House of God (cf. 1 Tim 3,15), the Household of God in the Spirit (cf. Eph 2, 19-22)"[56]. It goes further to demonstrate the importance of the family and the relevance of the concept as the most appropriate model for the Churches in Africa by saying that

> in a family which is conscious of this mission, all the members evangelise and are evangelised. In many answers to the *Lineamenta*, there is a strong emphasis on the notion of the Church as the Family of God among human beings. It is felt that Africans can be more easily enabled to experience and to live the mystery of the church as communion by utilising to good advantage the African's understanding of family, especially as regards the values of family unity and solidarity. The Church is a living family made up of bishops, priests, men and women religious and lay persons. Through baptism every Christian becomes co-responsible for the

---

[55] Lieven Engbanda Lingonge, The Church as the Family of God. A Guide in the Praxis and Ethics of Reconciliation and Peacemaking in the Democratic Republic of Congo, Chicago 2004, p. 46.

[56] *Instrumentum Laboris*, 25, in: http://afrikaworld.net/synod/inlaboris.htm (visited on January 30, 2012).

proclamation of the gospel[57].

Similar views were raised by Cardinal Hyacinthe Thiadoum, Archbishop of Dakar, Senegal, and General Rapporteur of the African Synod 1994 in his *Relatio ante disceptationem.* He reiterated the deep desire of the Churches in Africa to perceive the purpose of evangelisation to be the building up of the family of God on earth. He traces this position to

> the profound Christian and African values of *communion, fraternity, solidarity* and *peace.* [...] Since the whole of humanity is in a sense God's family, this image also opens evangelization out to its universal dimensions: welcoming all peoples and each person into this great family, as a conscious member or as one moved by the Spirit[58].

It could be said that the aim of finding an identity for the ecclesiae in Africa is to help achieve the goals of evangelisation by creating the necessary structures for it and by involving all the agents thereof. The Churches in Africa were in search of a metaphor that symbolises the love for life and the most appropriate image is the family, represented by the woman with the baby in the arms. Another Synod Father, Bishop Bernard Bududira of Burun/Burundi made an intervention that in a way demonstrates the heart beat of many a Christian in Africa. He does not only present the concept Family of God as a desired ecclesial model but rather he goes further to indicate some consequences of such a self-identity. He says *inter alia*

> the image of the Church, based on the references of the Word of God and which finds anthropological resonance in African culture must first of all make people understand that everybody who is baptized [...] now forms a new family of whom God is the Father and supreme Ancestor. In this view of the Church, the ultimate and absolute reference of the African Christian – instead of being his tribe or ethnic group ideologized and absolutized by politics – will always and everywhere be 'the only God and Father of everybody who is in everybody' (Eph 4, 6). The second consequence of the view of the Church as family of God is the sense of co-responsibility in evangelization and as witness of evangelical life. In the African mentality, when one belongs to the same family, one feels tied by the same solidarity of fate. In a Christian sense, we would say linked by the same vocation, called to life by the same father and providence. Hence contributing to the success of a member of the family becomes the success and pride of all, whereas being the cause of failure of a member of the family is failure and shame for all the members. The privileged bond from which this sense of co-responsibility must stem in the conception of the Church as family of God, the privileged place where this sense of co-responsibility blooms is the nuclear family, the

---

[57] Ibid., 25f.
[58] Cardinal Hyacinthe Thiandoum, The Gospel, Inculturation and Dialogue, in: OR, 20th April 1994, p. 8.

> neighbourhood, the professional environment where living ecclesial communities are formed and act [....] To prevent complementarity and co-responsibility in the 'living ecclesial communities' from resulting in confusion, it would be useful to recall that even in traditional African communities the roles and assignments were done according to specific accepted rules. It is important in 'living ecclesial communities' – in a natural environment of life – that non-ordained ministries be recognized and provided for, and the mandates specified[59].

On Friday, 22nd April 1994, in the Aula of the Synod, the Synod Fathers heard the *Relatio post disceptationem* delivered by the Rapporteur, Cardinal Hyacinthe Thiandoum, Archbishop of Dakar, Senegal, on the issue of the Church as Family of God, he said:

> The African sense of family solidarity affords a valuable base on which to build an ecclesiology of the Church as 'Family of God' on earth. In this ecclesiology, Living Christian Communities form cells within which love of God is inseparable from love of neighbour, and in which the tendencies of disunity – egoism, tribalism, etc. – are discerned and overcome[60].

On his part, Bishop Albert Kunene Obiefuna, the then bishop of Awka, Nigeria, commented thus: "the *Instrumentum laboris* in paragraph 25 thus summarizes the many references to the African family in these words:

> 'it is felt that Africans can be more easily enabled to experience and to live the mystery of the Church as communion by utilizing to good advantage the African understanding of the family especially as regards the values of family unity and solidarity. What the Instrumentum laboris says is quite in order but must not be over-estimated. The truth remains that the typical African lives the family life and also his Christian life in the context of his or her tribal work. They are usually caught up in the clan and tribal interests. Similarly, the Church, whether we look at it from the inter-diocesan, diocesan, parish or station level is seen and valued from the point of view of is relationships and benefit to the clan, tribe, town or village. Where the Church is built, where the parish centre is situated, where the Bishop comes from, where he lives, are all more important than what they are and stand for. ... The Church is indeed a family. Its boundaries extend beyond the clan and the tribe. The typical African, even if he or she be a Catholic, does not consider that. Indeed the African Christian with his exaggerated ethnicism finds it difficult to accept the truth that the man or woman in India who is a Christian is much more a brother or sister than the non-Christian brother or brothers or sisters in the natural family (Gal 5:10). The mentality is so pervasive that the saying goes among the Africans that when it comes to the crunch, it is not the Christian concept of the Church as family which prevails but

---

59 Bishop Bernard Bududira, Burun, Create Living Church Communities, in: OR, 4th May 1994, p. 7.

60 OR, 25th May 1994, p. 9.

> rather the adage that 'blood is thicker than water'. And by water here one can presumably include the waters of Baptism through which one is born into the family of the Church. Blood relationship is more important even for the African who has become a Christian[61].

The reality to be faced is that blood relationship is very important even to the Ghanaian or African who has become a Christian. Bishop Obiefuna is not against the concept Church-as-family. On the contrary he supports it and gives suggestions as to how it could be promoted. He cautions, however, that the African Christian should not be considered without his or her tribal, cultural or clan background. According to paragraph 25 of the above-mentioned document it is felt that Africans can be more easily enabled to experience and to live the mystery of the Church as communion by utilising to good advantage the African understanding of the family, especially as regards the values of family unity and solidarity[62]. As much as he agrees with the view stated in *Instrumentum Laboris,* he firmly states that the typical African does not live his or her family and/or Christian life outside the tribal context. In other words, the values mentioned in the statement quoted above do seldom work beyond the tribe and ethnic group. They are usually connected in one way or the other to the clan and tribal interests[63]. It may be true to say that the African lives his Christian life within the context of tribe and clan. However, the phenomenon may not apply to Africans alone. Every human being lives his faith within the context in which he was born and brought up. The problem arises, however, when the socio-cultural traits outweigh the Christian value of communion. Neither the statement "blood is thicker than baptismal water" nor the statement "baptismal water should be thicker than blood" serves the purpose of the Gospel. Identity is an important value in the history of mankind. It does not, however, have to be ideologised.

Cardinal Jozef Tomko, for instance, warns against absolutising family solidarity which has the possibility of encouraging corruption and nepotism in society. For religious and priests, he says, absolutised solidarity could pose serious dangers especially in the administration of ecclesiastical goods. He recalls the context of the various countries by saying that

> it is often the case that countries in this continent contain an agglomeration of peoples, cultures and languages who have generally lived their separate destinies until quite recently. In the context of a modern state, it is sometimes the case that various family and tribe solidarities find themselves in conflict; a number of the social and political problems of the continent are attributable, in part, to this element. .... The Church in Africa should be able to present itself before men as the 'family of God', a 'people made one with the unity of the

[61] Bishop Albert Kanene, Present the Church as Family to Christians in Africa, in: OR, 27th April 1994, p. 9.
[62] Ibid.
[63] Ibid.

Father, the Son and the Holy Spirit[64].

The voices presented above all agree that the image most appropriate to the Church in Africa is Church-as-family of God. The criticisms are meant to serve as wake-up calls to issues which could mar its beauty. Looking at the image from the point of view of cultural values alone will be unsatisfactory. Rather it should be seen in the light of the mission of the Church to evangelise and to heal the wounds of society. Such a contextual constellation offers the concept its place in the ecclesiological map of the Church.

5.2.4 The Church-as-Family of God as Symbol of Hope

At the time of the Synod in 1994, Africa had just experienced divisions in many countries. Added to that is the general notion of Africa as a continent full of calamities, hunger and misery. In the civil society and in the Church an enormous variety of situations were experienced that went a long way to buttress the presentation of Africa as a dark continent. The Synod seized the opportunity to speak a word of hope to the continent. Africa is not just a shattered continent, but one of values and future. Against this backdrop the model "Church-as-family" was given a renewed consideration and became one of the cherished fruits of the Special Assembly[65]. In the post-synodal exhortation, *Ecclesia in Africa*, Pope John Paul II observes:

> The Synod Fathers acknowledged it as an expression of the Church's nature particularly appropriate for Africa. For this image emphasizes care for others, solidarity, warmth in human relationships, acceptance, dialogue and trust. The new Evangelization will thus aim at building up the Church as family, avoiding all ethnocentrism and excessive particularism, trying instead to encourage reconciliation and true communion between different ethnic groups, favouring solidarity and sharing of personnel and resources among the particular Churches without undue ethnic consideration[66].

For the first time after the 4th Century the Church formally receives this image as an ecclesiological self-understanding. It was really a synod of hope and resurrection because also for the first time after the 15th century in the history of the Church in Africa that an attempt was made to develop an ecclesiological image that gives special consideration to the particular context of the black continent. One could say that it was for the Church in Africa a re-awakening of

---

[64] Cardinal Jozef Tomko, Situation of the Church in Africa and Madagascar – Some Aspects and Observations, in: OR, 27th April 1994, p. 20.
[65] Cf. Nicholas Fogliacco, The Family: An African Metaphor for the Trinity and Church, in: Cecil McGarry and Patrick Ryan (eds.), Inculturating the Church in Africa. Theological and Practical Perspectives, Nairobi 2001, p. 133.
[66] *Ecclesia in Africa*, no. 63.

the lived-reality among the Christian brethren in the first three centuries of Christianity in North Africa.

The illustration above hints to the fact that the metaphor "Church-as-Family" is neither a creation of the Special Assembly for Africa of the Synod of Bishops (1994) nor is it the prerogative of the Church in Africa to call itself family of God. The Synod was "the last straw that broke the camel's back" – it was the last and immediate instance that gave the concept its formal place[67] in the ecclesiological self-understanding of a continent.

In the documents produced after the synod one experiences an almost over-proportional frequency of usage of the term family either alone or in combination with other words. The bishops used the concept thirty-three times in their "Message of the Synod". In their write-up they emphasised the importance of the family as the cell of society and highlighted it as the foundation upon which the social edifice of Africa is built[68], namely "the care for others, solidarity, warmth in human relationships, acceptance, dialogue and trust"[69].

In talking about the family, the Synod fathers had three types of it in mind: the Christian family, which is seen as the core of the ecclesial community, the natural family – understood to be the extended family, and the Holy family, which is the model of all Christian families. Interesting to note is also the view shared by the Synod Fathers that the human race and as a matter of fact the universal Church is a family of God. The relationships within the one family of God are seen first of all in the use of the former as a metaphor and secondly in their roots in a certain affinity of feelings, in the sharing of thoughts and deliberations, and in affections and interests. Since the Church is located in different cultures, the community of believers called the one big family of God does not characterise uniformity but rather communion in diversity. It is the reason why the word family can be broken down to various degrees and it will still be compatible with the understanding of Church-as-family.

5.2.5 Why not House of God?

A recall of the discussions in chapter two of this study shows that some cultures and languages in Ghana derive their concept of family from the term house. In addition to the points given above, scholars such as Michael H. Crosby and Elisabeth Schüssler Fiorenza are in favour of the house-of-God metaphor. The argument of Crosby, for instance, is that the house as a metaphor is a necessity

---

[67] I say „formal place" because the documents of Vatican II use the concept family at various points to describe the Church, even though the acclaimed ecclesiological image thereof is the people of God. See LG 6, 27, 32, 51. The fraternal love among Christians – all who are children of God and form one family in Christ – is mentioned here. "Nam omnes qui filii Dei sumus et unam familiam in Christo constituimus (cfr. Hebr. 3,6), dum in mutua caritate et una sanctissimae Trinitatis laude invicem communicamus, intimae Ecclesiae vocationi correspondemus et consummatae gloriae liturgiam praegustando participamus".

[68] See *Ecclesia in Africa*, no. 80.

[69] Ibid., no. 63.

for the Church just as every human life needs air to live or the way water is a necessity to fish. He contends that the house was the fundament for the early Church in the same manner as it was for economics at the time when Jesus lived. Therefore, "just as air and water are assumed for those entities dependent on them, so it must be assumed that at the time of Jesus [...], 'house' was the center of economics and political life, as well as religious and ecclesial life"[70]. If one would want to take an image that best describes the Church's nature, based on the life of the early Church, Crosby posits, then it should be the metaphor of Church-as-House of God. Elizabeth Schüssler-Fiorenza, on her part, admits the fact that the early Christians saw themselves as a new family. However, their self-understanding took its institutional shape in the house Church[71]. In the first letter to Timothy, the author also used the duty of the man in a household to illustrate the responsibility of the overseer or bishop. He, the bishop or presiding elder, the author of the letter writes further, must be "a man who manages his own household well and brings his children up to obey him and be well behaved: how can any man who does not understand how to manage his own household take care of the Church of God?" (1Timothy 3, 4). This is ample evidence of the possibility of using the metaphor or model Church-as-House of God rather than Church-as-family of God.

A bone of contention is the disagreement among scholars as to which interpretation of the term household is nearest in meaning to the concept of the early Church and how this inspired them to live their Christian life[72]. In addition to the above given point is the patriarchal understanding of *bayith* and *oikos* – house in Hebrew and Greek respectively – which has the possibility of evoking emotions among the feminist groups who may see such a metaphor as a way of perpetuating male dominance in the Church.

Furthermore, the house bears a temporal significance. In traditional Ghana, for instance, many houses are built of mud and/or wood. The rains come and destroy them. They thus lack the character of longevity or permanency required of a family. In the eyes of the Ghanaian, the name of a family dies or disappears when no single member of the descent still lives. Even though this phenomenon is relatively seldom it does take place. Many houses, however, collapse in a year and are either rebuilt or the ruins are left unattended. Furthermore, a house has walls with clearly demarcated boundaries. To widen it, one would either have to pull down certain structures or build a new one. The accomplishment of this task is associated with material resources and work. A

---

[70] Michael E. Crosby, House of Disciples; Church, Economics, and Justice in Matthew, New York 1988, p. 11. See also Edward Tengan, House of God, 1997, p. 70.

[71] See Elizabeth Schüssler-Fiorenza, In Memory of Her. A Feminist Theological Reconstruction of Christian Origins, New York 1983, p. 251.

[72] See Edward Tenga, House of God, 1997, p. 68-70. Cf. M. E. Crosby, House of disciples, 1988, p. 33f. One could say that the Jewish term *qahal* – congregation - which is almost nearest in meaning to the Greek concept of *ecclesia*, could be used here to illustrate the inter-relationship within the community of Christian believers. The problem here is that some scholars are hesitant to put the two at par. Crosby contends that though the formal gatherings of people had religious undertones, the original meaning of ecclesia was devoid of inherent religious connotations.

family grows through birth – a gift of God. Another nuance associated with the house metaphor in Ghana is the danger of seeing the house unit as a closed one. Its relationship to other units cannot be shown by the visible structures. Using the house as the metaphor for the Church in Ghana could bear the risk of overburdening the Church also with an atomistic feature or orientation. It must be remarked at this juncture that the family in Ghana also has a certain amount of the character of the house described above. It is a unit or institution with properly delineated lines of authority, ancestry and religious tradition. This view corresponds with that of the "Church as Institution", in which clearly defined hierarchical structures and precise clarifications on membership are made. The difference between the two, however, is that in the case of Church as Church-as-family it is not the juridical aspect that is emphasised but rather the dynamic relationship among its members. It is a vibrant reality, constituted by persons with their own worth and freedom who bring into realisation the unity in a community and complement one another reciprocally[73] through interactions. To talk about the Church-as-family of God is to deal with the freedom of individuals, who commune with God and one another in love and solidarity. It also entails dealing with all those elements that make human life in a community meaningful.

By their nature families are intertwined with others in a network of relationships. There is hardly a Ghanaian family that exists without relationship to other units in the clan or village. It functions not just for its own good but prepares its members for the service of other relatives or people from the homestead and guests. The preference of the family image to that of a house for the Church in Ghana is the fact that the former brings out one important element of the Church very clearly: communion through deaconry.

Furthermore, brothers and sisters of an individual in Ghana are more than those of a household or house. A Ghanaian in Germany for instance calls his fellow Africans brothers and sisters. If he or she is in another African country, then the brothers and sisters there are all those from Ghana. The relation shifts from situation to situation independent of house or household. Notwithstanding the merits of the house as an ecclesial model that of family is more encompassing, admirable and appropriate for the Church in Ghana.

5.3 The Church-as-Family in Search of Appropriate Evangelisation Method

The consequences for the Church in Africa in its inability to develop an ecclesial model – before the advent of the African Synod 1994 - that paid particular attention to the spiritual and pastoral needs of the faithful based on their cultural and historical contexts was that it had to take over the models brought to it from the missionaries. It is, therefore, no wonder that these images

[73] See F. Bechina, Die Kirche als „Familie Gottes“, 1998, p. 30. The original text is: „Wie die natürliche Familie sei die Kirche aus Personen von eigener Würde und Freiheit konstituiert, die die Einheit in Gemeinschaft und gegenseitiger Ergänzung verwirklichen“.

also bore the cultural elements of the countries of origin of the respective missionary congregations[74]. The implication for the Church in Ghana, the case study of this research is that such ecclesiological models seemed not to have gained deep roots in the various societies and cultures, since most of the metaphors could not be translated properly into the languages of the local faithful and hence lost their desired meaning and impact.

Since the various ecclesial models were accompanied by corresponding methods of evangelisation, it is important at this point to recall some of them and the associated perceived consequences thereof. It must be said that the more insight that was gained into the values of cultures and peoples, the more the terms were changed to reflect the spirit of the time. The implication also is that the appropriation of the concept "Church-as-Family" of God also goes with the use of a corresponding evangelisation method.

5.3.1 Adaptation, Accommodation and Indigenisation

The term adaptation has played an important role in missiology and liturgy for a very long time. It was used synonymously with the term "accommodation" [75]. Both terms formed the framework of ecclesial implantation and evangelisation adopted by the Church in its early stages of mission in Africa, Latin America and parts of Asia. Although the terms do not have clear-cut definitions, the missionaries or pastoral workers who employed these concepts attempted to fit all the elements of the Christian life – pastoral, ritual, didactic and spiritual – into the customs of the faithful being evangelised. For instance, in cases whereby the missionaries were not sure of the translation of a particular word in a given language, the Latin version was used. Even today among the *Frafra* of Northern Ghana, the Latin word *gratia* – meaning grace – is still left to function in the translation of the prayer *"Hail Mary"*. The word grace cannot be directly translated into *Gurune*. The nearest in meaning to it is *wine sɔm*. One would have expected the translation of the first sentence of the prayer "Hail Mary full of grace" to be *Fara Maria, fom piri la Wine sɔm* rather than the old translation undertaken by the early missionaries, namely, "*Fara Maria, fom piri la gratia*". Now "*wine sɔm*" means approximately "God's blessing". For the *Frafra*, God's blessing is all that the human being needs in his everyday life. This is different from the verb *"ka mã̆ãle"*, which signifies the act of blessing, for instance by a priest. Even though *Kã'ã* and w*ine sɔm* are closely related, the latter is a substantive and the former a verb. *Wine sɔm* embraces the whole human life and signifies the dependence of the human person on God, the giver of every good thing. *Kã'ã* or *Ka mã̆ãle* on the other hand is related to a particular spiritual need of the person at a given point in time and the religious act performed to fulfill this need. Due to the fact that the missionaries and their pastoral workers were not too sure of the most appropriate word to use, they opted for the Latin form, *gratia* – it was adaptation.

---

[74] Cf. F. Nwaigbo, Church as Communion, 1996, p. 45.

[75] Cf. Constitution on the Sacred Liturgy *Sacrosanctum Concilium*, 37-40 (hereafter SC).

Another case study is the use of the word priest in the liturgy and scripture reading among the *Frafra*. They have priests who take care of the spiritual needs of the believers of the traditional religion. These are called *tin'dããn dɔma.* The singular is *Tindããna*[76]. In the biblical and liturgical literature of the said *Frafra* in the Navrongo-Bolgatanga diocese, the word Priest and High Priest are still found in their English version and not *Tindããna* or *tin'dããndɔma.* This is because of the fear that the faithful could fail to perceive the difference between the two terms: a traditional priest and a priest in the Jewish tradition or even Jesus as High priest. The solution to the problem could be to add the prefix "*Wine*", God, to *tindããna* and the problem would have been solved. If attention were paid to the translation offered here, a priest in the liturgy and bible will be called thus *Win'tindããna.* The specification above may sound discriminatory since the traditional priests are also performing a religious function with God as the Supreme Being. It could also imply some sort of spiritual arrogance when the Christians decide to accord their priests with a godly character to the neglect of the others. What cannot, however, be forgotten is the language imperialism which tacitly takes place in the former. Furthermore, the openness of the traditional Ghanaian culture allows the specification without the fear that "Win' t*indããna* will not be wholeheartedly accepted by the people in question. The people also understand the concept in their own language. The traditional priests would appreciate the place of their counterparts in other religions and religious traditions, thereby making it possible for the affected parties to dialogue.

The examples above depict adaptation and accommodation as one-way-traffic approach to the liturgy and missiology in what was branded as "mission territories". The Christian faith was "made to fit into a particular culture without the former being open for change"[77]. It is the reason why the approaches have been heavily criticised by many theologians in our days. It is also treated as an outdated model of evangelisation and pastoral work. The impression is that adaptation and accommodation appear to convey "rather an extrinsic relation between the Christian life"[78], the gospel message and a particular culture. As a missionary terminology the term adaptation can convey the impression that modifications should be characterised as having a transitory and external nature[79]. Aylward Shorter perceives it as containing within itself "the seeds of perpetual Western superiority and domination"[80]. In the report of its workshop after the publication of the *Instrumentum Laboris* for the first African Synod 1994, the Catholic Theological Association of Nigeria (CATHAN) writes, "the

[76] Every culture in Ghana has made provision for someone who takes care of the spiritual needs of the citizens. They bear different names according to the language and culture in question.

[77] Joseph Osei-Bonsu, The Inculturation of Christianity in Africa, Frankfurt a. M., 2005, pp. 14f.

[78] Arij Roest-Crollius, Inculturation, in: S. Karotemprel (ed.), Following Christ in Mission: A Foundational Course in Missiology. Bombay 1995, p. 111.

[79] See Congregation for Divine Worship and the Discipline of the Sacraments, The Roman Liturgy and Inculturation, January 25, 1994, par. 4.

[80] Aylward Shorter, African Christian Theology, Maryknoll-New York 1977, p. 150. See also J. Osei-Bonsu, The Inculturation of Christianity in Africa, Frankfurt a. M., 2005, p. 15

Church in Africa rejects the theology of adaptation, which is no more than 'nativizing' the Roman Church. Rather, the African Church opts for a theology of inculturation and incarnation"[81]. In other words, an ecclesiological metaphor is good enough for the Churches in Africa if it can strip and distance itself from a model that inhabits imperialism and theological superiority. CATHAN acknowledges and appreciates the immense contribution of the Western missionaries who brought education, medical services and contributed generally to enhance the quality of life of many Africans. The association, however, notes that missionary work in the past paid little attention to the importance of African culture in Evangelization. The consequence is that the language, concepts, and world-view in which the Christian message was presented were foreign. The impact of evangelisation on the people and its reception by them is, according to CATHAN, "less effective than it could have been"[82]. The observation made by CATHAN re-echoes the desire of many African Christians that the liturgy and way of life in the Churches in Africa should assume the cultural and world outlook of the people concerned. It is interesting to note that neither adaptation nor accommodation was mentioned in *Instrumentum Laboris*. One could interpret the position of CATHAN as a signal to Rome to allow African rites in the liturgy rather than interfering into the daily life of the local Churches.

Closely related to adaptation and accommodation is indigenisation. It is also used to illustrate the connectedness between the Gospel and culture in the evangelisation process. Unlike adaptation which shows a foreign dominance, indigenisation attempts to "express the Christian message in the categories of thought of the native, or the insider[83]" without necessarily cutting links with the external environment, namely the universal Church, nor avoiding to borrow elements from it. However, the leadership is in the hands of the local people also called the indigenous people. An example can also be found in the political life of Ghana. Kwame Nkrumah, the first president of the country, introduced the indigenisation of industries. Apart from restricting the contribution of "outsiders" to just certain areas of the life of society and only for particular purposes, the concept makes reciprocal learning difficult. It is also a one-way-traffic just like adaptation and contributes only negatively to the achievement of the goals of communion and solidarity. Rather than interdependence the model supports the monad-mentality and self-sufficiency. Another disadvantage is inadequate allowance for internal renewal within a system. This is because anything foreign is looked at first of all with skepticism and as a threat to the already existing system. Furthermore, the natives may not sufficiently know how much social change affects their social structure[84], which may call for re-adjustment in life style and approach.

---

[81] Catholic Theological Association of Nigeria (CATHAN), Statement, in: Africa Faith and Justice Network, African Synod, Maryknoll – New York 1996, p. 51.
[82] Ibid. p. 50.
[83] Cf. J. Osei-Bonsu, Inculturation of Christianity, 2005, p. 15.
[84] Ibid., p. 15. See also A. Shorter, African Christian Theology, 1977, p. 150.

5.3.2 Incarnation: God crosses Borders

The concept incarnation is the first attempt to give a biblio-theological foundation to the relationship between the gospel and cultures based on John 1, 1 &14: "In the beginning was the Word, and the Word was with God and the Word was God [....] The Word became flesh and dwelt among us". The theology of incarnation denotes the reality of Christ's coming into human nature. God's presence among human kind is personal and visible as denoted by the words *έσκήνωσεν* and *σκηνόω* which literally mean that God "pitched his tent" or "took up residence" among the human race. In other words, Jesus dwelt among us, by coming into a particular culture and history, thus assuming "the concrete historical realities of a particular people, i.e. the Jews. He became part of the history, culture, traditions and religion of his people and partook of them"[85]. It is also worth considering that Jesus was influenced by his society through the act of nurture.

A certain theological thought is being introduced here, namely the theology of incarnation. The word represents the mystery of the Eternal Word – Jesus' insertion into a particular history and into a particular socio-cultural context. Incarnation is seen in this sense as a process rather than a *fait accompli.* And in respect to evangelisation it is the "enfleshment of the Word"[86] in the hearts of the people, who are cultural in nature. This can be seen from the context of the encyclical *Slavorum Apostoli* in which Pope John Paul II talked about "the incarnation of the Gospel in native cultures and also the introduction of these cultures into the life of the Church"[87]. The encyclical was written to commemorate the eleventh centenary of the missionary work of the Saints Cyril and Methodius. The tone of this encyclical finds resonance with that of *Evangelii Nuntiandi,* which talks about the evangelisation of cultures, and with *Ecclesia in Africa,* where Pope John Paul II repeats his theology of incarnation in combination with inculturation for the purpose of evangelisation, whereby the former is reflected upon as a process by which the content of the latter "takes flesh" in the various local cultures[88]. The conclusion is that in the attempt to relate the Gospel to culture, incarnation of Christ should be the starting point.

Incarnation is construed by some scholars as a product of socio-cultural contextualisation and history. An example is M. L. Stackhouse who asserts that "the doctrine of the incarnation suggests that the very reality of the only true and transcendent God took the risk of contextualization in a very human, very concrete, very contextual person"[89]. He places this doctrine at par with the thought of the Church as the Body of Christ, "the incarnate presence of the

---

[85] J. Osei-Bonsu, Inculturation of Christianity, 2005, pp. 15f.
[86] Ibid.
[87] John Paul II, Encyclical Letter *Slavorum Apostoli* (2nd June, 1985), 21.
[88] Cf. *Ecclesia in Africa*, 59 and Paul VI, *Evangelii Nuntiandi,* 20.
[89] M. L. Stackhouse, Contextualization, Contextuality and Contextualism", in: R.O. Costa (ed.), One Faith, Many Cultures: Inculturation, Indigenization and Contextualization, Maryknoll-New York 1988, p. 4f. See also Osei-Bonsu, Inculturation of Christianity, 2005, p. 16.

living Christ"[90], which assumes different forms and shapes in the various cultural contexts in the world. In this regard it can be said that just as Christ took on the human nature with all its associated characteristics except sin (cf. Heb. 4,15), so must the Church seek to accept and use the cultural elements of the respective peoples except those elements that are obnoxious and are seen not to be compatible with Christianity[91]. This view is supported by E. Hillman, who asserts that

> the action of God in history is the paradigm of the Church's action. What God has done through Jesus Christ once and for all in the historico-cultural terms of a particular people, the Church must do among all the tribes and tongues and peoples and nations, who, with their varied experiences and myriad cultures, constitute the whole of humanity in its spatio-temporal extension[92].

Some other theologians concede that the primary incarnation took place once and for all through Jesus Christ. In other words, the incarnation of the *Logos* – the fact of the Word becoming flesh – is unique in nature, because there was and is just one and only one incarnation in the person of Jesus Christ, the Son of God, which happened within the cultural setting of Palestinian Judaism. Joseph Ratzinger, now Pope Benedict XVI, in his contribution at the first African Synod 1994 reiterated the importance of a correct understanding of incarnation, which he describes as a historical event, which is "unique and unrepeatable: the Son of God became incarnate once and for all time in a specific man, Jesus of Nazareth, born in Bethlehem, who died and rose in Jerusalem"[93]. He posits that incarnation is not delineated but rather implies permanent link with this particular history described above. Other important elements in his view are the paschal mystery and the pneumatological dimension. He conceives incarnation, therefore, to comprise "the binding force of the unique historical event, the paschal transformation [...] and the universality of the risen Christ"[94]. Herein lies the difficulty when applying incarnation as a method of evangelisation. The word of God taking flesh in the hearts of the people and for that matter in their cultures can be talked of in intrinsic analogical sense[95] to inculturation but not as a historical process of evangelisation.

---

[90] Ibid.

[91] Cf. SC 39.

[92] E. Hillman, Missionary Approach to African Cultures, in: T. Okure, P. Van Thiel, Inculturation, pp. 62f.

[93] Joseph Ratzinger, Correct, Complete Theology of Inculturation is Necessary. OR 17th April 1994, p. 15.

[94] Ibid.

[95] Osei-Bonsu, Inculturation in Christianity, 2005, p. 17

5.3.3 Inculturation: Giving Evangelisation a Cultural Dimension

The insertion of the Church in a particular culture thus falls under a different category. It is called inculturation in many circles. The concept denotes a dialectical process, involving the interpretation of the gospel message by the people of that culture. It is not Christianity – as way of living the Christian faith – which has to find expression in another culture, "but rather the Gospel message: the Christ event – Jesus' life, death and resurrection as interpreted by a living faith community, which belongs to a bigger society with its own values or ideals"[96]. The former category, namely, expressing Christian and ecclesial life in a particular culture, falls under the general rubric of ecclesial identity called contextualisation. This concept has already been examined at the beginning of this chapter. In dealing with inculturation, the recipients of the gospel message get actively involved in remodeling their lives and society to make them fertile grounds for the seed of the Word of God to be sown. It is the true way of purifying cultures of obnoxious elements which may have the tendency of not enhancing dignified human living.

According to Paul VI the concept inculturation is more than the evangelisation of cultures. He entreats that effort should be made not to forget considering "the person as one's starting-point and always coming back to the relationships of people among themselves and with God"[97]. A significant leap is made here. Whereas many a times inculturation is looked at in relation to the evangelisation of cultures, Paul VI pays attention to the maker of cultures, the human beings, and their creator in the center of affairs. It is not just about the insertion of the Gospel message into a particular culture but rather the process by which the recipients of the Word of God are enabled to find a relationship with God and with one another. The conversion of the human heart leads mostly to a change in his way of life, which could lead to remolding of his culture. Paul VI remarks as follows:

> the kingdom which the Gospel proclaims is lived by men [and women] who are profoundly linked to a culture, and the building up of the kingdom cannot avoid borrowing the elements of human culture or cultures. Though independent of cultures, the Gospel and evangelization are not necessarily incompatible with them; rather they are capable of permeating them all without becoming subject to any one of them[98].

The concept inculturation originates from the cultural anthropological term called *enculturation*. The former is, however, used mostly in the ecclesial world and has thus acquired a pastoral-theological significance distinct from the latter. The connotation of enculturation is the learning process by which an individual

---

[96] Catholic Theological Association of Nigeria, Statement, 1996, p. 51.
[97] Paul VI, Apostolic Exhortation *Evangelii Nuntiandi* (8 December, 1975), 20.
[98] Ibid.

gets initiated into his or her culture[99]. The Yogyakarta Research Seminar defines inculturation as:

> the process by which an ecclesial community lives its Christian faith and experience within a given cultural context, in such a way that these not only find their expression in elements of the local culture, but also become a force that animates, reshapes and profoundly renews that culture, so as to create new patterns of communion and communication within that culture and beyond it[100].

Since one of the aims of developing an appropriate ecclesiological model for the Church in a particular society is to enable it to undertake its evangelisation mission more effectively, it is imperative that the image should possess a character that can ensure sustainability and acceptance by the faithful involved. The concept is one such pastoral approach to ecclesial life that has the probability of being accepted by most Catholics especially in Africa. In the *Lineamenta* to the first African Synod 1994 it is stated that "the Church in Africa will have to tackle inculturation as a matter of necessity and urgency in her evangelizing mission"[101]. It goes further to show the dispensability of inculturation in the proclamation of the Gospel as outlined in *Ad Gentes* nr. 22. Mention is also made of the importance given to the concept by Pope Paul VI in his Apostolic Exhortation *Evangelium Nuntiandi*, nr. 20. The statement from John Paul II, who never ceased telling the bishops of Africa during their visits *ad limina apostolorum* "to face up to the exigencies of inculturation which he sees as an essential and indispensable task in the Church's evangelizing mission in Africa today"[102] also got prominence in the document. As was seen in the introduction to this study, the *Lineamenta* questions on inculturation did not make mention of "authentic cultural values" but only concentrated on the possibilities of abuses. How can one talk about integration of cultures and/or cultural values in Christianity, if one does not know what they are?

At the Synod itself, however, the concept was considered as one very important element of the proclamation of the Word of salvation. The premise surrounding this view is the demand on each particular Church and every baptised person to welcome the good news down to the roots of their cultures and then to carry it to the ends of the world. In the Message of the Synod presented by the fathers of the Synod, it is stated that Evangelisation which is limited only to the dimension of proclamation without considering inculturation leads to disfiguring the former[103]. The Synod Fathers further observe that it is

---

[99] Cf. F.-V. Anthony, Ecclesial Praxis of Inculturation, 1997, p. 43.
[100] Yogyakarta Research Seminar is quoted in: F.-V. Anthony, op. cit., 1997, p. 45.
[101] Special Assembly of the Synod of Bishops for Africa, The Church in Africa and her Evangelising Mission towards the Year 2000: "You shall be my Witness"" (Acts 1,8). *Lineamenta*, Vat. City 1990, no. 27.
[102] Ibid.
[103] Cf. Message to the Synod, no. 13: OR, 11th May, 1994, p. 6.

> the baptized person who receives from the risen Christ the mandate of to bring evangelization to its terms and who responds to it [and] becomes in his turn a witness. He evangelizes the cultural roots of his person as of his community and takes up the socioeconomic and political challenges in order to be able to express the message in his own words and in a new dynamic of life which transforms the culture and society[104] (*Message of the Synod, 17*).

In his Post-Synodal Exhortation *Ecclesia in Africa*, Pope John Paul II recapitulated the views of the Synod Fathers and added that the concept inculturation is "the process by which 'catechesis takes flesh in the various cultures". This, he argues, has two dimensions: It is "the intimate transformation of authentic cultural values through their integration in Christianity and the insertion of Christianity in the various human hearts"[105]. Since no further explanation is given in the above statement, inculturation would be interpreted to mean the internalisation and personalisation of the Word of God which gives birth to the profession of the faith in Jesus Christ and which shows forth in daily life within a socio-cultural context. The explanation given above makes it possible to place Christianity at par with authentic cultural values. In his book "Anatomy of Inculturaion. Transforming the Church in Africa", Laurenti Magesa illustrates a remark which is said to be attributed to one elderly Christian from West Africa. The elderly man was asked why people in his area supposedly did not adhere strictly to the teachings given them by the missionaries. His reply was: "We eat everything they give us, but we digest it in our own way"[106]. According to Laurenti Magesa, the digestion refers to the way the faith is appropriated. And so he comments that "the Christian faith cannot be assimilated by people of a given culture unless it is digested by that culture"[107]. The process of food digestion and assimilation takes place in a particular body in the same way as culture and for that matter the process of inculturation is to a given cultural framework. The view of the elderly man quoted above is representative of the sentiments on the African continent. In the *Instrumentum Laboris*, which resulted from the responses to the questions raised the *Lineamenta*, it is stated that

> the image of seed absorbing food from the ground which it transforms into itself shows that "the synthesis between culture and faith is not just a demand of culture, but also of faith. A faith which does not become culture is faith which has not been fully received, not thought through, not fully lived out". Inculturation is the evangelization in depth of every aspect of the individual and societal life of a people; it is – as one Particular Church put it – "Jesus leading the community in a new dance

---

104 Ibid., p. 7.
105 *Ecclesia in Africa*, 59.
106 Laurenti Magesa, Anatomy of Inculturation. Transforming the Church in Africa, New York 2004, p. 7.
107 Ibid.

and drumming a new rhythm"[108].

The emphasis is on the Gospel message which is in contact with a particular culture and serving as catalysts of renewal and animation for dialogue within the culture itself and beyond. Through inculturation authentic cultural values are transformed "through their integration with Christianity"[109] and elements of the culture(s), lived and expressed in ways particular to them, are also introduced into the Church. Among many ordained ministers in Ghana, the word inculturation has direct link with the celebration of the liturgy. Unfortunately little attention is given to inculturating other aspects of ecclesial life such as the promotion of discussions using the principles of African Palaver, developing an inculturated celebration of the sacraments, giving a cultural dimension to canon law in the particular Church and the building up of leadership structures drawn from the valuable traditional principle of service and solidarity. It is surprising to observe that although the Fathers of the Synod acknowledged the field of inculturation to embrace theological, liturgical, catechetical, pastoral, juridical, political, anthropological and communal dimensions, they proposed that "a special attention should be paid to liturgical and sacramental inculturation, because it directly concerns all the people who are already participating in it"[110]. This proposal was not taken up in "*Ecclesia in Africa*", probably because of the practical implication such a move could have for the universal Church. It could mean, for instance, allowing all or at least the Churches in Africa to develop their own liturgical forms and ways of sacramental celebration, with the consequence that control may no more be possible or uniformity will be lost. The former archbishop of Kumasi, Ghana, Peter Kwasi Sarpong, for instance, questions the appropriateness of the present theological understanding of sacrifice to the faithful of his former archdiocese as presented in the Roman Mass format. He is proposing that pastors on the African Continent should be given the freedom to develop formats that would be better understood by the faithful. Using the *Asante* culture and tribe as example, he notes that "the reading of Scripture and the homily could be more effective after the Holy Communion"[111]. This practice would allow an uninterrupted flow of the Mass. Following the Ghanaian cultural practice, the listener is more open to the message after he has eaten than when he is still hungry. A further format worthy of consideration is the posture to be taken during the proclamation of the Gospel. In the traditional Ghanaian cultures the listeners sit down when the Chief or an elderly/prominent person speaks. It is a sign of respect and also indicates that the listener is not in a hurry to go away.

---

[108] Special Assembly for Africa of the Synod of Bishops, Instrumentum Laboris, 17.

[109] *Ecclesia in Africa*, 59.

[110] Message to the Synod, 18: OR, 11th May 1994, p. 7. Archbishop Peter Kwasi Sarpong of the Kumasi Archdiocese of Ghana in his contribution during the first African Synod lamented over the situation whereby inculturation is equated to liturgy. In his view, "inculturation embraces the totality of human life, including morality, spirituality and forms of religious life". See OR, 27th April, 1994, p. 16.

[111] Ibid.

Since Jesus is seen as teacher, Lord and King, then the faithful would want to accord him the honour that he deserves. The Roman Mass format, however, demands that the faithful stand when the Gospel is proclaimed. The fear of disturbing the Catholic uniformity may have its validity and importance in its own right. It is, however, worth noting that the Catholic unity will not at all be tempered with through inculturation.

The language in *Instrumentum Laboris* clearly shows that this issue was also discussed and thought of in the various Churches. Inculturation in the view of the African Churches presents the individual younger Churches, as they call themselves, as being "adorned with their own traditions", which "will have their own place in the ecclesiastical communion, without prejudice to the primary of Peter's See"[112]. As already stated, inculturation means more than liturgical and sacramental celebrations. It involves the Gospel message taking roots in the heart of the people and their culture. It will be a disservice to the process of inculturation if conversion of heart and lived-faith experience were not included. To limit the concept to liturgical and sacramental celebrations would also imply limiting the process of inculturation to the inner ecclesial sphere. But as it were authentic inculturation is part of an integral evangelisation process which leads to "maturity of faith, integration of faith and culture, doctrine and life, worship and daily living"[113]. The bishop of Bata, Equatorial Guinea, Bishop Anacleto Sima Ngua, in his intervention during the first African Synod 1994 expressed it as follows:

> Today, more than yesterday, and as never before, the African Church feels the need to integrate its faith and its traditional culture in the same movement of dual fidelity: fidelity to those traditional values, and also to the evangelic message. In this context, the task of inculturation is imposed on its own. And it is imposed from its own people and from outside Africa as an effort for conversion, change in mentality and assimilation of a reality which permits, more and more, greater opening[114].

A study of the contributions from the Fathers of the African Synod 1994 and the documents thereof demonstrate a yearning for the appreciation of the cultural values of local Churches in order to enhance the proclamation of the Gospel, the living of the Christian faith, which again cannot be delineated from the relationship between the individual Christian and God on the one hand and the relationship of the Christians among themselves on the other. In short, inculturation helps in the building up of an ecclesial body which has the identity of the people in question and God as the head. It is about the creative and vibrant encounter between the good news of Christ and local cultures. Gregory I. Olikenyi confirms this position by writing that "the message of the gospel can be relevant in Africa only if it is articulated using cultural symbols containing values and meanings compatible with those of the gospel proper to the African

---

[112] *Instrumentum Laboris*, 17.

[113] Ibid., 22.

[114] Bishop Anacleto Sima Ngua, Searching for its own Identity, in: OR, 20th April, 1994, p. 12.

culture or cultures"[115]. The assumption, however, is that care will be taken not to import everything called cultural into the Church. Inculturation demands a painstaking "investigation into those aspects of the culture that are very much alive"[116] and still meaningful to the people, otherwise it can yield negative results. It must also be remarked that inculturation is the way that the Church lives out its life in order to make it possible that the Gospel message may be more easily understood and received by the people in Ghana. It is, however, a subset of contextual ecclesiology.

In the light of the discussions above, the various ecclesiological models can be placed in the rubric of theologies that were developed in context of time, socio-cultural, political and religious occurrences. The self-understanding of the Church in Ghana as family is, in the light of the deliberations undertaken thus far, a response to a systematic analysis of the concerns of the faithful of a country and of a continent at a time, namely, to have an image that incorporates in its being and nature the love for life and that offers the Church an impetus for evangelisation. There is thus a correlation between the proclamation of the Gospel message and the building up of a family where life begins. The model Church-as-family does not apply only to Ghana or Africa but also to the universal Church at large. This was the image of the first Christian communities. Even the whole of humanity is seen in a sense as God's family. The concept thus opens evangelisation out to its universal dimensions and on the whole befits the Church in Ghana because of the profound meaning family has for the people and the practical implications that are intensely felt and immediately understood when the concept is used.

---

[115] Gregory Ikechukwu Olikenyi, African Hospitality. A Model for the Communication of the Gospel in the African Context, Nettetal 2001, p. 81.

[116] Ibid.

CHAPTER SIX

THE THEOLOGY OF CHURCH-AS-FAMILY

6.0 Introduction

The concept Church-as-family is considered in many circles as the African contribution to ecclesiology[1]. There are two aspects to this assumption: the origin of the concept and the ecclesiological exposition. From the discussions undertaken in this study so far, it is difficult to wholly accept the first aspect of the assumption. This is because the concept does not have its origin in Africa but rather traces its roots to the community of Jesus. It also impressed upon the life of the Church for a very long time. However, over centuries the concept was left without specific theological content and exposition from the magisterial office of the Church. The contribution of the African Church is the re-awaking of the consciousness of the universal Church to the "availability and suitability" of such a concept as an appropriate ecclesiological image. The issue worth considering is how the model "Church-as-family" is to be understood.

Common to the various views offered on the concept is that the Holy Trinity is the basis for such a model. It could thus be said that it has a Trinitarian component. The Synod Fathers of the African Synod 1994 expressed a great desire to Pope John Paul II that theologians in Africa should "elaborate the theology of Church-as-family with all the riches contained in this concept, showing its complementarity with other images of the Church [...]. Meanwhile we encourage the development of an African ecclesiology on the Church-as-family of God"[2]. The proposal was accepted by John Paul II and reproduced in *Ecclesia in Africa*, nr. 63. The above-mentioned Synod Fathers suggested a framework for further development. In their Message of the African Synod, the bishops stated that

> the Church-Family has its origin in the Blessed Trinity at the depths of which the Holy Spirit is the Bond of Communion. It knows that the intrinsic value of a community is the quality of relation which it makes possible. The Synod launches a strong appeal for dialogue within the Church and among religions[3].

Building the ecclesiology of the Church-as-family on a Trinitarian theology helps to correct the dangers of particularistic tendencies that could be associated with such a concept[4]. The persons in the Holy Trinity cross borders of their godliness to share fellowship with the human race in their creation and salvific

[1] Cf. F. Bechina, Die Kirche als "Familie Gottes", 1998, p. 384.
[2] Propositions, nr. 8, quoted in: Africa Faith and Justice Network, The African Synod. Documents, Reflections and Perspectives, Maryknoll – New York 1996, p. 89.
[3] The Special Assembly for Africa of the Synod of Bishops, Message of the African Synod, 20: OR 11th May 1994, p. 6.
[4] E. Orobator, Contemporary African Ecclesiology, 1996, p. 271.

acts. Secondly they are united in their being and deeds and this could be an example for the Christian Church-as-family to remain united and focused on bringing all of humanity to experience life and love in the one true God. The Trinitarian foundation of the Church-as-family helps in the actualisation of the *Imago Dei* inherent in the Church and the human person.

Two other important elements emanating from the theology of the church-as-family of God are communion/community and dialogue. These concepts also have their respective implications as will be seen in the rest of this chapter.

6.1 Understanding Communion in the Church-as-Family of God

The mention of the word communion arouses the notion of community and traces its roots back to the Latin and Greek words *communio* and *koinonia*, respectively[5]. Important to community is the interaction that takes place, characterised by mutual interpersonal relations and intimacy among the members. The fundamental form of communion can be explained through the phenomenon of the Word becoming flesh and dwelling amongst the human race, which makes it possible for the latter to share fellowship with God the Father, the Son and the Holy Spirit[6]. The individual members in the Church and of the human family as a whole also share fellowship with one another (I John 1,3). Associated with communion is the component of communities, which also interact at various levels. The communion of believers and communities could be seen thus as "a fellowship of diversities of roles and persons"[7].

At the sixth General Congregation of the Special Assembly for Africa (1994), Anselme Titianma Sanon, the Bishop of Bobo-Dioulasso/Burkina Faso speaking on the topic *the Church is communion, family and brotherhood*, expressed his joy over the return of the tradition of the Church communion in the life of the Churches. The ecclesiae in Burkina Faso and the others in the rest of Africa, he said, give various expressions to communion according to their respective socio-religious experiences under the concepts of Church-family, Church-brotherhood, basic Christian community, basic family community, living ecclesial community etc. He perceives all these forms of articulating communion in the various Churches as important "since in the Church, each people, race, language and nation, culture as well, has its own place. Each member has its own place and role towards the communion of the whole"[8]. For, as he further remarks, "we have the same faith but not the same ways"[9]. The statement from Anselme Titianma Sanon further underscores the importance of pluriformity as a way of allowing the faithful in each particular Church find the most appropriate means of translating the well-treasured tradition of

[5] Cf. H. Vorgrimler, Neues theologisches Wörterbuch, 2000, p. 118.
[6] Cf. ibid., p. 118.
[7] Cardinal Hyacinthe Thiandoum, the Gospel, in: OR, 20th April 1994, p. 9.
[8] OR, 27th April 1994, p. 14.
[9] Ibid.

communion into the ecclesial life of their particular Churches in the form that best suits their socio-cultural and religious experiences, without hampering the realisation of oneness or unity in the Lord.

In short, communion enhances interaction and widens the physical and mental boundaries associated with a unit, without necessarily fostering uniformity. Rather it lives on the colourfulness of unity in diversity. It emphasises the vertical relations with God and throws light on the importance of the horizontal dimension of the members therein – as brothers and sisters. The concept is thus an appeal to reconsider the nature and being of the Church, to bring to fruition the mandate it has received from the ancestor Jesus Christ. This mandate could be termed as *Missio Dei,* the purpose of which is to bring all God's children into the one big family of God.

6.1.1 Communion, Collegiality and Fraternity in the Church-as-Family

An important issue emanating from the discourse on communion in the Church-as-family is the relationship between the local Churches and the universal Church. Will the local Churches be so independent that the treasured "unity" of the Church may be lost? On the 14th of April 1994, Cardinal Jozef Tomko, the then Prefect of the Congregation for the Evangelisation of Peoples raised similar fears in his speech on the situation of the Church in Africa and Madagascar. He first of all praised the sense of community in the respective African cultures and religiosity, which, he said, "helps Christians develop the ecclesial sense of communion and unity"[10]. He proceeded to illustrate how certain discussions went against the spirit of communion thereby causing a sense of suffering, "just as one suffers when a member of one's own family or father is offended"[11]. He remarks further:

> On a broader scale such a sense of community links up with the concept of the Church as family of God and is expressed in a deep sense of communion with the universal Church and with its centre which is encountered in the African communities. How often one notices a sense of suffering during certain discussions that go against that communion, just as one suffers when a member of one's own family or father is offended. **One could almost say that the African soul is not only *"naturaliter Christiana"* but *"naturaliter Catholica"*** as well. **It is certain that 'anti-Roman' feeling has no origin or home in Africa; the ground is not even appropriate for it, it is a foreign commodity**[12].

The fears of Cardinal Tomko can be observed in his attempt to appeal to the emotions, using the language of praise so that Africans themselves will no more be attempted to present the opposite side of the issue. He further presents a narrow view of African understanding of communion, which does not begin

[10] OR, 27th April 1994, p. 18.
[11] Ibid., p. 18.
[12] OR, 27th April 1994, p. 18. The bold marking is mine.

with the big unit but is realized first of all in the smallest social unit but expands to include even the environment and creatures. A demonstration of this is found in the exchange of greetings, whereby the condition of health of the neighbours and the livestock is enquired but the starting point is the individual in question and the immediate family members. Even though the cosmological dimension of the African is not trivial to him in anyway, equally important is the individual who shares fraternity and common fate with fellow human beings and with all of creation.

Two things are being mixed up in the views of Cardinal Tomko as presented above: catholicity and Roman catholicity. Whereas the first concept would illustrate solidarity and unity with all Christians, thus allowing for particularity of the individual Churches, the second concept over-emphasises the attachment to Rome. The danger with this second variation is the cementation of uniformity which hardly pays attention to pluriformity or the "colours" of the particular Churches. In the understanding of family in Ghana the place of the family representative or earthly father is usually not questioned. In a situation where the importance of the leader of the family, clan or village is brought to the discussion table means that there is something fishy. In none of the documents or interventions during the African Synod 1994 was the importance of the seat of St. Peter as the point of coordination of unity within the Catholic Church questioned. It is the more surprising that Cardinal Tomko made communion with the Seat of Peter a topic of discussion. Since the successor of the apostle Peter is a brother among the brethren, communion automatically means acting in concert with him. Considering the fact that religion is being used by some political leaders on the continent to manipulate the masses, one would have expected Cardinal Tomko to first of all emphasise the binding force of the faithful namely the faith through Jesus Christ, which brings them to build one big family of God. Since no family is without a head – in the Ghanaian sense of the word – there can be no Catholic Church without the Successor of Peter being at the realm of affairs.

It is imperative that the Christian life be lived is such a way that all human beings are seen as children of God. They all deserve love and support in their daily life. There is the need to stress God as the Father of all, who has given us Jesus as our brother. This has the higher propensity of promoting the feeling of relatedness, solidarity, warmth and love, which begins in the smallest cell of the bigger community. The Christian Church, just like the family, is the place where the individual baptised person expresses intensely his vertical and horizontal relationships. Through their actions the Christians bring to realisation the vision aptly captured in Isaiah 26:7b, namely, "my house shall be called a house of prayer for all peoples".

Returning to the statement made above by Cardinal Tomko that the soul of the African is *naturaliter Christiana* and *naturaliter catholica,* it can be said that the observation is too much of a generalisation. It is not correct to say that the African soul is by nature Christian and naturally catholic. Granted that his position were true, the whole continent would have been christianised by now.

The figures presented in chapter two of this study indicate, however, that the opposite is true. Ghana has a pluralistic landscape of religions. The formulation "the soul of the African is *naturaliter Christiana* and *naturaliter catholica*" especially in terms of Rome, would mean that all those biologically born Africans, who are not Christians are as a matter of logic not really African. Furthermore, if an individual person does not belong to the Roman Catholic Church, he is also not African enough. The deduction from Cardinal Tomko's statement is that the true African soul must be Christian and catholic. The statement discriminates and segregates. In other words, rather than promoting communion his statements has the potential of severing the already existing differences and discords in the African society.

Taking the understanding of family in Ghana as the starting point one would say that communion can be lived out in different forms: the sharing of brotherhood of the family heads could be a sign for intensive collegiality among the Church leaders. Such as the extended family or clan is a family of families, so is the Church a community of communities. The founder of them all is the ancestor, Jesus Christ. Furthermore, the celebration of the Eucharist promotes communion and brotherhood. This does not take place only among those gathered at the altar of God but includes even the countless faces throughout the world who have toiled to ensure that the "gathered congregation" has bread and wine for their spiritual journey. They pray thus not just for themselves alone but also for all of humanity, signifying their connectedness to all of creation. Celebrating communion in the form illustrated above could bring about a widening of the mental and emotional borders of the individual members of the Church-family.

6.1.2 The Church-Family as Force of Integration

The choice of the word communion, which demonstrates relation or relatedness in the society, is perhaps the appropriate concept, so that the Church in Ghana can restore the unity and harmony it partly helped to destroy, namely, the unity and coherence among and within families. Delving back to the analysis in chapter two of this study, religion has been seen in many respects as a two-edged sword, namely, it disintegrates and integrates. An analysis of the history of Christianity in Ghana shows that families have been torn apart and at the same time have held together by it. On a whole, religion has been a source of alienation of many a Ghanaian from his or her cultural roots, particularly upon the arrival of the Islamic and Christian missionaries in the country. The adherence of a family head or even a chief to a certain religion meant the conversion of all his "subjects". Refusal of one to belong to the same religion meant defiance of authority, with its telling consequences on him or her. Peter Sarpong affirms this point, even if he does it cautiously by his introduction of the phrase *unintentional disruption of culture(s)*. According to him the

> missions might have been unintentionally culturally disruptive; the missions remained a structure apart from the local population. Africans

> who came to profess the doctrines of the missions were adopted, body and soul, into a new way of life and were regarded by their non-Christian kinsmen as outcasts[13].

The new converts found themselves alienated from society and felt that they were not fully accepted.

Other voices supporting the above-mentioned issue argue that "if you meet in one and the same family members of different denominations, there is generally a very simple reason for that: they attended different denominational schools"[14]. Whereas the traditional religion led them to the common shrine, the Christian religion brought them to different Churches or "altars".

It will, however, be a disservice to religion and especially to the Christian religion in Ghana to reflect upon it as only having a disruptive character. It has also helped and still helps to hold families and communities together, thereby aiding the Ghanaian society to some degree to live out its community ideals. Max Assimeng sums this up by citing L. J. Lewis[15] who says *inter alia* that "the Church [...] has been an integrating influence bringing men and women together and providing power for unifying society by giving that inner core of unity to life which makes men and women prove against the stresses and changes in human society"[16]. Two things occur: there is the disruption of social relationships on the one hand and the support of community life, which gives impetus for regularising social relationships and for cohesion in society, on the other hand. In other words, the adherence to a common religion or confession has led to families and communities seeing their common bond and unity, thus performing their noble functions of social integration and cohesion[17]. One of the contributions of the model Church-as-family of God in this framework is to enlist the dynamic forces of relations among celebrating Christian communities and evokes the sense of unity, solidarity, trust and the sharing of love within the Church.

Care must be taken, however, not to romanticise this image of Church-as-family. A. E. Orobator cautions against an uncritical acceptance of the model because of what he calls "certain disturbing practices" that may jeopardise the ability to live out the values of community and "*relationality*". Orobator calls the threats variously as "ethnocentrism, tribalism or restricted love"[18]. *Ecclesia in Africa* (nr. 63) describes the situation as "exaggerated ethnocentrism". It must be observed that this situation is not particular to Africa or Ghana for that matter. The danger of not going beyond the borders of one's abode is a human phenomenon. In some countries the phenomenon may be depicted as "extreme

[13] Cf. ibid., p. 85.
[14] Forms of Service: The Ghanaian Voice, Accra 1968, p. 78.
[15] L. J. Lewis was with the Colonial Department of the University of London Institute for Education.
[16] Cf. M. Assimeng, Religion and Social Change, 1989, p. 96.
[17] Cf. Ibid., pp. 95f.
[18] Cf. Agbonkhiameghe E. Orobator, The Church as Family. African Ecclesiology in its Social Context, Nairobi 2000, pp. 35f.

nationalism". Whether it is extreme tribalism, ethnocentrism or nationalism, the situation needs re-examination since they all lead to restricted love. Orobator is not against tribal or national identities, since these identities could help bring dynamism and colours into the Church. It would, however, be a contradiction in terms to define the Ghanaian as a community person in essence, whose relatedness does not go beyond his immediate family or tribe. As already illustrated above, the individual and his relationships in his cosmos – his relationship to God, to the living-dead and to the living – get a special treatment in the tradition of communion. Each person is a recognised distinctive moral being[19], and relationships between him and others or between him and God and/or the ancestors take precedence over all other things. This notion of relatedness has been examined already in chapter two expressed vividly in a comparison made by John Pobee: Whereas René Descartes says *cogito ergo sum* – "I think, therefore, I am", the average Ghanaian would say that "I am related, therefore, I am"[20]. As already mentioned above, it is not just the collection of individuals who are important but also the individual person and his or her cultural context. Our attention here is thus drawn to the individual Christian in the ecclesial body of Ghana, to his personal life history and the particular cultural background, which have determined to a great extent his thought and life patterns, respectively. Communion ecclesiology, illustrated through the model Church-as-family of God upholds these cherished values of relationships of the individual Christian. It can, therefore, be expected that the family, conceived as the most basic community in society, where a person can develop his individuality and personhood, is of great interest to the Christian in the Church-family. Since no family stands alone but is rather connected to other families in the village, which in turn is linked to others in the bigger society, the Church can use this model to promote communion from the Small Christian Community level up to the universal Church. The community does not only put stress on its particularity but goes further to consider its commonness with others.

6.2 Life and Organization of the Church-as-Family

The theology of the Church-as-family of God also calls for a conceptualisation of the life and authority structure within it. Every human institution requires a certain amount of functional and organisational structure. In the deliberations above life of the Church-family is seen to be that of a shared fate, of fraternity and collegiality. The presumption here is that leadership promotes the building up of community of brothers and sisters with an authority structure. The leaders

---

[19] Cf. ibid., pp. 77-79.

[20] John S. Pobee is quoted by F. A. Oborji, Building Relationships in Pluralistic Communities, 2003, p. 161. See also John S. Pobee, Grundlinien einer Afrikanischen Theologie, Göttingen 1981, p. 43. He wrote in respect to the Akans but this trait has resonance in the whole of Ghana. "Während Descartes für den Menschen des Westens sprach, wenn er sagte *cogito ergo sum* – ich denke, darum existiere ich – gilt für den Akan-Menschen (Ghanaer) cognatus ergo sum – ich bin blutverbunden, deshalb lebe ich, oder: ich lebe, weil ich zu einer Familie gehöre."

and members alike bear similar amount of responsibility and loyalty to the family. The ensuing deliberations will thus pivot around the spirit of communal life.

6.2.1 Participation in the Church-Family

The logical consequence of appropriating the concept of family as a contextual ecclesiological model is the question of how the individual members participate in it. Since the image is closely linked to everyday life of the faithful, it is the expectation that words will also be translated into action. Participation is based on the premise that every individual member in the particular set-up has his/her own vocation and ways of contributing to the welfare of the unit in question. Without wanting to reduce the human person to a functional creature, it can be said all the same, that even the baby also contributes to life in the family. It cries eats and smiles. That brings life in a particular way into the social unit. Even though the possibility of passivity of some family members cannot be denied, the general desire of the members of a Ghanaian family is that every individual will contribute his quota to the success of life in it. The expectation is also that nobody will be discriminated against or even be forgotten of in the job sharing. This way of life could help the Church-family in the organisation of its life.

As already seen earlier on in this study, there is the inclination to the creation of a priest-centered Church with its hierarchical undertones. Participation in decision-making, leadership and structuring of the life in the Church-as-family of God needs a re-thought. It would imply reading the signs of the times and interpreting them in the light of the gospel[21] together with the rest of the brothers and sisters in the one Church-family. This could take place in fraternal discourse built on the model of African palaver: it is a spirit of discourse undertaken among members of a family or clan. The affected members share their views on the topic. The dangers of exclusion or discrimination is reduced or avoided in the process. A discourse of this kind undertaken in fraternal spirit of respect for one another does not in any way play down authority but rather gives weight to the importance of the latter, since no African palaver is undertaken without a leader who coordinates it and makes the final decision in concert with the elders.

In sharing his views on participation in the Church-as-family of God Cardinal Laurean Rugambwa, Archbishop emeritus of Dar-es-Salaam, Tanzania, observed on the 15th of April 1994 that the lay leaders have to be involved "in our Church government structures"[22]. He was appealing to the Church authorities of the respective local Churches to design structures that make room for more participation of the members therein. Bishop Anselme Titianma Sanon, the bishop of Bobo-Dioulasso/Burkina Faso, on his part, proposes that a canon law should be tolerated, which takes into account the

---

[21] GS 4.

[22] OR, 4th May 1994, p. 7.

socio-cultural dimension of the particular Church undertaken in the spirit of unity in diversity[23]. This would also mean allowing lay people to take up functions that do not necessarily lead to disequilibrium in the theological orientation and tradition of the Church. An intensified involvement of the laity with commensurate leadership responsibility would fulfill in the Ghanaian sense the feeling of being tied by the same fate. In theological language it could be said that the members are bound by the same vocation. The implication for the individual baptised members is that the fate, vocation or mission of the Church becomes part of their personal vocation. It can be taken for granted that the individual Christian communities and their members want to help in the building of the kingdom of God. This is only possible through co-responsibility and not through passive consumption of the services of some selected members.

The Archbishop of Mwanza, Tanzania, Archbishop Anthony Mayala, dares to challenge the wrong perception of some of his fellow bishops who think that they are those who have an apostolic mission and all others share in it. In his view, despite the unflinching efforts of the lay faithful who have founded and sustained many parishes and out-stations,

> the ingrained institutional hierarchical model of the Church and the pre-Vatican II mentality are still a great obstacle for many of the People of God in understanding and affirming the role of the lay faithful as being agents of proclamation. Even this Synod seems to imply this way of thinking when it says: "The apostolic mission of the Bishops is shared by priests, men and women religious and lay persons, each with his or her own sphere, (*Instrumentum laboris*, n. 26)"[24].

His argument is in line with the spirit of Vatican II, according to which the bishops share together with the other members of the Church in the mission of Christ. The difference is seen in the diversity of ministry but not in the mission. Rather than seeing the bishops as the fountain from which all ministries in the Church flow, emphasis needs to be put on the Church as family of God anointed to proclaim the message of redemption to all people. The arduous task of being the salt of the earth and light for the world does lie in the hands of all the members of the Church and not of an individual head[25]. Viewed from this angle reliance will no more be on institutional structure but rather on the power of the Holy Spirit who shares God's grace among the rank and file of the faithful. There is no particular member of the Church who has a different source, where his or her charisma originates, although the gifts may be varied and particular to him or her. There is, therefore, no need for monopolisation in ministry. That will mean making some members, because they are not ordained ministers to bury their talents in a napkin. The end loser will be the Church community. Since the goal of charismas or ministries is the good of the Church community,

---

[23] OR, 27th April 1994, p. 14.

[24] OR, 4th May 1994, p. 10.

[25] Cf. Decree on the Apostolate of Lay People *Apostolicum Actuositatem* (18th November 1965), 2f (hereafter AC).

through which it witnesses to the reign of God on earth, all should be encouraged to *put their hands on the plough.*

Pope John Paul II said in his speech to the participants of a Symposium on "Th*e Participation of the Lay Faithful in the Priestly Ministry*" organised by the Congregation for the Clergy on 22nd April 1994 that the Church in its totality lives in a "missionary communion" which is to be understood in the sense of an organic communion, identical to that of a living body. The leading principles in such a communion are the "diversity and complementarity of vocations and states of life, ministries, charismas and responsibilities"[26]. This presents an organic and dynamic outlook of the Church and that means non-static vision for any apostolate in the Church which has the power to give life and joy to the members. For the enhancement of this organic communion, he reiterated, the "particular gift of each of the Church's members must be wisely and carefully acknowledged, safeguarded, promoted, discerned and coordinated, without confusing roles, functions or theological and canonical status. Otherwise the Body of Christ is not built up nor does its mission of salvation correctly develop"[27]. However, he cautioned that the various gifts, charismas and offices should be well harnessed and treated with respect, thereby according all Christians with equal dignity and recognising the intrinsic missionary vocation of all baptised[28]. This is another way of saying that the various ministries and offices should be respected and promoted without anyone claiming superiority over the other.

6.2.2 Authority and Ministry in the Church-as-Family

The communal life in Ghana, as already seen above, has its essence and vibrancy in the principle of participation but it does not take the character of "an undifferentiated cast of confused roles"[29]. The role play is also in concert with the head of the family or clan, who is the symbol of authority. The person in authority gives orientation to the activities in his community and ensures fairness not only in the sharing of "wealth" but also in the performance of duty. He is also aware that his family does not stand alone but is connected to other families belonging to the same ancestry.

The Ghanaian family head or leader of a community is noted to be a good listener even if he has the onerous task of making the final decision. The Chief, for example, acts only in concert with his council of elders, who supposedly seeks the opinion of the people before gathering for the decision-making. In respect of the Church, we observed that any ecclesial arrangement which is not able to take this into consideration will mean a failure to allow for the active involvement of all the members of the "Church-family". The implication would be to deny the theory of ministry in the Church its true

---

[26] OR, 11th May 1994, p. 3.

[27] Ibid.

[28] Cf. LG 17 and 32.

[29] E. Orobator, The Contemporary African Ecclesiology, 1996, p. 275.

meaning: ministry does not confine "itself to the role and functions of ordained ministers"[30] but rather expands to include the exercise of charismas as understood and experienced in the history and tradition of the Church. Since the elder or leader does not only have authority but also responsibility, those in Church leadership have the function of ensuring order, of guaranteeing unity and of ensuring that knowledge is properly transmitted.

Analysis of the authority system in the traditional Ghanaian society, as undertaken in chapter two of this research, shows that seniority determines mostly authority in normal day life. When, for instance, an argument arises in public, the elder or the eldest is seen to be right. The aim, first of all, is to ensure harmony and to allow room for dialogue and consultation. However, the elder of the two will surely be reprimanded in private, when it is found out later that he was in the wrong. Although this phenomenon is not bad in itself, it has to be used with care. The issue is of particular interest to many theologians, not only in Ghana but in Africa as a whole especially because of the existence of clericalism, understood "as the obsessive and excessive monopoly of power, initiative and control of the ecclesial community based on one's membership in the class of ordained ministers"[31]. The danger (of clericalism) is manifold: initiatives and participation could be smothered, dialogue and/or consultation may not be practised and this could lead to alienation of various lay groups and individuals in the Church and it could also lead to infantilisation of the faithful. Due to the concept of priests in the traditional religion and the special honour that they enjoy in society, the priests, religious and bishops in Ghana will continue to be respected. They are the leaders of their parishes and dioceses. The lay faithful get disgruntled when these leaders no more serve in their office as shepherds but rather become wolves in sheep skins. The reciprocal respect will also dwindle when the members of a Christian community do not feel treated as equal members of the family of God. If the Church takes over this social unit for its self-understanding then the treasure of the traditional authority system in which service, fairness and love are written with capital letters needs to be revisited. The Church must be cautious not to do wholesale importation of what is called Ghanaian. The prophetic role of the Church calls for a critical examination of things and to give the social system a human heart. This is part of the *mission Dei* entrusted to the Church and the Church-family would help the biological unit called family heal its wounds. It is part of reading the signs of the time and elucidating it in the light of the gospel.

Another important observation about the authority structure of the Ghanaian family is that it does not originate from the top, that is, it is not hierarchical[32]. It springs from the centre, perceived here as the ancestral figure. All members build a net around the ancestor. The role of the family head in this constellation is to arbitrate and to officially represent the unit in legal and religious matters. His duty can be summarised to be that he works to promote

[30] Ibid, p. 41.

[31] A. E. Orobator, The Church as Family , 2000, p. 43.

[32] A. E. Orobator, Contemporary African Ecclesiology, 1996, p. 275.

life. As an earthly father and leader he could be described as a brother in service of the family. He has taken over the mantle from his father, who was also a brother among brothers. In other words the eldest in the family or clan also had some people older than him. He can't therefore make the family serve him nor can he be a dictator. That will be against the tradition of the family. In the same way the ordained minister at whichever level could be seen as an "elder" brother, who is called to serve his fellow brothers and sisters. One of the greatest legacies of the Church-as-family of God is service handed over to it by its ancestor, Jesus Christ. He came to serve but not to be served. He asked his disciples emphatically to do the same. Luke 22, 24-27 illustrates this point vividly:

> An argument also began between them about who should be reckoned the greatest; but he said to them, "Among the gentiles it is the kings who lord it over them, and those who have authority over them are given the title Benefactor. With you this must not happen. No; the greatest among you must behave as if he were the youngest, the leader as if he were the one who serves. For who is the greater: the one at table or the one who serves? The one at table, surely. Yet here I am among you as one who serves![33]

As a human institution one cannot deny the human tendencies to lord it over others. This will be against the tradition and legacy of the Church received from the great ancestor, Jesus Christ. Separation and disunity are also against the spirit of the Church-as-family of God, since they are totally against the wish of the one who founded this family, namely Jesus Christ.

6.2.3 Small Christian Community: the Smallest Church-as-Family of God

The building up and development of the Small Christian Community (SCC) or Basic Christian Community[34] is one way of actualising the Church-as-family. The notion of SCCs in Africa dates back to the early 1960s in Zaire (today D. R. Congo). The Nyarombo Parish, in Musoma Diocese, Tanzania, followed up in 1966. A resonance was found in 1971 in Lusaka Diocese, Zambia, in St. Charles Lwanga Parish. A systematic formation and development of the concept was, however, first initiated by the Association of Member Episcopal Conferences in Eastern Africa (AMECEA) in 1973 as a way of making the Church in East Africa realise itself as a local Church. It was reflected upon as a response to a quest for pastoral orientation.[35]

---

[33] The translation is taken from The New Jerusalem Bible, Standard edition, London 1985.
[34] In other places the concept is also termed as Basic Ecclesial Community, Living Ecclesial Community or Basic Family Community. These concepts were listed by Bishop Anselme Titianma Sanon, Bishop of Bobo-Dioulasso/Burkina Faso in his intervention during the Sixth General Congregation of the Special Assembly of the Synod of Bishops for Africa. Cf. OR, 27th April 1994, p. 14.
[35] Cf. A. E. Orobator, The Church as Family, 2000, pp. 23f. and F. Nwaigbo, Church as Communion, 1996, p. 290.

Whereas some African theologians reflect upon it as a "new way of being Local Church"[36] it is worthwhile to also consider it as the manner in which the Church-as-family contextually lives out its identity in the various local *ecclesiae* in Africa. Aylward Shorter proposes that:

> African Christians want a simpler and more congenial Church, not one in which they feel estranged by western forms that are irrelevant to their own cultural environment. They want a greater measure of participation, of community experience and of communion with the Church's leaders[37].

The concept of Small Christian Communities brings the elements of solidarity and participation into fruition, which draw their strength, in the context of Ghana, from the relational values of family and community. In these Christian communities the Church of Christ fully manifests itself in legitimately organised cells of faith,

> which in so far as they are united to their pastors, are also quite appropriately called Churches in the New Testament (Acts 8:1; 14:22ff; 20:17ff). In these communities [...] Christ is present, through whose power and influence the One, Holy Catholic and Apostolic Church is constituted[38].

The individual basic communities know that they are in communion with other communities with like interests which come together to build the parish. This cell of faith, however, takes care of their emotional and sometimes material needs which cannot be met by the bigger community. SCCs enable sharing in family life and bring about actualisation of belonging to small communities which are part of a larger one. Through this the "*Church as community of communities*" is being built.

The Synod Fathers, in their deliberations in 1994 in Rome, also recognised that the division of Church into "communities small enough to foster close human relationships"[39] was one sure way of making the Church-as-family fully realise its potential. Their views of such Christian communities are that they will become places of evangelisation for the faithful themselves

> so that subsequently they can bring the Good News to others; ...communities which pray and listen to God's Word, encourage the members themselves to take on responsibility, learn to live an ecclesial life, and reflect on different human problems in the light of the Gospel. Above all, these communities are to be committed to living Christ's love for everybody, a love which transcends the limits of the natural solidarity of clans, tribes or other interest groups.[40]

---

36 A. E. Orobator, The Church as Family, 2000, p. 24.
37 See Ibid., p. 26.
38 LG 26.
39 *Ecclesia in Africa,* 89.
40 Ibid., 89.

In the history of the Church in Ghana it is observed that in the past the pastors were totally responsible for life and ministry in the parish and many people thought that nothing could happen without them. For most people the priests were the Church and the general perception that "Father-does-and-knows-best" seemed to have been accepted by the parishioners or at least by most of them. The parish was mainly his concern and property. The parishioners did not have to mingle in his affairs[41]. The concept "Church-as-family" helps to correct this phenomenon through the Small Christian Communities. It is the establishment of a Church at the grassroots where the faithful come together for reflection on and sharing of the Word of God and for active participation in the life of the Church and society. The faithful are also able to share their faith, joys and sorrows with one another. The sharing that takes place provides impulses for the living out of their faith. In most dioceses the SCCs' concept is replaced with the so-called "Renew" programme. The communities are then called "Faith Sharing communities". However, the principles of the Small Christian Communities are still in place. In any case both expressions describe the basic Christian communities as the kernels of the Church or primary ecclesiastical nucleus, the activities of which are "connected to the participatory and collegial structure of the parish as a *communion of communities*"[42]. And since dialogue forms an indispensable component of a communion, the Church-as-family becomes a dynamic community of dialogue and of strengthened human relations.

6.2.4 The Place of Women in the Church-as-Family

Characteristic of the contemporary world is the growing awareness of the dignity of the woman not only in the Church but also in society at large. In the book of Genesis it is stated that "God created man in the image of himself, in the image of God he created him, male and female he created them" (Gen 1,27). God remains the source of life for man and woman. The dignity, freedom and intelligence of any person do not depend on the gender but on God, the creator of heaven and earth. The history and tradition of Ghana, however, show that over a long period of time women have not enjoyed the above-mentioned *essentials* of their humanity to the fullest. The Ghanaian woman, like her contemporary African sisters, is challenged to become more conscious of her social, cultural, economic and political dignity, her life-giving role and rights of participation in the social life and development of the country. In addition to playing her important role as social catalyst, she should also assume her rightful dignity and not allow it to be determined by others.

The Ghanaian society is predominantly patriarchal, implying that authority is traced to male descendants and that more males than females are at

[41] F. Nwaigbo, Church as a Communion, 1996, p. 286.

[42] Healey Joseph, Towards a New Way of Being Church: Pastoral Implications of the Small Christian Community Model of Church in the World Church Towards the 21st Century, in: African Christian Studies 7 (1991) 9.

the realm of affairs in the various spheres of life. It is known, for example, that in most cases women "are not involved in decision making and [some] are themselves still convinced that men are, and should always be, their leaders"[43]. This is not absent in the Church, which is largely male dominated, especially in the hierarchical leadership but not in ministry or exercise of charismas.

One of the greatest values of the Ghanaian family is that it has a listening ear, it is consultative and discussions form part of its inner dynamics. The Church is thus called to re-examine these elements and to see how they can be incorporated into the life of the Church-as-family. The Church needs to develop an art of listening to the plight of women and if possible the male members need to help the female counterparts develop a spirituality which is proper of their nature as such. A. E. Orobator notes that

> the art of listening to the conversations going on in the community called church involves listening to the conversations of women: their pain and sorrow, their joys, hopes and dreams. This process of listening ultimately enriches the Church's fulfilment of its mission[44].

The Ghanaian women themselves can and should tell their own story. Not even Western feminists can do it for them. Their concerns are not just the development of adequate mechanisms of socio-economic, political, cultural and religious empowerment but are also the building up of structures of permanent nature, which will offer them an enabling environment, where they can relate their own stories. The women are also offering something to this family of God to which they belong and they are not and should not be satisfied with just being spectators or be content with only carrying out the directives of the clerics.

The men but also those women who are still ignorant need to recognise that the women are also called to participate in building the Church-as-family of God. They are not to be called upon "to do work which others cannot do"[45]. They can in their own right and as part of the family do a lot of things for the good of others. As women they bring in their "feminine genius" in the giving of love and healing where divisions and destructive forces prevail.

The Church is a liberated family, which has as its agenda the integral liberation and salvation of all people and the renewal of social structures. It must thus "continue to play its prophetic role and be the voice of the voiceless"[46] beginning in its own house. It lies at the very heart of the Gospel message to seek the integral development of everybody, especially the poor and marginalised in society. This connotes the Church delving into the sphere of history and culture to help "cleanse" them of biases against women. The Ghanaian woman needs to be given her rightful and God-given place in the Church and society at large, and the model Church-as-family of God is

---

[43] L. Magesa, Anatomy of Inculturation, 2004, p. 29.
[44] A. E. Orobator, The Church as Family, 2000, p. 40.
[45] Barbara Emmanuel, African Women in the Church as the Family of God, in: http://www.sedos.org/english/barbara.htm (visited on 5th November, 2011).
[46] *Ecclesia in Africa,* no. 106.

appropriate because it has the character of ensuring that none of its members is denied the dignity proper to him or her.

6.2.5 Solidarity and Hospitality in the Church-as-Family

Two other important elements worth considering in the theology of the Church-as-Family are the values of solidarity and hospitality. An analysis of the life of the early Christians indicates that the followers of Jesus "sold their goods and possessions and distributed the proceeds among themselves according to what each one needed" (Acts 2, 45). This way of life finds expression in the ecclesiology of Church-as-Family of God under the heading of SOLIDARITY. This concept has been seen in *Ecclesia in Africa* as one of the remarkable elements of family in Africa that makes the former an appropriate ecclesial metaphor. In the spirit of solidarity the Church in Ghana can be compared with the good Samaritan presented in *Ecclesia in Africa*. The Church does not only see the situation with the eyes of a prophet but goes on to alleviate the pains of the affected people. More than that, the Church is invited to offer assistance to those people in need. In eschatological terms one could talk about the realisation of the *Visio Dei* – eschatological vision of God, whereby pains are no more and all live happily together under the authority of God, the father.

The ecclesia in Ghana has been nursed by its sister Churches in Europe and North America for a very long time. It thus knows the importance of standing by those in need. In this context the Church is being called upon not just to awaken the conscience of the politicians and non-governmental organisations to the plight of the suffering masses, but more so it is to get deeply involved in bandaging the wounds of the injured, to dialogue for the liberation of the oppressed and to create an enabling atmosphere at its bosom where people can find security and trust. It shares with them in their various conditions and identifies itself with them.

Furthermore, solidarity finds its place in primary evangelisation, whereby people come into contact with the word of God for the first time and desire to get immersed into it. Since the announcers of the Word of God were once themselves searchers of it, they can feel the thirst and hunger of those who are looking for it and so they seek to create the necessary conditions for its proclamation and reception. This is also a sign of solidarity lived in context – it is evangelisation in deeds. Solidarity understood within the context of Church-Family is dancing with those who are happy, weeping with those in sorrow, offering cushion to the oppressed and solace to the neglected. In short, solidarity means translating the Gospel message in John 1, 4, which says that the Word became flesh and pitched his tent among the human race, shared their joys and sorrows, brought good news to the oppressed and afflicted and freedom to those in bondage.

Added to the thought of solidarity is the cultural value of hospitality which expresses itself in providing a home for the "searchers of the Word", who are seen here as "guests". The term "hospitality" has its origin in Latin. It is from *hospitium/hospitalitas* which stem from *hospes*[47]. The word connotes an encounter between a host and a guest. The Greek equivalent is *philoxenia* – to welcome a stranger – or simply *xenia.* According to Walter T. Wilson, *Xenia* in Greek or *hospitium* in Latin is the only alternative to marriage in the Greco-Roman antique, where people of different political or kin groups established cooperative relations with one another[48] and encompassed "the whole process of shared friendly relationship"[49] between host and guest. Hospitality is concretised in the Ghanaian culture by the exchange of friendly greetings, drinks especially water, food and gifts, not excluding the exchange of information. It is a process and regardless of whether the guest and host have known each other hitherto or not, the latter has the duty to make the former comfortable. This value stands out as one of the vital elements of the Ghanaian culture that has withstood the test of time. It is seen by Elochukwu E. Uzukwu in his article, *Missiology Today: The African Situation,* as having held so well that "it could be described as a way of being an African"[50]. Ezukwu made the statement as valid for African. This means that Ghana, a subset of the continent, will not be alone in the application of this method in its evangelizing mission.

Ghana has been described earlier on in chapter two as a multi-cultural and -ethnic society. This component of the society also affects the life of the Church. Many parish communities, especially those in towns and cities, are made up of people from different ethnic groups. First of all, members of the Church who have newly arrived will look for a community of Christian worship. Such people need a welcoming atmosphere in which they can feel at home, in order to forget the hassle of the day, and in order to concentrate on their worship with the other members of their spiritual family. The second group of people are those who have come into contact with the Gospel for the first time and are longing for deeper experience with it. Hospitality towards them is inevitable and implies not just the way the Word is delivered but more so, it embodies how they are received into the Church, characterised by the creation of a homely atmosphere, where the guest or visitor can tell his or her story. The practice of *amania* by the *Akan* or *to mãsim* by the *Frafra,* by which the host declares his preparedness to listen to the guest, could be an example for the Church. The gesture of the host creates trust for the exchange of information, which is of primary importance in evangelisation. It is not enough for the Church to show that it has a message for the people. It must also show that it has an ear for the questions that bother the seekers. Through this process the Church in Ghana would then be in the position to develop appropriate pastoral and evangelisation methods to respond to the various situations at hand.

---

[47] Cf. Walter T. Wilson, Gastfreundschaft, in: Hans Dieter Betz et al. (Hg.), Religion in Geschichte und Gegenwart, Band 3, Tübingen [4]2000, 475.

[48] Cf. Ibid.

[49] G. I. Olikenyi, African Hospitality, 2001, p. 83.

[50] Cf. Elochukwu E. Uzukwu, "Missiology Today: The African Situation", in: Elochukwu E. Uzukwu (ed.), Religion and African Cultures. Inculturation – A Nigerian Perspective, Enugu 1988, p. 158.

The spirit of hospitality in the Ghanaian understanding of the word also connotes the pardoning of the mistakes of the guest. The *Frafra* of Ghana have a saying that *sããna nini karigɛ mɛ ge ba kayɛti* – meaning, "the eyes of the stranger are big but they cannot see [well]". They need time to get used to the new social and cultural environment. This exercise takes time and demands patience from the stranger/guest and the local inhabitants/host. Every person was perhaps also a visitor somewhere and sometime ago. Some family members could also be going through the same process somewhere else. Showing hospitality, therefore, is a sign of solidarity with all people who are on a journey. The Church is also on a pilgrimage. It is a stranger or visitor in some countries and needs to have an understanding heart and a listening ear of the host. Hospitality is as real as family and that means everybody experiences it in one way or the other. In other words, anybody can be a host or a guest at any given time. In a case where the family plays host to an individual or group of individuals, "every member of the family is directly involved; all the members of the family play different but complementary roles"[51]. Within the framework of this discussion the Church-family is the host, and this demands the involvement of all members to make sure that the "guests" perceived here as seekers and new converts feel at home. In a Church with a long tradition of members associating pastoral care of the faithful with Church leadership especially the ordained ministers, the concept "hospitality" can bring about a shift in mentality and attitude, thereby fostering participation and use of talents in the Church. The task of the Church in the area of hospitality is to create an atmosphere where people feel belonging to it and wanted and can express their quest for God; where people can find refuge and trust to tell their "faith story" and where the right thing is given to them – the Word of God.

Associated with solidarity and hospitality are the elements of sharing and co-operation among family members. As the saying goes, "charity begins at home" and the members of the Church in Ghana, i.e. individuals, parishes and dioceses, will have to learn to share and co-operate with one another. Through the sharing among themselves, it will be ensured that no one is really needy. Co-operation is a facet of the Ghanaian cultural value system that is very much cherished and used. The *Akan* talk about *nnoboa*; in *Krobo* it is called *katsu* and in *Gurune kããribã*. The Church can use it to harness resources and to benefit from synergy effect of such a system.

These two cultural values – sharing and cooperation – which emanate from the communal feeling of the Ghanaian, serve as cushion in times of difficulties, thereby enriching the whole community. The Church can make use of these in its ecclesial system. Ghana has four archdioceses, fifteen dioceses and one apostolic vicariate. Experience has shown that apart from the exchange of personnel, there is hardly any other form of sharing especially in economic terms. Partnership and/or cooperation among parishes and dioceses are almost zero. It is common knowledge that some parishes and dioceses in Ghana are poorer than others. Also parishes within a particular diocese do not have

[51] G. I. Olikenyi, African Hospitality, 2001, p. 104.

proportionate economic resources. The use of the principle of solidarity and sharing would imply awakening the conscience of the pastors together with that of their lay leaders to the need of cooperating with other parishes and dioceses. Those who are better off financially could think of helping those in need. This principle would have been in line with that of the Pauline communities where the richer ones helped the others with their prayers and economic resources. In doing so, the Church would show to the rest of the world that the concept of Church-as-Family is neither theological cosmetics nor intellectual gymnastics but rather a lived-reality in the context of the culture of the people. Instead of having partnership with only sister parishes in Europe and North America, the local parishes and dioceses could create a financial pool to help each other and get into partnership as a concrete forum in which they live out solidarity. The sharing should begin with the priests, religious and bishops. For instance, priests who are in richer parishes could give up a certain percentage to those in poorer parishes. Pastoral and social projects could also be developed using similar principles. The spirit of solidarity learnt already in the natural family would demand that the religious leaders be sensitive to the needs of their confreres and co-sisters in order to curb the existing economic and social discrepancies.

The advantage of solidarity, hospitality, sharing and cooperation is the possible reduction of ethnocentrism and particularism, which could make way for unity in diversity. Furthermore, solidarity strengthens the much revered communion already examined in this study. If the various dioceses and parishes in Ghana could begin to cooperate and work together as one family, it would be a testimony to the fact that the Catholic Church is at once both universal and particular. It is made up of different cultures and people but they form one big family of God. If the Church can in any way help transform the Ghanaian society, it has to begin with itself, since charity begins at home.

Solidarity and hospitality should not be considered as the signing of a blank check for some people or Church communities to again become dependent on others. The scenario should not be created that the host remains a host to the guest nor should one community perpetually depend on the other for its survival. Solidarity should be able to bring about self-reliance and hospitality makes the erstwhile "stranger" or "utterly other" become a brother or sister in the one family of God.

6.3 Interaction and Dialogue in the Church-family

It is perhaps one of the most difficult issues in the development of a contextual ecclesiology based on the understanding of family in Ghana, namely, the issue of dialogue in the Church-as-family itself, dialogue among the Christian Churches and communities and dialogue with other non-Christian religions. The problem has its roots in the celebration of faith and the perception of religion in the traditional family system. Religion and religious practice are matters for family members, sometimes only of nuclear family members. If one member should bring in "foreign gods" into the family, his actions may be tolerated but no dialogue takes place. The same is true when it comes to other religions. There is co-existence and "reciprocal" respect at the personal level but no dialogue in the Western sense of the word. Interaction takes place and it can be said that each person "dances out his religion". It is the way of dancing out the faith or religion that attracts and not so much the idea of dialogue.

In ecclesiological discussions so much emphasis is laid on ecumenical and inter-religious dialogue to the neglect of intra-ecclesial interaction. This issue will also be considered here.

6.3.1 Intra-Ecclesial Interaction

One way of looking at the Church in Ghana is that it is a family of families. A pictorial presentation of the phenomenon can be illustrated as follows: if the parish is considered as an extended family, the various Small Christian Communities or the Outstations serve as the nuclear families. These all build the family of God united in spirit and truth. The next step is the diocese with its many parishes, which all build the diocesan Church-family, thus building a communion of brothers and sisters. Again one could take the aggregation of the various dioceses in the country as an extended family, thus making it possible for the use of the expression the "Church-as-Family in Ghana". Here again the Church wins the image of family of families. The relation can be zoomed to the level of the universal Church.

Important at all the levels is the interaction that takes place among the communities and the members therein. Considering that the country is made up of various languages and cultures, it would not be an exaggeration to assume the existence of prejudices and antipathy of some kind. Interaction at the various levels would bring about the actualisation of the ideals of relatedness inherent in the understanding of family in Ghana. Furthermore, interactions at parish, diocesan and national levels could bring about a greater appreciation of the differences in the various "families of God", which is an enrichment for the Church. Prejudices also wane in the course of time and the "strange neighbour" gets the status of a brother or sister in the spirit of Gal 3, 26-28, where it states that all the baptised are children of God united through their faith in Christ Jesus.

6.3.2 The Church as Family in Ecumenical Dialogue

It is not uncommon in Ghana to find in many families and/or compound houses that members therein belong to different Churches. At the level of inter-personal interactions and relationships they do many things in common and see themselves as one people. Confessional difference comes to play when they want to pray to the same God through their brother and Lord Jesus Christ. Since Ghana has over 3000 Churches and Christian communities, the question is what amount and type of dialogue is needed? When it comes to the interaction among the Catholic Church with other Christian Churches and/or communities the term ecumenism or ecumenical dialogue is used. The concept "Ecumenism" has its origin in the Greek word *oikos,* which can be expounded to form the term *Oikoumene* and implies the totality of the inhabited earth[52]. In this context, ecumenism would mean the collaboration among the various Churches on earth as one universal Church. In the everyday language it is the co-operation among and/or between Christian denominations. The process of ecumenism, described by the Vatican II as "ecumenical movement", entails "the initiatives and activities encouraged and organized, according to the various needs of the Church and as opportunities offer, to promote Christian unity"[53]. An important observation of the decree on ecumenism is the way the term Church is used. In some instances the concept comprises the Catholic Church in singular and in other times it signifies the various Churches and Christian communities. This is an expression of the willingness to collaborate and to dialogue.

The Christian religion has experienced in its history until now elements of dissensions wherever the Church has been implanted. Ghana has not been spared these regrettable incidents of inter-denominational "antagonism" which have in no small way deformed inter-denominational dialogue and collaboration[54] and hampered Christian unity. The tactic of "divide and convert" used by the missionaries created tension within families, clans and villages and presented no good image of Christianity[55]. The need for ecumenical dialogue in Ghana lies especially in the need to live the Gospel message of love and unity as is the wish of Jesus. It also has relevance in the urgency of the time to save families, clans, villages and towns and in fact the country as a whole from falling apart due to confessional or denominational differences.

As already seen in chapter four of this study the most outstanding aspect of Catholicism is its wholeness. By its "catholicity" the Church is challenged to "at all costs avoid falling into a sectarian mentality. Being 'catholic', this Church must be open to all God's truth, no matter who utters it"[56]. It is a paradigm shift from defence of doctrines, which for ages has kept the various denominations apart from each other, to sharing of faith and perspectives which has the potential of opening up new horizons in respect of the individual and group experiences of God. The truth remains "that all who have been justified by faith in baptism are incorporated into Christ"[57] and form a big community of Christians, notwithstanding the differences in doctrines and hierarchical structure. It is thus no more an option but rather an imperative to undertake ecumenical dialogue and collaboration.

---

[52] Cf. Solomon Okezie Obasi, Evangelisation and Modernity. Cultural Issues as Missiological Imperatives in *Ecclesia in Africa*, Rome 2002, p. 158.
[53] UR 4.
[54] A. E. Orobator, The Church as Family., 2000, p. 125.
[55] Harris W. Mobley, The Ghanaian's Image of the Missionary. An Analysis of the Published Critiques of the Christian Missionaries by Ghanaians 1897-1965, Leiden 1970, p. 144.
[56] A. Dulles, Models of the Church, 2002, p. 3.
[57] UR 3.

The dialogue and collaboration under consideration are not the preserve of the experts who may confine it to the field of theological and doctrinal intricacies. The existence of a Church "goes beyond the quest to achieve a doctrinal rapprochement between differing denominations"[58]. It is the task of the whole Church, the laity as well as the clergy, theologians as well as non-theologians. It is the task of everyone, each person performing his task according to the talent he has[59], be it in daily Christian living or in theological studies.

In the ecumenical process efforts should be made to avoid expressions, judgements and actions of all forms that could hinder mutual relations with the brethren of other denominations. It is a demonstration of respect to those who share the same faith in the one Lord. True ecumenical dialogue at this level could lead to dissolution of misunderstandings inherited from ages past[60]. There is the need to show clearly the similarities and authentic differences which unite and divide the Christian denominations: the elements that bind the big Christian family of God and the particularities of the individual "nuclear families". Especially in Ghana where Churches or Church communities and sects spring up almost every month, there is the need to emphasise that everything is not the same. A pastoral help would be to encourage the members of the different Churches to consciously discuss what they see as being particular of their denomination which makes them different from the other Church-families. They should also be encouraged to find out what they have in common with each other and why religious antagonism is a disservice to the Church. Since unity does not imply uniformity, the individual Church-families still have their individuality, as already stated above, but they recognise the importance of communion and relatedness. This ecclesiological practice could help to free the ordinary Christian from falling into dismay. Through this process "the people are liberated, transformed from within and are made new"[61] and human relations tend to improve between and/or among members and communities. Ecumenical dialogue has the potential to unveil those who stand behind religion to satisfy their own whims and caprices. It does away with fear and suspicion of the intentions of the other.

It must be noted, however, that dialogue with other Churches and ecclesial communities is not a substitute for the proclamation of the Word of God nor is it an alternative. It is an imperative to announce the good news of Christ. Ecumenism is part of giving witness to the Gospel message. The exercise of one implies the other. They are intrinsically interwoven and should not be separated from each other. There are issues that are of greater concern and demand concerted efforts to combat them: poverty, oppression, ignorance and disease, just to mention a few. Christians are being called in the spirit of ecumenism to work towards their abatement or reduction. Ecumenical dialogue

[58] A. E. Orabotor, The Church as Family, 2000, p. 126.
[59] Cf. Ibid., p. 5.
[60] Cf. S. O. Obasi, Evangelisation and Modernity, 2002, p. 163.
[61] Ibid.

makes the preaching of the gospel more authentic and effective especially for those who are searching: it gives them some level of security. It also helps the dialogue participants to live out their faith in a practical way and be convinced about it. In fact, a Catholic in ecumenical dialogue begins to delve more deeply into the mystery of faith and may even become more catholic than before. The other non-catholic Christian opens the eyes of the Catholic counterpart – and vice versa – to other ways of experiencing God[62] that differ from his own. They throw light onto each other's path, thereby giving new insights for improved Christian life. This enriches the individuals and the Church as a whole, and brings about greater unity and appreciation of each other.

Without underrating the importance of the influence of personality clashes of the respective Church leaders and their preparedness to encourage their members to participate in ecumenical activities, the ecclesiological model of a particular Church can also contribute in a great way to the intended dialogue or hinder it. The image of Church-as-family stands *inter alia* for unity and harmonious human relations. Since the Christians all have experience of family life, they would most probably find it easy to transfer their knowledge of family to Church. The term family thus offers the Church an opportunity to develop its system for effective dialogue.

6.3.3 The Church-as-Family in Inter-Religious Dialogue

The analysis of religion in Ghana in chapter two indicated that the institution underwent a dramatic change upon the advent of Christianity and Islam on the soils of the country. Before this time, the perception of God was influenced by the religious practice proper to the traditional religion. The latter also provided for the unity of purpose within the respective villages, clans or families. Islam and Christianity brought in new perspectives and flavour in the religious arena of the country and introduced a new dimension in the way the Ghanaian related to his creator. A disturbing factor, however, is that their presence in Ghana also put asunder some families, clans and villages. This issue has been mentioned a number of times in this research already. Chinua Achebe, the Nigerian novelist, illustrated this incident in the following manner: "The white man came quietly and peaceably with his religion. We were amused at his foolishness and allowed him to stay. Now he has won our brothers and our clan, we can no longer act as one. He has put a knife on things that held us together and we have fallen apart"[63]. The phenomenon could be described as follows: when someone got converted to Christianity or Islam without the rest of the family, he or she was isolated in some way. It was more or less like abandoning his or her roots. Furthermore, the various missionary societies from the different denominations took up territories in the country. These regions thus won the character of the said missionaries. The school a person attended was very much linked to the

[62] Cf. ibid., p. 164.

[63] Chinua Achebe, Things Fall Apart, in: Gabriel Maduka Okafor, Development of Christianity and Islam in Modern Nigeria, Würzburg 1992, p. 101.

Church he belonged to. This attitude of "divide and convert", which is not different in character from the "divide and rule" method of the colonial masters, was a contradiction to what the Church is committed to, namely, the continuation of the mission of Jesus to gather the children of God who are scattered abroad (John 11,52).

The accusation against Christianity in Ghana concerns especially its disrespect for anything called traditional and/or cultural, which it hitherto termed fetishism. Christianity confronted the Ghanaian with a world view different from what he was formerly familiar with and threatened the cultural and structural equilibrium of the society. This phenomenon could be described as a "slap in the face" of the traditional religion. Islam on its part adopted the principle of assimilation through the trading activities of its adherents and so gradually gained roots in Ghana. The *Dagbon* culture (*Dagbani* – see appendix I, no. 19), for example, is so much islamised that an outsider can hardly differentiate between what is particular to or original from the culture itself and what is borrowed from Islam.

Gabriel Maduka Okafor in defending the missionaries argues that they "made a correct appreciation of the fact that West African religions were much more closely integrated with West African culture"[64]. His argument cannot be accepted on a wholesale. First of all, it is almost impossible to talk of West African religions. The fact that the traditional religion is expressed in different forms at different places does not make it plural. If that were the case then Christianity and Islam would also have to be referred to in plural, namely, Christian religions and Islamic religions. After all there are so many denominations and movements of both religions but they are referred to respectively in singular. Secondly, every religion is a product of culture in one way or the other. To separate the two will be an impoverishment of the social structure. Just as the African Traditional Religion is very much connected to culture, so is Christianity too. To accept the argument of Okafor will mean that the missionaries' aim was to transport the Western culture to the West Africans or Ghanaians and not a religion –although the fact of exportation of culture cannot be wholly denied.

It is undeniable that the missionaries were ignorant of the local customs. Their intolerance of anything that was in contrast or contrary to their world view(s) and/or the Christian doctrine, however, calls for a second examination. In defending the missionaries we would say that they were children of their time and so acted within a certain frame of mind. As children of our time, however, we have to correct things by engaging in inter-religious dialogue, which Pope John Paul II observes as "one element in the mission of the Church"[65].

---

[64] Gabriel Maduka Okafor, Christianity and Islam in West Africa. The Ghana Experience, Würzburg 1997, p. 80.

[65] Pontifical Council for Inter-religious Dialogue, Dialogue and Proclamation, 6. See http://www.vatican.va/roman_curia/pontifical_councils/interelg/documents/rc_pc_interelg_doc_19051991_dialogue-and-proclamatio_en.html (visited 25th November, 2011).

Dialogue in the context of religious pluralism means to undertake "all positive and constructive inter-religious relations with individuals and communities of other faiths which are directed at mutual understanding and enrichment"[66]. The consequence for a pluralistic society like Ghana is that a pragmatic engagement with the current religions and institutions at a table of mutual respect will have to be undertaken, keeping in mind the particularity and peculiarity of each. Through it the Church-as-family reaches out to a larger population and contributes in no small way to the promotion of fraternal co-existence of all peoples[67]. Dialogue unites the great human family here on earth and represents most fully the kingdom of "a huge number, impossible for anyone to count, of people from every nation, race, tribe and language" (Rev 7:9). It also moves the parties-in-dialogue towards God.

The call to respect, to peacefully co-exist and to collaborate with the traditional religion or other non-Christian religions in Ghana does not mean the neglect of witnessing about the faith the individual person has. This point was also made in respect to ecumenism but in a different form. Inter-religious dialogue and the proclamation of God's saving work in our Lord Jesus Christ are two sides of the same coin: dialogue leads to understanding the other, brings about respect for the other and appreciation of his otherness. Evangelisation is the proclamation of the message of Christ to all those who would want to listen to it. There can, therefore, "be no question of choosing one and ignoring or rejecting the other"[68]. The Gospel needs also to be proclaimed to the followers of these religions, for they also have the right to know and experience the depth of the power of the Word of God. And those who accept the good news of Christ are to be led "to baptism and the Christian life"[69].

The good news in Ghana is that one does not experience serious religious clashes in the country. In many families and/or households people are living together with different religious orientations. They do everything together except when it comes to matters of worship. It is a demonstration that doctrinal differences or religion as a whole should not be a cause of separation and tension among them. The doors of the Christian schools are open to all without religious discrimination, just as some Islamic schools are also open to all. This is inter-religious dialogue in practice and no religious leader(s) should do anything to hamper the collaborations between their adherents nor should any individual or individuals obstruct in anyway their peaceful co-existence. In times when a particular religion is looked down upon fanaticism and radicalism spring up. The situation gets worse when tribal sentiments come into play. Since the Church-family expresses the love for life and is promoter of communion and unity, efforts should be made to bring all to the round table

---

[66] Ibid., 9.

[67] Cf. *Ecclesia in Africa*, no. 137.

[68] Pontifical Council for Inter-religious Dialogue, Dialogue and Proclamation, 6. See also http://www.vatican.va/roman_curia/pontifical_councils/interelg/documents/rc_pc_interelg_doc_19051991_dialogue-and-proclamatio_en.html (visited 25th November, 2011).

[69] *Ecclesia in Africa*, 74.

where issues can be called by name and dealt with in the spirit of love and peace. This will be one way of living out its identity as Church in the context of culture and history of Ghana.

CHAPTER SEVEN

EPILOGUE

7.0 Introduction

The analysis undertaken in this study so far has shown that the image of the Church-family of God carries with it a perception that supersedes a mere human organisation or free association of people. It has its foundation in God. This thought finds correlation with that of Peter Neuner who rejects the theological consideration which only sees the Church as a mere gathering of the faithful. Rather he considers the Church as a "work of the Holy Spirit, in which the Word of God and his salvation are tangible. That is why the Church is more than just an assembly of people, a *congregatio fidelium*, a gathering of believers"[70]. It is understood as a community of brothers and sisters held together by the intense interpersonal relationship that exists amongst them through the power of the Holy Spirit. They journey with the three Divine Persons towards a common everlasting destiny of life, thereby presenting God as the strength and core of the image of Church-as-family.

In the concluding part of this study an analysis of the similarities and dissimilarities between Church and family as two subjects in discourse will be undertaken. This is done with the assumption that both concepts have something to share with each other. The term family as a social unit and concept contributes to an enrichment of theological discussion. It becomes in that way a "*locus theologicus*", in which the discussion about God and the community dedicated to him assume an enviable place in a socio-cultural concept. The Church on its part serves as theological capital that helps highlight the importance of the social unit called family. It also highlights some disturbing elements associated the family as a social reality. These issues will be discussed under the heading the Church and Family in Discourse. This will be followed by the challenges facing the Church-as-Family of God if it has to live according to its Christ given mission. The final issue will be a revisit of the element of the composition of the Church and the question of the non-baptised Church-goers. The step is aimed at also making a social issue an instance of theological discussion. It is a sign of the time which draws the attention of the Church to a reality which could put a question mark on the seriousness of its evangelisation efforts. A brief summary of some salient issues in this study will draw down the curtains on the research. The dance of life, however, continues on the other side of the stage.

---

[70] P. Neuner, Die heilige Kirche, 2002, p. 80. The translation is mine. The original text is as follows: Die Kirche wird geglaubt als Werk des Geistes, in der Gottes Wort greifbar und sein Heil offenbar wird. Darum ist die Kirche mehr als nur ein Zusammenschluss von Menschen, eine congregatio fidelium, Versammlung der Gläubigen.

7.1 The Church and Family in Discourse

The use of the model Church-as-Family of God shows its appropriateness in the level of compatibility of Church and family and the possible trade-offs, through which similarities and dissimilarities, and the symbiotic relationship between the two concepts can be discerned. On the one side, a theological concept assumes the elements of a sociological entity and develops its self-understanding out of it. On the other side, a socio-cultural unit, here family receives its God-given dignity and functions as the school of life.

In the human family life originates almost wholly from within and mostly by conception and birth. In other words, the natural family is a unique type of human community whose members are connected to one another mostly by blood-ties and/or marriage and are therefore linked to one another by a constant and invariable pattern of mutual relations. They support and stand by one another in times of difficulties. In the Church-as-family of God the members come from outside, brought into the fold through baptism. It is a non-baptised individual who exists already as a person and who is later called by God to faith and baptism. The discernable similarity is the element of life. Upon their coming together God becomes their Father and all of them are brothers and sisters, who share their joys and happiness, sorrows and worries with one another. The dissimilarity is the way the memberships increase. The size of the natural family gets augmented through marriage, procreation and/or adoption. In the Church-as-family of God it is a question of rebirth and regeneration exercised through a sacramental act called baptism. The new life imparted on the baptised flows entirely from the "Church's womb".

Relatedness is also a feature that is available in both units. The analysis of the family in Ghana in chapter two showed that the family is made up of the living-dead, the living and those who are yet to be born. The daily act of relating is, however, in respect to the living. The other two subjects of relation namely the living dead and the yet to be born belong to what is called the realm of the transcendence. One relates to them with some amount of awe. They are perceived to be with God and possess a certain amount of transcendence. God is considered to be the Supreme Being and is also an assumed reality. One does not, however, deal directly with him because of his "awesome otherness". Rather the individual's relation to him is made possible by the mediation of the ancestors who are considered to be next to him. In the case of the Church-as-family of God relationships are defined at two levels: vertically with the three Divine Persons – Father, Son and Holy Spirit and horizontally with the fellow members in the Church. Both of them are, however, very important. Even though the saints are generally considered as part of the Church and play an important role in the life of the latter, they are not the intermediaries between God and humans: Jesus is the only mediator.

Discernable interchangeable roles and features between Church and family are not only found in Ghana. Studies have shown that many other societies and cultures also pay attention to the discourse between the two concepts. A quotation from Toinette Eugene[71] is a propitious exposition on this:

> The church in the black tradition has been an extended family, while the family, in many instances, has been in fact a "domestic church". Church and family together have nurtured our suffering race and preserved us through all the ordeals of our history[72].

The black families, according to T. Eugene, do not only support family members and other black people under oppression, but are also structurally open and socially active towards all those in need, up to and including positive, reconstructive engagement with their own oppressors. "Theologically and ethically, the black family," regardless of whether it finds itself amid success or coming out "from within fierce struggles, provide[s] a paradigm of Christian family identity that incorporates kingdom values of mutual sacrifice, inclusion, patience, endurance, and hope and trust in God"[73]. Here the good values of the Church as family and those of the natural family as domestic Church are intermarried thus giving the latter a new flavour of a kind.

The Ghanaian family, clan or village is based on the principle of "ancestorship". The ancestor serves as the center of unity and he also functions as the pivot around which life is organised[74]. In respect of the Church one would also raise the question of who Jesus is or could be within the framework of understanding the Church-as-family in Ghana. It could be argued that a contextual Ghanaian ecclesiology cannot be delineated from Christology. Been baptised in the name of the Holy Triune God, the Christians are born into a community of love and life and are made brothers and sisters of Jesus Christ, the "brother-ancestor" as Charles Nyamiti expresses it[75]. Why is the concentration on Jesus as ancestor and not on the Holy Trinity as such? The answer lies in the Ghanaian perception of an ancestor. He must be someone who had lived on earth before and so belongs to the category of the living-dead. An ancestor is said to be closer to God and can mediate between the living and the Supreme Being. One other special character of an ancestor is that he must have lived a life worthy of emulation. Within the framework of the Ghanaian concept of Church-as-family of God, Jesus could be classified as an ancestor in respect of his mediator role, his love for life and his exemplary life. He has also left a legacy behind. This pedigree forms the basis for Church-family ideal and tradition.

---

[71] Toinette M. Eugene wrote an essay "Lifting as we Climb." In this essay she quoted from her fellow African American scholar, J. Deotis Roberts, on the nature of the African American Catholic community. See Lisa Sowle Cahill, Family. A Christian Social Perspective, Minneapolis 2000, p. 111.

[72] Ibid.

[73] L. S. Cahill, Family, 2000, p. 12.

[74] Cf. E. Orobator, Contemporary African Ecclesiology, 1996, p. 272. See also Bénézet Bujo, African Theology in its Social Context, Nairobi 1992, pp. 75-92.

[75] Cf. Charles Nyamiti, Christ our Ancestor, Gweru/Zimbabwe 1984.

The ancestorship of Jesus must, however, not be understood in the sense of blood relationship but rather on the basis of his salvific and mediator role. It is this categorisation which gives the concept of ancestor new vigor in Jesus. Those who gather around the "ancestral shrine" are no more just people from a particular tribe or clan but rather all those who follow him. The gathering is an answer to the *Verbum Dei* – the word God, which again is the means of communication between God and his family. This "event" does not take place only at one particular point but rather all over the world. The members of one unit, however, feel bound to those of other sister units. In other words, the common ancestor is the binding force of the various nuclear families who build a common extended family. Perceiving this view in ecclesiological terms the situation could be described as follows: the Small Christian Community, the Parish or Diocese could be understood as families in their own right. These in turn are united automatically with the universal Church, which has the same tradition and ancestor, in the person of Jesus Christ. The determining factor for their common roots at any time in history is the common ancestor. His place within the universal Church-as-family of God does not, however, affect the way life is arranged within the individual family units. Through the understanding of family in Ghana the horizon of the Christian is widened to include also the universal Church, thereby illustrating the catholic dimension of the metaphor.

The similarities of the two concepts could be summed up as follows: the Church-as-family and the natural family stand for the gift and promotion of life. They both reach out to other institutions in society and are interrelated. Since they are set out to serve others, they should do well to bring out the communicative and communion aspects of the human society.

7.2 Challenges of the Church-as-Family

Admittedly there are occasional excessive forces which stand in the way of a healthy family life. These forces surface in the form of extreme familial and tribal loyalties as observed in chapter six of this study. The scenario under consideration also prevails many times in Ghana. Changes also occur in the various family types. These complex relationships, however, do not make the family to be viewed as an institution with lesser importance but rather accentuate its usefulness for social life. Since the various institutions in a social structure act in concert to bring about the needed development therein, the expectation is that the family of God would give impetus to the natural family, when the latter has difficulties. This would highlight the Church as sacrament, which functions to heal and transform[76]. The proposal of the family model is thus a challenge to the local Church in Ghana to build networks good enough to facilitate dynamic relationships between the different ethnic and social groupings in the country, in order to free the Church of ethnic and tribal biases

[76] Cf. Maurice Schepers, The Ecclesiology of the Church as Family of God: A Systematic Approach, in: Theology of the Church as Family of God. Tangaza Occasional Papers/ No. 3, p. 26f.

prevalent in a country with different cultures and languages[77]. The situation in which the appointment of bishops and parish priests is tainted by quarrels and animosity because of the tribal background of the candidates is a disservice to the society at large and the Church in particular. If the Church, which is supposed to unite and heal the wounds of the people, is also engaged in actions that can bring about divisions in the society, who would then help the ailing society? The metaphor of the family is in this case a challenge to the Church to reconsider how it lives out its character and task as salt of the earth and light of the world. An *ecclesia* that should portray and live out unity, love and solidarity gives life to the natural family and serves as cushion in times of social upheavals. It is in this case both a moral and theological instance.

On its part the family could be of great service to the Church by its function as the smallest or domestic Church, as a place of prayer and lived-faith and as a community in which relationships are nurtured and renewed by Christ. In this way the natural Christian family takes part in building up the kingdom of God[78]. In the words of L. S. Cahill, seeing the family as domestic or miniature Church or e*cclesia domesticae* is to talk about "the reign of God in human society" which is opened up to the "neighbour, stranger, and enemy in a new family of sisters and brothers in Christ"[79]. By so doing the family serves the Church and the world, since this model can serve as the mechanism for evangelisation and at the same time offer an opportunity for the development of a family ethic that is "socially transformative"[80]. In order to fulfil the task of social transformation, however, Christian families have to structure their internal relations in a form that is based on the ideals of Christian spirituality and supported by the principle of reciprocal service.

John Paul II reflected in his Apostolic Exhortation *Familiaris consortio* that the Church as *ecclesia domestica* is called upon to experience the communion which is authentic and to bring to perfection the human relationships to prevail among the various members thereof. According to John Paul II

> the Christian family constitutes a specific revelation and realization of ecclesial communion, and for this reason too it can and should be called "the domestic Church". [...] [The Christian family is] "a school of deeper humanity": this happens where there is care and love for the little ones, the sick, the aged; where there is mutual service every day, where there is sharing of goods, of joys and of sorrows[81].

---

[77] Cf. *Ecclesia in Africa*, 63.

[78] John Chrysostom (ca. 349-407), bishop of Constantinople, considered the family as very important in Christian formation. He is said to have been categorical in demanding that Christian families should see the service to the poor as part of their God-given duty. See L. S. Cahill, Family, 2000, p. 83.

[79] Ibid.

[80] Ibid.

[81] John Paul II, Apostolic Exhortation *Familiaris Consortio* (22nd November, 1981), 21 (hereafter FC).

In the spirit of *Lumen gentium* and *Familiaris consortio* the family is a living image and historical representation of the mystery of the Church[82]. It could, therefore, be said that the social mission of the Christian family is found within the boundaries of the Church's identity and mission.

Another challenge posed by the understanding of family in Ghana to the ecclesia as a whole is how to define the relationship between the Catholic Church-family and the other Christian Churches and Christian communities in Ghana on the one hand and the relationship between the Christian Church-family and other religions in the country. In the traditional family system only members gather at the "ancestral tomb" or family shrine. Religion is in this case a family affair. The logical consequence is that non-members are excluded from religious gatherings. This perception depicts the family as closed system and could pose a problem to ecumenism and inter-religious dialogue. The Gospel message has the power of transforming cultures and purifying thought patterns. This makes it possible for the Church-family to engage in dialogue with Christians of other denominations and people of other religious confessions. This is because God is the father of all and the creator of heaven and earth. The members in the Church-family know that the Christian Church is bigger than the Roman Catholic Church and all Christians are supposed to witness to the Gospel of Christ. These other Christians are also their brothers and sisters of the one father through Jesus Christ and by the power of the Holy Spirit. If the whole of humanity is seen as the biggest family of God, it becomes easy to understand that non-Christians are also children of God but belong to different nuclear families. This makes it possible to share and dialogue.

Within the Church-as-family in Ghana the danger of exclusion and the nuances associated with the concept of person are disturbing. The Archbishop emeritus of the Archdiocese of Kumasi, Ghana, Most Rev. Peter Sarpong observes that the concept Church-family used to describe the Christian community in Africa is beautiful. He quickens to caution that such a concept which demonstrates the sense of caring, of sharing, of concern and love, could also pose a risk if not handled with care. This is due to the fact that the elements mentioned above usually apply more often than not to members within the same community. Persons outside the cultural or language group of the individual are regarded as if they were non-persons. They are seen as strangers and this phenomenon "has been the cause of the worst atrocities in Africa and has led to the negative aspects of tribalism and ethnicity"[83]. The challenge of the Church is to use the Word of God to restore the dignity of every person as a child of God. The word stranger is a human construct which creates borders in social interactions. The effect of these borders which are nourished by the incidence of fears and lack of knowledge leads to the postulation of an inhuman construct called non-person as a way of describing his or her "otherness". The Christian

---

[82] Cf. LG 11 and FC 49.

[83] Peter Sarpong, Conclusions, Expectations of the Synod, in: The African Synod. Documents, Reflections, Perspectives, compiled and edited by the Africa Faith and Justice Network, Maryknoll-New York 1996, p. 224.

view of the human person is that he is created in the image and likeness of God. It implies, therefore, that nobody can be a non-person. Through the theology of the Church-as-Family of God the Christian therein is being challenged to positively reform his cultural mentality to make it compatible with the Gospel message which he preaches.

It must be said that every entity has its boundaries. The same is true with relational concepts. Joseph Ratzinger, now Pope Benedict XVI, asserts in his book entitled *the Meaning of Christian Brotherhood* that brotherhood of any kind creates a frontier. "In Plato, if the community of the state bestows brotherhood, then the foreigner, the *barbaros*, is regarded as a non-brother; Xenophon's brotherhood of friends not only unites friends, but also divides off those who are not friends"[84]. Here Ratzinger quotes Plato and Xenophon, who used the word brother not just in reference to children of the same parents but also in respect to fellow citizens (by Plato) and friends (by Xenophon). The intention of Ratzinger here is to show the boundaries inherent in the use of terms connoting relations. In his view "all unions involve the separating of those who are united together from others"[85]. He is quick to add that Plato and Xenophon did not specifically refer to this differentiation. However,

> if, for example, the people united in one *polis* form a brotherhood, the ethos within that *polis* will necessarily differ from the attitude toward those outside it, who are not brothers: Ethical responsibility is different within the 'extended family' than outside it[86].

The same applies to people belonging to the same homestead or what he terms the *polis*. Their attitude to one another differs from that towards non-members just the same way as a person's responsibility towards members of the family is likely to be more intensive than his responsibility for outsiders[87]. It is a fundamental tension in human life, which applies to every social group including the Church-as-family.

The proposal of this study is that there can be no non-persons in the diction of the members of the Church since they all belong to one big family. The only differences should be those offered by natural, cultural and societal backgrounds such as race, language, temperament and mentality. These elements should, however, be seen as contributions to the enrichment of the Church and not to its impoverishment.

7.3 Baptism and the Case of Non-Membership in the Church-Family

The expression "members of the Church" has been mentioned a lot of times in this study without detailed exposition. These are those who profess their faith in Jesus Christ, the risen Lord and have been initiated into the community by

---

84 J. Ratzinger, Christian Brotherhood, ^{2}1993, p. 5.
85 Ibid.
86 Ibid, pp. 5f.
87 Cf. ibid., p. 6.

baptism. In response to the question concerning the membership of the community called Church, Pope Pius XII answered unequivocally in his encyclical *Mystici Corporis Christi* in the year 1943, mentioned already in this research, that only those are members who have been baptised and who remain united with the Catholic Church[88]. The views expressed in this encyclical resemble those of Robert Bellarmin who saw the Church with a clearly defined membership. He further postulated the Church to be as visible as the kingdom of Venice. Apart from the fact that it is very juridical with great emphasis on full communion with the Catholic Church through the Stool of Peter, it also stresses on the celebration of the liturgy and sacraments as necessary components for full communion or membership with the Catholic Church. One of such sacraments is the baptism.

The code of canon law stipulates that only the person who has not yet been baptised, may receive baptism[89]. It is the initiation into the Church-family and a marked public profession of faith in Christ. In short baptism forms the basis for belonging to the Church. The stipulation of the canon above indicates that those who profess their faith in Jesus Christ and (expressly) ask for baptism may be baptised[90]. It could be deduced that restrictions in whichever form may have to do with political, social and historical developments. The implication is that, if one were to go by the act of professing one's faith in Jesus alone, many more people would have been or felt being full members of the Church than it is now.

This issue may not be bracketed out in the Church-as-family: it may be excluding some people as members even though they would gladly belong to it. Taking a stride back to chapter two of this study, it was observed that a term like cousin, even though relational in nature, is being frowned upon in most cultures in Ghana. The basis of this phenomenon is that the terms brothers and sisters portray a much "closer relationship within the family [...]. There is no clear boundary, even at the tribal level, where people can say that they do not belong to the same family"[91] in one way or the other. The fact remains that the person is either accorded or not accorded with the title brother or sister. The consequence of the discussion here is that the outer boundaries of family in Ghana are perhaps difficult to define due to analogous forms arising from particular circumstances and needs. It may be easy in one culture to have these boundaries clearly defined. In another culture, however, the situation may not be the same. In any case the concept of family is generally a double-edged sword: it embraces many into its fold but also has the element of exclusion. Returning to the ecclesial life in Ghana, a situation is found whereby certain groups of people are categorically excluded from becoming full members of the

---

[88] MCC 22.

[89] *Codes Iuris Canonici* (1983), Can. 864: "*Baptismi capax est omnis et solus homo nondum baptizatus*".

[90] The point made here is in respect of adult baptism. Even in respect of infant baptism the parents still have to ask for the sacrament for their child.

[91] L. Lingonge, The Church as the Family of God. 2004, p. 72.

Church. This is especially the case with persons who want to be baptised but are denied it because before they heard of the Gospel of Christ they lived in the so-called polygamous marriages: this phenomenon applies to both men and women. The present practice in Ghana is that if the man is not prepared to dismiss the other wives or if the second and third wives are not ready to leave their man then they would not be baptised. Only the first wife may be accepted for baptism without any problem, however, with the consent of her husband. This is irrespective of the stipulation in can. 864 of CIC 1983.

The partners in polygamous relationships are people who hitherto either belonged to another religion or were simply not baptised (due to the family or life situation) but who now have the desire to be baptised and the opportunity to belong to the family of God. Interestingly, no one hinders them from offering the Church communities their services or participating in social and communal activities of the parish or out-station nor does anyone refuse to accept the Church dues they pay. They may only not be baptised nor be given Christian burial. The Church-family literally refuses new members and that means it refuses re-birth in the Spirit and/or it selects who may experience the rebirth. This practice is against the cherished value of love for life of the Ghanaian traditional family. Will such non-baptised also be called brothers and sisters, or are they cousins, strangers or visitors?

The author of this study is no supporter of polygamy and does not propose that monogamy as a Christian value should be undermined. The question is, however: If baptism is considered as a sacrament of initiation through which one becomes a full member of the Church, are some people not being excluded as such because of a given cultural practice and because of their previous way of life partly moulded by their traditional background? Which pastoral effort has been undertaken by the Churches in Ghana to address the plight of such people? The Ghanaian traditional family value of hospitality could be applied here to heal wounds and to bring joy to the respective seekers. In *Ecclesia in Africa,* no. 74 Pope John Paul II wrote that there are millions in Africa today who are still not evangelised. Therefore

> the Church is faced with the necessary and urgent task of proclaiming the Good News to all, and leading those who hear it to Baptism and the Christian life.... For the baptized the great challenge will always be that of leading a Christian life in conformity with the commitments of Baptism, the Sacrament which signifies death to sin and daily resurrection to new life (cf. Rom 6, 4-5).

Baptism, he says,

> is not simply a seal of conversion, a kind of external sign of indicating conversion and attesting to it. Rather, it is a Sacrament which signifies and effects rebirth from the Spirit, establishes real and unbreakable bonds with the Blessed Trinity, and makes us members of the Body of Christ,

> which is the Church. Therefore a journey of conversion that did not culminate in Baptism would stop half-way[92].

If the statement from Pope John Paul II is to be taken literally and seriously then the Churches in Ghana will have to reconsider the current practice of denying certain members of the society this very important sacrament of initiation. Another aspect worth considering is the perception of polygamy as relationship in perpetual sin rather than seeing it as cultural value. If all those in such relationships are living in (perpetual) sin, it implies automatically that their children are also products of sin. How would one explain it to these people? If, however, monogamy is a value just as polygyny, then ecclesiological discussions would have to take place, paying attention to this important element in the traditional Ghanaian family structure. Further to the theological discussions is the development of a pastoral approach that addresses this problem, with the aim of making the Christian message find a home in the hearts of the ordinary people. It is thus a challenge to the bishops in Ghana to seek a particular canon law with a concrete ecclesiological substance for the country – an ecclesiology that embraces all children of God and shows love for life. These people desire to participate fully in the life of the Church and to experience an end to their journey of conversion. Unfortunately, they have been refused this opportunity of receiving life in Jesus Christ through the active profession of faith in him. The value of the Church-family as lover of life could be useful here.

If Baptism is very important to make the conversion a complete one, if it is the Sacrament that signifies and effects rebirth in the Spirit, if it establishes the real and unbreakable bonds with the Holy Trinity, why are some people denied it? The first argument is found in *Ecclesia in Africa*, no. 74, where it is stated that baptism as "new life in the radical newness of the Gospel also involves certain breaks from the customs and culture of whatever people in the world, because the Gospel is never an internal product of a particular country but always comes from outside, from on high". An important theological question is: would Jesus have asked these people to bring their collection to his community, spend time to work for him but to go away when it comes to being his followers? Seen from a soteriological perspective, it is important to question whether Jesus is not great enough to heal the wounds of these children of God and to save them despite the polygamous relations.

As hinted above, this problem also has a pastoral connotation. Polygyny and monogamy are two values appealing to two respective cultural and religious systems: the Ghanaian traditional culture/religion and the Church/Western culture, respectively. To allow the baptism of the man and of all the wives would mean the acceptance of polygyny in the Church. This could have other implications in canon law and understanding of the sacraments. Not to allow them to be baptised will also mean a denial of their full membership of the family of God, which is discrimination in no uncertain terms and a sign of

[92] *Ecclesia in Africa*, 73.

disrespect of an important element in the traditional Ghanaian family structure and system. It could be argued that the Church should concentrate on bringing the people to believe in the Word of God, rather than attempting to *sacramentalise* its life. As much as this argument may have weight, the question is why then baptism as a sacrament is given so much importance in the Church.

Baptism is not only an act of initiation but also a sign of repentance. Since through the act of rebirth sins are also forgiven, refusal to baptise those in polygamous relationships is a denial of such people to experience the love and mercy of God at the bosom of the Church. Using the case of "living in perpetual sin" as an argument for the denial of baptism would mean throwing dust into the eyes of the people. It is rather a sheer demonstration of lack of courage to tackle this cultural issue, which has also great theological explosiveness. The consequence of the prevailing sacramental practice is that the statistics of the Church in Ghana represent only a fraction of those who believe in Jesus, attend liturgical celebrations and participate actively in other aspects of the Church's life. It does not include those non-baptised but "active or non-active participants". Are these people in polygamous relationships non-members, half-members or full members of the family-of-God? The issue at stake is that a person is either a member or a non-member of a group. If the observation by Peter Sarpong in respect of non-person is anything to go by, then the Church in Ghana is failing in its moral responsibility to integrate all children of God into one family and to give all human beings the dignity accorded to them from creation. To be able to preach with a prophetic voice that all human beings are equal before God and that there are no non-persons, the Church-as-family of God must show it in action.

If those husbands and the "Not-first-wives" in polygamous families are non-members, the essence of the proclamation of the word of God would be questioned. Is God the loving father? Are they being punished because they were not fortunate enough to be born into a certain religious tradition and cultural setting? Is it not an exploitation of these people, if the Church accepts their material and human resources but refuses their full participation and membership in the Church called family?

7.4 Brief Summary

From the discussion in this study it was found out that theology as a discipline and ecclesiology for that matter cannot be undertaken in a vacuum but rather in the context of the historical and socio-cultural developments of this world, of a given society and time. The discipline is perceivable in this form to the addressees of the various cultural set-ups and epochs. To sum up: theology is always in context.

The concept of "Church-as-family" is a response to the quest of many that the Church should pay attention to the culture and traditions of the people among whom it wants to take roots, thus making itself comprehensible to the members therein. In the context of Ghana the image provides a forum for life characterised by communion or community in which people relate to each other, share their joys and sorrows and celebrate their faith in God. Their cultures and the elements therein, which were hitherto condemned as fetish and irreligious, receive a new understanding. A social concept becomes a focus of theological reflection.

Since family represents life and dynamism, the concept gives the Church in Ghana hope for the future. The joy is great when new members are born. One can, therefore, not have a more appropriate image than the family, which describes the life and being of the *Ecclesia* in Ghana. The perception that God is the one who gives and sustains life of the family in Ghana, the spread of the Gospel message finds fertile grounds. It is interesting to observe that no single missionary congregation made any attempt to give a concept of God to the Ghanaian. The names of God they found in the various cultures were left to bear up till now. This buttresses the religiosity of the Ghanaian populace and the God-relatedness of the individual members.

A contextual ecclesiological reflection of the Church in Ghana would demand a cosmological world look. As a person in relation to others, the Ghanaian perceives the world from three angles: his relation to the transcendent, the relation with the living and his relatedness to the environment. This world view also affects the way he treats the environment and his everyday life.

It has also been observed thus far that the Ghanaian family is made up of the living-dead, the living and the yet-to-be-born. An ecclesiological model that does not take the above-mentioned factors into consideration may not be encompassing enough for him. Taking the Ghanaian understanding of family as the starting point, the Church-as-Family is made up of the saints who are the living-dead, the baptised perceived as the living and the catechumens seen as the yet-to-be-born. He has a relatedness to all these and above all to God his creator, who has given all humans the mandate to take care of his beautiful creation. The image is a reality that presents the individual member of the Church-as-family as a person who has the desire to participate in the life of other people, "to share in the joys and sorrows of the community in which he is an indispensable part. [He] participates in its ceremonies and rituals, discharges [his] tasks and duties to the community, kindred and clan, and at the same time claims his rights and privileges as a member of the community"[93]. In short, the model Church-as-family gives impetus to the individual Christian and the Church as a whole to strive for unity and to promote quality life for all mankind.

The principles of palaver and authority structure, which is non-hierarchical in nature and which is grounded in the ancestor, are good ingredients for the life of a Church that has had a long history of hierarchy. The place of the bishop within the Church-Family becomes that of service and coordination. In this constellation the individual members could see themselves as brothers and sisters of the same family, with every one of them having a

[93] F. Nwaigbo, Church as Communion, 1996, p. 217.

specific role to play. They also know that though they are many, they are one family in Christ.

In respect to the point made above, the Church-as-family of God is conceived as a Church for the people and a lover of life, realised through the dynamics of relationships and/or interactions among the family members and with non-members. It is committed to create communion; it seeks to build up a multi-ethnic community of believers, where there is no "Jew or gentile", but one family of God based on one faith, love and charity. Extended even to the field of politics, the Church has been described by some scholars such as John Pobee as "the guardian angel of African nationalism because of her insistence on the worth and dignity of the individual, whether white or black, red or yellow"[94]. This was made possible by the Gospel spirit of unity which breaks cultural and ethnic barriers, thus eradicating or avoiding all forms of isolationism. Cultural, ethnic, national, social and religious divisions should be matters of the past and, therefore, must not be allowed to prevail in this Church-as-family of God.

The image is associated with a difficulty: how much of and how many cultural elements of the concept would have to be sieved in order not to confuse the metaphorical meaning of the term, that is, its applied form with the original context. As already observed no culture is perfect and not everything Ghanaian is good for a healthy and successful Church life. The nuances in the image would thus have to be filtered out and challenged by the Word of God, which has the power to transform society and to bring about renewal. The Church-family is the instrument of Christ for this wonderful task; it is the beacon of hope and life not only for the people of Ghana but also for the whole of humanity.

Culture is universal but articulated differently in the various societies, according to the dynamics thereof. The Church is also universal but exists within particular cultural contexts, which influence its life. The encounter between Church and culture leads to a tradeoff without any of them losing its real identity. This is contextualization – a conjunction between culture/anthropology and theology, between family and Church. It is, as it were, giving the Church an identity particular to the society without the former losing its catholicity.

[94] J. S. Pobee, Kwame Nkrumah, 1988, p. 106.

APPENDIX I

Ethnological Map of Ghana (1999)

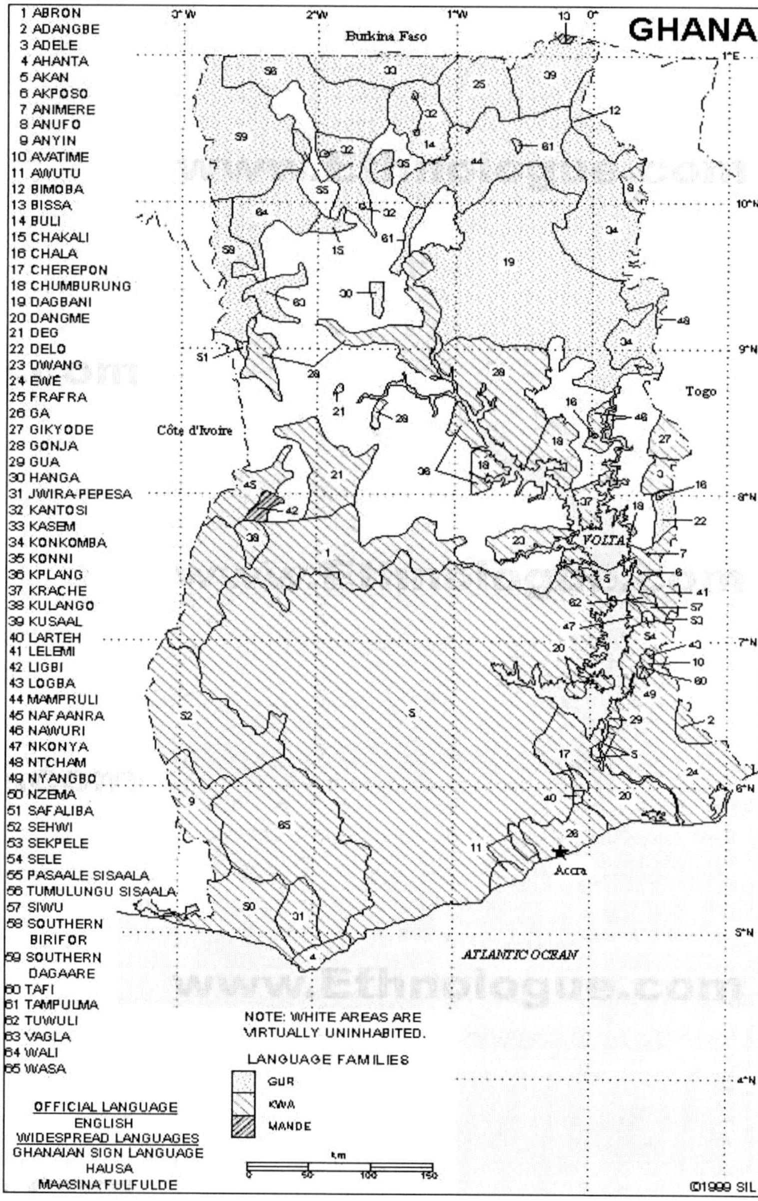

NOTE: Hausa is not a Ghanaian language even though it is widely spoken in the country.

SOURCE: http://www.ghanaweb.com/GhanaHomePage/tribes/map.html (visited on 20th April, 2012).

BIBLIOGRAPHY

Pontifical Documents

PIUS XII, Ecyclical letter *Mystici Corporis Christi* (29th June, 1943): AAS 35 (1943), 193-248.

PAUL VI, Message to the People of Africa, *Africae Terrarum* (29th October, 1967): AAS 69 (1967), 1073-1102.

--- Apostolic Exhortation *Evangelium Nuntiandi* (8th December, 1975): AAS 68 (1976), 6-76.

JOHN PAUL II, Encyclical Letter *Slavorum Apostoli* (2nd June, 1985): AAS 77 (1985).

--- Encyclical Letter on the Permanent Validity of the Missionary Mandate *Redemptoris Missio* (7th December, 1990): AAS 83 (1991), 249-340.

--- Post-Synodal Apostolic Exhortation *Ecclesia in Africa* on the Church in Africa and its Evangelization Mission towards the Year 2000. (14th September, 1995): AAS (1996), 5-82.

Synodal Documents

SPECIAL ASSEMBLY OF THE SYNOD OF BISHOPS FOR AFRICA, The Church in Africa and her Evangelising Mission towards the Year 2000: "You shall be my Witness"" (Acts 1,8). *Lineamenta,* Vatican City 1990.

--- *Instrumentum Laboris* Vatican City 1993.

---- Message of the Synod, in: L'Osservatore Romano, (Weekly Edition), 11th May, 1994, pp. 6-9.

SYMPOSIUM OF EPISCOPAL CONFERENCES OF AFRICA AND MADAGASCAR, The Church as Family of God. *Instrumentum Laboris*. Pastoral Letter, Accra 1998.

Documents of Diocesan Synods

ABADAMLOORA, Lucas, Acts of the first Synod Navrongo-Bolgatanga Diocese 2002, Navrongo 2002.

BAMILE, Paul, The Acts of the Wa Diocesan Synod, Wa 1999.

PALMER-BUCKLE, Charles Gabriel, Acts of the First Synod of the Catholic Diocese of Koforidua. "The Church as Family of God and Its Evangelising Mission in the Catholic Diocese of Koforidua, Kukurantumi 2004.

--- Acts of the Second Synod of the Catholic Archdiocese of Accra 2009. "Renewing the Church and Fulfilling our Vocation and Mission in the Catholic Archdiocese of Accra in preparation for its 125th Anniversary", Accra 2009.

Secondary Literature

XIV. Internationaler Kongress für die Familie, Bonn 1989 e.V. (ed.), Familie ist Zukunft, Bonn 1989.

ABOAGYE-MENSAH, Robert K., Mission and Democracy in Africa. The Role of the Church, Accra 1993.

ACHEBE, Chinua, Things Fall Apart, in: Gabriel Maduka Okafor, Development of Christianity and Islam in Modern Nigeria, Würzburg 1992.

ADEGBOYEG, Oluwole, NTOZI, James P. M. and SSEKAMMATE-SEBULIBA, John B., The African Family: Data, Concepts and Methodology, in: Aderanti Adepoju (ed.), Family, Population and Development in Africa, London 1997.

ADEPOJU, Aderanti and MBUGUA, Wariara, The African Family: An Overview of Changing Forms, In: Aderanti Adepoju (ed.), Family, Population and Development in Africa, London 1997.

AGYEMANG, Dominic K., Continuity and Change in Africa. The Paradox of Development, Accra 1996.

ALBERIGO, Guiseppe, A Brief History of Vatican II (Breve Storia del Concilio Vaticano II – 1959-1962) translated by Matthew Sherry, Maryknoll-New York ^{3}2009.

ALLAN, Graham, Introduction, in: Graham Allan (ed.), The Sociology of Family. A Reader, Oxford 1999, pp. 1-11.

ANDERSON, Michael, The Sociology of the Family, Harmondsworth 1980.

ANTHONY, Francis-Vincent, Ecclesial Praxis of Inculturation. Towards an Empirical-Theological Theory of Inculturizing Praxis, Rome 1997.

ARDAYFIO-SCHANDORF, Elizabeth (ed.), Family and Development in Ghana, Accra 1994.

ARINZE, Francis, Reflecting on Church as Family. Introduction to the Symposium organized by the Association of Nigerian Priest and Religious in Rome on the "Church as the Family of God", Rome 19th February, 1995.

ASSIMENG, Max, Religion and Social Change in West Africa. An Introduction to the Sociology of Religion, Accra 1989.

AWEDOBA, Albert K., Culture and Development in Africa, Legon 2002.

BARBER, Karin, The Anthropology of Texts, Persons and Publics. Oral and written Culture in Africa and Beyond, Cambridge 2007.

BARCLAY, John M. G., The Family as the Bearer of Religion in Judaism and Early Christianity, in: Halvor Moxnes (ed.), Constructing early Christian Families. Family as Social Reality and Metaphor, London, New York 1997, pp. 66-80.

BARTON, Stephen C., Discipleship and Family Ties in Mark and Matthew, Cambridge 1994.

---- Relativisation of Family Ties in the Jewish and Graeco-Roman Traditions, in: Halvor Moxnes (ed.), Constructing Early Christian

Families. Family as Social Reality and Metaphor, London and New York 1997, pp. 81-100.

BECHINA, Friedrich, Die Kirche als „Familie Gottes“. Die Stellung dieses theologischen Konzeptes im Zweiten Vatikanischen Konzil und in den Bischofssynoden von 1974 bis 1994 im Hinblick auf eine „*Familia-Dei*-Ekklesiologie“, Rome 1998.

BENNEH, George, Family and Development in Ghana. An Overview, in: Elizabeth Ardayfio-Schandorf, Family and Development in Ghana. Proceedings of International Training and Research Workshop Held at the University of Ghana, Legon on 14th – 18th December 1992, Accra 1994, pp. 5-12.

BENSON, Edward White, Cyprian: his Life, his Times, his Work, London and New York 1897.

BEVANS, Stephen B., Models of Contextual Theology. Revised and expanded edition, Maryknoll-New York 2007.

BOH, Katja, European Family life Patterns – a Reappraisal, in: Katja Boh et al. (eds), Changing Patterns of European Family Life: A Comparative Analysis of 14 European Countries, London 1989, pp. 265-90.

BRANICK, Vincent P., The House Church in the Writings of Paul. Zachaeus Studies: New Testament, Wilmington 1989.

BUJO, Bénézet, African Theology in its Social Context, Nairobi 1992.

--- On the Road toward an African Ecclesiology. Reflections on the Synod, in: Africa Faith and Justice Network, The African Synod. Documents, Reflections, Perspectives, Maryknoll – New York 1996, pp. 139-51.

BULMAN, Raymond F. and PARRELLA, Frederick J., From Trent to Vatican II. Historical and Theological Investigations, Oxford 2006.

BURGESS, Ernest W., The Family as a Unity of Interacting Personalities, in: Family (1926) 7: 3-9.

BURGUIÈRE, André /KLAPISCH-ZUBER, Christiane/SEGALEN, Martine/ZONABEND, Francoise, A History of the Family Vol. 2. The Impact of Modernity (transl. into English by Sarah Hanbury Tenison, Polity Press 1996).

CAHILL, Lisa Sowle, Family. A Christian Social Perspective, Minneapolis 2000.

CATHOLIC THEOLOGICAL ASSOCIATION OF NIGERIA (CATHAN), Statement, in: Africa Faith and Justice Network, African Synod, Maryknoll – New York 1996.

CHEAL, David, The One and the Many: Modernity and Postmodernity, in: Graham Allan (ed.), The Sociology of Family. A Reader, Oxford 1999, pp. 56-85.

CLERICI, Luigi, The Church as Family: African Church communities as Families of Jesus and of God, a Biblical and Ecclesiological Reflection, in: African Christian Studies 11(1995), 27-45.

CROSBY, Michael E., House of Disciples; Church, Economics, and Justice in Matthew, New York 1988.

D'ANTONIO, W. V. and J. Aldons, Families and Religions. Conflict and Change in Modern Societies, Beverly Hills 1983.

DE GRAFT JOHNSON, K. E., Family Research: The Ghanaian Situation, in: Elizabeth Ardayfio-Schandorf (ed.), Family and Development in Ghana. Proceedings of International Training and Research Workshop Held at the University of Ghana, Legon on 14th – 18th December 1992, Accra 1994.

DEMEL, Sabine, Zur Verantwortung berufen. Nagelprobe des Laienapostolats, Freiburg i. Br. 2009.

DFERRARI, Roy J., The Fathers of the Church. A New Translation. Saint Cyprian Treatises volume 36, New York 1958.

DOLPHENE, Florence Abena, The Emancipation of Women. An African Perspective, Accra 1991.

DOZON, Jean-Pierre, "Africa: the Family at the Crossroads" quoted in: André Burguière/Christiane Klapisch-Zuber/Martine Segalen/Francoise Zonabend, A History of the Family Vol. 2. The Impact of Modernity (transl. into English by Sarah Hanbury Tenison), Polity Press 1996.

DUJARIER, Michel, The African Synodical Tradition, in: Guiseppe Alberigo and Alphonse Ngindu Mushete (ed.), Towards the African Synod, Nijmegen 1992, pp. 1-13.

DULLES, Avery, Models of the Church, New York 2002.

--- A Half Century of Ecclesiology, in: Theological Studies 50 (1989), pp. 419-22.

DUNN, Geoffrey D., Early Christian Fathers: Tertullian, London and New York 2004.

ELA, Jean-Marc, My Faith as an African, trans. John Pairman Brown and Susan Perry, Maryknoll – New York and London 1989.

ELSER, Philip F., Family Imagery and Christian Identity in Gal 5:13 to 6:10, in: H. Moxnes (ed.), Constructing Early Christian Families. Family as Social Reality and Metaphor, London and New York 1997, pp. 121-49..

EVANS-PRITCHARD, Edward Evan, Nuer Religion, Oxford 1956.

FOGLIACCO, Nicholas, The Family: An African Metaphor for the Trinity and Church, in: Cecil McGarry and Patrick Ryan (eds.), Inculturating the Church in Africa. Theological and Practical Perspectives, Nairobi 2001, pp. 120-35.

GENERAL SYNOD BOARD FOR SOCIAL RESPONSIBILITY, Something to Celebrate. Valuing Families in Church and Society, London 1995.

GNILKA, Joachim, Paulus von Tarsus. Apostel und Zeuge, Freiburg i. Br., Basel and Wien, 1996.

GOOD, Esther N., Contexts of Kinship. An Essay in the Family Sociology of the Gonja of Northern Ghana, Cambridge 1973.

GRAND' MAISON, Jacques, The Modern Family. Locus of Resistance or Agency of Change? in: Andrew Greeley (ed.), The Family in Crisis or in Transition, New York 1979.

GRANDFIELD, Patrick, The Church as *Societas Perfecta* in the Schemata of

Vatican I. Church History, 48(1979), pp. 431-46.
GRANDFIELD, Patrick, The Rise and Fall of *Societas Perfecta,* in: Peter Huizing and Knut Walf (eds.), May Church Ministers be Politicians? (English language editor Marcus Lefébure), *Concilium* 157 (1982), pp. 3-8.
GROVES, Charles Pelham, The Planting of Christianity in Africa, vol. 1, London 1948.
GYEKYE, Kwame, African Cultural Values: An Introduction, Philadelphia and Accra 1996.
HALL, Douglas John, Professing the Faith: Christian Theology in a North American Context, Minneapolis 1993.
HAMERTON-KELLY, Robert, God the Father. Theology and Patriarchy in the Teaching of Jesus: vertures of Biblical Theology, Philadelphia 1979.
HEALEY, Joseph, Today's New Way of being Church. Pastoral Implications of the Small Christian Community Model of Church in the World Church towards the 21st Century, in: AFRICAN CHRISTIAN STUDIES 7(1991), pp. 63-77.
--- Church-as-Family and SCCs. Themes from the African Synod, in: African Ecclesial Review 37 (1995), pp. 44-46.
HELLERMAN, Joseph H., The Ancient Church as Family, Minneapolis 2001.
HELLWIG, Monika K., Sacraments, in: Michael Glazier and Monika K. Hellwig (eds.), The Modern Catholic Encyclopedia, Minnesota 1994.
HETTLAGE, Robert, Familienreport. Eine Lebensform im Umbruch, München 1992.
HILBERATH, Bernd Jochen, Zwischen Vision und Wirklichkeit. Frage nach dem Weg der Kirche, Würzburg 1999.
--- Kirche als Communio. Beschwörungsformel oder Projektbeschreibung, in: ThQ 174 (1994), pp. 45-65.
HILDEBRANDT, Jonathan, History of the Church in Africa, Achimota [4]1996.
HUBER, Hugo, The Krobo. Traditional Social and Religious Life of a West frican People,
Fribourg 1973 (St. Augustin 1963).
INTER-REGIONAL MEETING OF THE BISHOPS OF SOUTH AFRICA (IMBISA), Our Bishops Want Family on Synod Agenda, in: Africa Faith and Justice Network (ed.), African Synod, Documents, Reflections and Perspectives, Maryknoll, New York, 1996.
ISRAEL, Joseph, The Church as Family: A Theological Pastoral Study with Reference to African Synod, Dissertation ad Doctoratum in Facultate Theologiae, Rome 1998.
JACOBSON, Arland D., Divided Families and Christian Origins, in: Ronald A. Piper (ed.), The Gospel Behind the Gospels: Current Studies in Q 75 (1995), pp. 360-81.
JENNI, Ernst, 'āb Vater, in: Jenni Ernst/Westermann, Claus (ed.), Theologisches Handwörterbuch zum Alten Testament (THAT), Band 1, [6]2004, col.1-17.

--- 'āḥ Bruder, in: Jenni Ernst/Westermann, Claus (ed.), THAT, Band 1, [6]2004, Col. 98-104.
JEREMIAS, Joachim, Neutestamentliche Theologie, Gütersloh [2]1973.
KAMALI, Sabih A., Religion in a Pluralistic Society, in: John S. Pobee, Religion in a Pluralistic Society, Leiden 1976.
KASPER, Walter, Kirche als Communio. Überlegungen zur ekklesiologischen Leitidee des II. Vatikanischen Konzils, in: Walter Kasper, Theologie und Kirche, Mainz 1987, pp. 272-289.
KENZO, Mabiala Justin-Robert, Religion, Hybridity, and the Construction of Reality in Postcolonial Africa, in: Exchange 33(2004), pp. 244-68.
KINGUNGA, Raphael, The Anthropology of Self-Person and Myth in Africa, Frankfurt a. Main 1996.
KOSKELA, Douglas M., Ecclesiality and Ecumenism. Yves Conga and the Road to Unity, Milwaukee 2008.
KRAFT, Charles, Christianity in Culture, Maryknoll-New York 1979.
KRONENFELD, David B., Fanti and the Analysis of Kinship Terminologies, Urbana and Chicago 2009.
KUADA, John and CHACHAH, Yao, Ghana: Understanding the People and their Culture, Accra 1999.
KUUIRE, Albert A., The Christian Faith in the Dagarti Culture, unpublished Licentiate Thesis, Institut, "Lumen Vitae", Université Catholique de Louvain, 1996.
LAKELAND, Paul, The Laity, in: Raymond F. Bulman and Frederick J. Parrella (ed.), From Trent to Vatican II. Historical and Theological Investigations, Oxford 2006, pp. 293-207.
LASSEN, Eva Marie, The Roman Family: Ideal and Metaphor, in H. Moxnes: Constructing early Christian Families, London and New York 1997.
LESLIE, Gerald R., Family, in: Edward Humphrey et al. (eds.) The American Peoples' Encyclopedia. A Modern Reference Work, New York 1970.
LINGONGE, Lieven Engbanda, The Church as the Family of God. A Guide in the Praxis and Ethics of Reconciliation and Peacemaking in the Democratic Republic of Congo. Chicago 2004.
LOHFINK, Gerhard, Jesus and Community. The Social Dimension of Christian Faith, (*Wie hat Jesus Gemeinde gewollt? Zur gesellschaftlichen Dimension des christlichen Glaubens*), translated into English by John P. Galvin, London 1985.
LOUKAS, Alexandra et al., The Family as a Unity of Interacting Personalities, in Luciano L'abate (ed.), Family Pyschopathology. The Relational Roots of Dysfunctional Behavior, New York 1998, pp. 35-59.
LUNEAU, René, The Expectations of the Catholic Church, in: Guiseppe Alberigo and Alphonse Ngindu Mushete (eds.), Towards the African Synod, Concilium 1992/1, pp. 83-87.
MALINA, Bruce J., The New Testament World. Insights from Cultural Anthropology, Louisville 1981.
MARKEY, John. J., Creating Communion. The Theology of the Constitutions

of the Church, New York 2003.
MASRI, Habib Iris, The Story of the Cops, Cairo 1978.
MAGESA, Laurenti, Anatomy of Inculturation. Transforming the Church in Africa, New York 2004.
MBITI, John S., African Religions and Philosophy, London 1969.
MEIER, John, The Brothers and Sisters of Jesus in Ecumenical Perspective, in: The Catholic Biblical Quarterly (CBQ), 54 (1992), pp. 1-28.
MEYER, Hans Bernhard, Liturgischer Leitungsdienst durch die Laien. Eine liturgiewissenschaftliche Grundlegung, in: Martin Klöckener und Klemens Richter, Wie weit trägt das gemeinsame Priestertum? Liturgischer Leitungsdienst zwischen Ordination und Beauftragung, Freiburg i. Br. 1998, 107-144.
MHAGAMA, Christian, Pauline Churches as God's Family. A Search from the Roots, in Cecil McGarry and Patrick Ryan, Inculturating the Church in Africa, Nairobi 2001, pp. 183-91.
MOBLEY, Harris W., The Ghanaian's Image of the Missionary. An Analysis of the Published Critiques of the Christian Missionaries by Ghanaians 1897-1965, Leiden 1970.
MOXNES, Halvor, Theology in Conflict, Studies in St. Paul's Understanding of God in Romans, NOVTSup 53, Leiden 1980.
--- What is family? Problems in Constructing Early Christian Families, in: MOXNES, Halvor (ed.), Constructing Early Christian Families. Family as Social Reality and Metaphor, London and New York 1997.
MUZOREWA, Gwinyai H., The Origins and Development of African Theology, Maryknoll – New York 1985.
NEUNER, Peter, Die Heilige Kirche der sündigen Christen, Regensburg 2002.
--- Yves Congar. Zwischen „nouvelle théologie" und II. Vatikanischen Konzil, in: Neuner Peter and Wenz Gunther (eds.), Theologen des 20. Jahrhunderts, Darmstadt 2002, pp. 174-91.
--- Katholische Identität im religiösen Markt der Möglichkeiten, in: Peter Neuner and Birgitta Kleinschwärzer-Meister (eds.), Ökumene zwischen 'postmoderner Beliebigkeit' und 'Rekonfessionalisierung', Berlin 2006, pp. 55-71.
NEUNER, Peter and KLEINSCHWÄRZER-MEISTER, Birgitta, Kleines Handbuch der Ökumene, Düsseldorf 2002.
NUKUNYA, G. K., Tradition and Change in Ghana. An Introduction to Sociology, Accra, 1992.
--- Tradition and Change: The Case of the Family, Accra 1992.
NWAIGBO, Ferdinand, Church as a Communion: An African Christian Perspective. Theology of the Local Church in the Light of the Second Vatican Council, Frankfurt a. M. 1996.
NYAMITI, Charles, Christ our Ancestor, Gweru/Zimbabwe 1984.
OBORJI, Francis Anekwe, Building Relationships in Pluralistic communities: An African Perspective, in: Studies in Interreligious Dialogue 13 (2003), pp. 158-174.

OBASI, Solomon Okezie, Evangelisation and Modernity. Cultural Issues as Missiological Imperatives in *Ecclesia in Africa*, Rome 2002.

OCHOLLA-AYAYO, A. B. C., The African Family between Tradition and Modernity, in: Aderanti Adepoju (ed.), Family, Population and Development in Africa, London 1997.

OKAFOR, Gabriel Maduka, Christianity and Islam in West Africa. The Ghana Experience, Würzburg 1997.

OKEKE, Hilary Odili, From "Domestic Church" to "Family of God": The African Christian Family in the African Synod, in: Neue Zeitschrift für Missionswissenschaft 52 (1996), pp. 193-207.

OLABIMTAN, Kehinde, 'Is Africa Incurably Religious' II: A Response to Jan Platvoet and Henk Rinsum, in Exchange 32 (2003), pp. 322-39.

OLIKENYI, Gregory Ikechukwu, African Hospitality. A Model for the Communication of the Gospel in the African Context, Nettetal 2000.

O'MALLEY, John W., Reform, Historical Consciousness and Vatican II's Aggiornamento, in: Theological Studies 32 (1971), pp. 573-601. Here p. 581.

--- Trent and All That: Renaming Catholicism in the Early Modern Era, Cambridge 2000.

--- Trent and Vatican II: Two Styles of Church, in Raymond F. Bulman and Frederick J. Parrella (eds.), From Trent to Vatican II. Historical and Theological Investigations, Oxford 2006, pp. 301-20.

OROBATOR, A. Emmanuel, Perspectives and Trends in Contemporary African Ecclesiology, in: *Studia Missionalia* 45 (1996) 267-281.

--- Leadership and Ministry in the Church-as-Family. An Essay on Alternative Models, in: Hekima Review 17 (1997), pp. 7-18.

--- The Church as Family. African Ecclesiology in its Social Context, Nairobi 2000.

OSEI-BONSU, Joseph, The Inculturation of Christianity in Africa: Antecedents and Guidelines from the New Testament and the Early Church, Frankfurt a. M., 2005.

p'BIKET, Okot, African Religions in Western Scholarship, Nairobi 1971.

PARRELLA, Frederick J., Conclusion: A Clash of Ecclesiologies, in Raymond F. Bulman and Frederick J. Parrella, From Trent to Vatican II. Historical and Theological Investigations, Oxford 2006, pp. 321-28.

Paul VI, Die Aufgabe, in: Yves Congar, Hans Küng und Daniel O'Hanlon (eds.), Konzilsreden. Was sagten sie? Wie wird die Kirche morgen sein? Die authentischen Texte geben Auskunft, Einsiedeln 1964.

PESCH, Otto Hermann, Das Zweite Vatikanische Konzil: Vorgeschichte – Verlauf – Ergebnis – Nachgeschichte, Würzburg 2001.

PLAVOET, Jan and RINSUM, Henk, Is Africa Incurably Religious? Confessing and Contesting an invention, in: Exchange 32 (2003), pp. 124-53.

POBEE, John S., Grundlinien einer Afrikanischen Theologie, Göttingen 1981.

--- Kwame Nkrumah and the Church in Ghana, Accra 1988.

--- Religion and Politics in Ghana. A Case Study of the Acheampong Era 1972-1978, Accra, 1992.

RATZINGER, Joseph, The Meaning of Christian Brotherhood, San Francisco ^{2}1996.

--- Zur Gemeinschaft gerufen. Kirche heute verstehen, Freiburg i. Br., Basel and Wien ^{2}2005.

REISS, Ira L., Family System in America, New York 1971.

ROH, Taeseong, Die Familia Dei in den Synoptischen Evangelien, Freiburg i. Br. 2001.

ROHRBAUGH, Richard L., Legitimating Sonship – A Test of Honor. A Social-Scientific Study of Luke 4:1-30; in P. F. Esler (ed.), Modelling Early Christianity: Social-Scientific Studies of the New Testament in its Context, London 1995, pp. 178-93.

ROEST-CROLLIUS, Arij, Inculturation, in: S. Karotemprel (ed.), Following Christ in Mission: A Foundational Course in Missiology. Bombay 1995.

RUSAM, Dietrich, Die Gemeinschaft der Kinder Gottes: Das Motiv der Gotteskindschaft und die Gemeinden der johannischen Briefe, BWANT 7/13 (133), Stuttgart 1993.

SALM, Stephen J. and FALOLA, Toyin, Culture and Customs of Ghana, Westport, Connecticut and London 2002.

SANDNES, Karl Olav, A New Family. Conversion and Ecclesiology in the Early Church with Cross-Cultural Comparisons, Berlin, Frankfurt a. M., New York, Paris, Wien 1994.

--- Equality within Patriarchal Structures. Some New Testament Perspectives on the Christian Fellowship as a Brother- or Sister-hood and a Family, in: MOXNES, Halvor (ed.), Constructing Early Christian Families. Family as Social Reality and Metaphor, London and New York 1997, pp.150-65.

SARPONG, Peter, Conclusions, Expectations of the Synod, in: The African Synod. Documents, Reflections, Perspectives, compiled and edited by the Africa Faith and Justice Network, Maryknoll-New York 1996, pp. 220-26.

--- Peoples Differ. An Approach to Inculturation in Evangelisation, Legon 2002.

SAUER, Hanjo, The Council Discovers the Laity, in ALBERIGO Giuseppe (ed.) History of Vatican II, vol. IV: Church as Communion. The Third Period and Intercession September 1964-September 1965 (edited in English by Komonchak, Joseph A), Maryknoll and Leuven 2003, pp. 234-67.

SCHATZ, Klaus, Allgemeine Konzilien – Brennpunkte der Kirchengeschichte, Paderborn, München, Wien and Zürich 1997.

SCHNEIDER, Benito, Kirche als Familie, Schönstatt 1975.

SCHOTT Rüdiger, Ehe und Familie in einer Gesellschaft westafrikanischer

Bodenbauer (Bulsa in Nordghana), in: Mensen, Bernhard (ed.), Ehe und Familie in verschiedenen Kulturen. Vortragsreihe 1981/82, Sankt Augustin 1982, pp. 55-74.

SCHÜSSLER-FIORENZA, Elizabeth, In Memory of Her. A Feminist Theological Reconstruction of Christian Origins, New York 1983.

SEGALEN, Martine, Historical Anthropology of the Family, Cambridge 1986.

SEMMELROTH, Otto, Die Kirche als Ursakrament, Frankfurt/Main 1953.

SETTLES, Barbara H., A Perspective on Tomorrow's Family, in: Marvin B. Sussman and Suzanne K. Steinmetz (eds.), Handbook of Marriage and the Family, New York 1987.

SGRITTA, Giovanni B., Towards a New Paradigm, in: Katja Boh et al. (eds.), Changing Patterns of European Family Life. A Comparative Analysis of 14 European Countries, London 1989.

SHORTER, Aylward, Christianity and the African Imagination: After the African Synod: Resources for Inculturation, Nairobi 1996.

SUOM-DERY, Eugene, Family as Subject of Moral Education in the African Context. Hamburg 2000.

Symposium of Episcopal Conferences of Africa and Madagascar, The Church as Family of God. Instrumentum Laboris. Pastoral Letter, Accra (no year).

TAUBIN, Sarah B. and MUDD, Emily H., Contemporary Traditional Families: The Undefined Majority, in: Eleanor D. Macklin and Roger A. Rubin (eds), Contemporary Families and Alternative Lifestyles, Beverly Hills 1983.

TENGAN, Edward, House of God. Church-as-Family from an African Perspective, Leuven 1997.

TROST, Jan, Do We Mean the Same by the Concept of Family?, in: Communications Research 17/4 (1990).

UKPONG, Justin S., A Critical Review of the *Lineamenta*, in: Africa Faith and Justice Network, The African Synod. Documents, Reflections, Perspectives, Maryknoll-New York 1996, pp. 32-42.

UZUKWU, Elochukwu E., The Birth and Development of a Local Church: Difficulties and Signs of Hope, in: Guiseppe Alberigo and Alphonse Ngindu Mushete (eds.), Towards the African Synod, *Concilium* 1992/1, 17-23.

--- Missiology Today: The African Situation, in: Elochukwu E. Uzukwu (ed.), Religion and African Cultures. Inculturation – A Nigerian Perspective, Enugu 1988, pp. 217-22.

VORGRIMLER, Herbert, Neues Theologisches Wörterbuch, Freiburg i. Br., 2000.

WAGNER, Harald, Dogmatik (STh), Stuttgart 2003.

WALLS, Andrew, Christian Scholarship in Africa in the Twentieth Century, in: Journal of African Christian Thought, 4/2 (2001).

WESTHEIMER, Ruth and YAGODA, Ben, The Value of Family. A Blueprint of the 21st Century, New York 1996.

WIEDENHOFER, Siegfried, Ekklesiologie, in: Theodor Schneider (ed.), Handbuch der Dogmatik 2, [4]Düsseldorf 2009.

WILSON, Patricia and PAHL, Ray, The Changing Sociological Construct of the Family, in: Sociological Review 36 (1988), pp. 233-66.

WILSON, Stephen G., „Voluntary Associations: An Overview", in: John S. Kloppenborg and Stephen G. Wilson (eds.), Voluntary Associations, London 1996.

WILSON, Walter T., Gastfreundschaft, in: Hans Dieter Betz et al. (Hg.), Religion in Geschichte und Gegenwart, Band 3, Tübingen [4]2000.

WÖSSNER, Jakobus, Soziologie. Einführung und Grundlegung, Köln [9]1986.

ZOÉ-OBIANGA, Rose, When will the Church in Africa become African?, in: Guiseppe Alberigo and Alphonse Ngindu Mushete (eds.), Towards the African Synod, Concilium 1992/1, pp. 88-92.

Internet Sources:

Congregation for the Doctrine of Faith, Letter to the Bishops of the Catholic Church on Some Aspects of the Church Understood as Communion, (28th June, 1992), accessible at: http://www.vatican.va/roman_curia/congregations/cfaith/documents/rc_con_cfaith_doc_28051992_communionis-notio_en.html (visited on 12th April 2012).

The Ethnological Map of Ghana. Accessible at: http://www.ghanaweb.com/GhanaHomePage/tribes/map.html (Visited 20th April, 2012).

THE FINAL REPORT OF THE 1985 EXTRAORDINARY SYNOD, The Church, in the Word of God, Celebrates the Mysteries of Christ for the Salvation of the World. Accessible at: http://www.sedos.org/english/magesa/htm. (visited 20th February, 2012).

EMMANUEL, Barbara, African Women in the Church as the Family of God. Accessible at: http://www.sedos.org/english/barbara.htm (5th November, 2011).

JACOBSON, Arland, Divided Families and Christian Origins. Accessible at: http://books.google.de/books?id=F_KbL5s6h_kC&pg=PA361&lpg=PA361&dq=Arland+Jacobson,,+Divided+Families+and+Christian+Origins&source=bl&ots=VjFMDY24Z3&sig=gO8XLa1eWc4ltSfzPX8NYKkMZNM&hl=de&ei=tArBTZ6vNZCe-QbfhNT5Aw&sa=X&oi=book_result&ct=result&resnum=1&ved=0CCEQ6AEwAA#v=onepage&q=Arland%20Jacobson%2C%2C%20Divided%20Families%20and%20Christian%20Origins&f=false (visited on 4th March, 2011).

MAGESA, Laurenti, Christology, African Women and Ministry. Accessible at: http://www.sedos.org/english/magesa.htm (visited on 22th June, 2011).

PONTIFICAL COUNCIL FOR INTER-RELIGIOUS DIALOGUE, Dialogue

and Proclamation, 6. Accessible at: http://www.vatican.va/roman_curia/pontifical_councils/interelg/documents/rc_pc_interelg_doc_19051991_dialogue-and-proclamatio_en.html (visited 15th November, 2011).

WIJSEN, Frans, Intercultural Theology and the Mission of the Church. Accessible at: http://www.sedos.org/english /wijsen.htm (visited on 10th March, 2012).

Special Assembly of the Synod of Bishops for Africa, The Church in Africa and her Evangelising Mission towards the Year 2000: "You shall be my Witness"" (Acts 1,8). *Lineamenta*. Accessible at: http://www.ewtn.com/new_evangelization/africa/synod/lineamenta.htm (visited on 26th February, 2011).

TARIMO, Aquiline, Ethnicity, Common Good and the Church in Contemporary Africa (25 Sept 2000). Accessible at: http://www.sedos.org/english/Tarimo.html. (visited on 17th January, 2012).